THE POLITICAL HISTORY
OF TUDOR AND STUART ENGLAND

The Political History of Tudor and Stuart England draws together a fascinating selection of sources to illuminate this turbulent era of English history. From the bloody overthrow of Richard III in 1485 to the creation of a worldwide imperial state under Queen Anne, these sources illustrate England's difficult transition from the medieval to the modern.

Divided into two parts, the first set of documents provides a political context to help interpret the reformation, regicide and revolution which occurred in tumultuous succession. The second set of documents is devoted to these upheavals, and reveals the politics in action that shaped their course.

Covering a period characterized by conflict and division, this wide-ranging single-volume collection presents the accounts of Yorkists and Lancastrians, Protestants and Catholics, and Roundheads and Cavaliers side by side. *The Political History of Tudor and Stuart England* provides a crucial opportunity for students to examine the institutions and events that moulded English history in the early modern era at first-hand.

Victor Stater is Professor of History at Louisiana State University. He is author of *Noble Government: The Stuart Lord Lieutenancy and the Transformation of English Politics* (1994) and *Duke Hamilton Is Dead! A Story of Aristocratic Life and Death in Stuart Britain* (US 1999) published in the UK as *High Life, Low Morals* (2000).

THE POLITICAL HISTORY OF TUDOR AND STUART ENGLAND

A Sourcebook

Victor Stater

Routledge
Taylor & Francis Group

LONDON AND NEW YORK

First published 2002
by Routledge
11 New Fetter Lane, London EC4P 4EE

Simultaneously published in the USA and Canada
by Routledge
29 West 35th Street, New York, NY 10001

Routledge is an imprint of the Taylor & Francis Group

© 2002 Victor Stater

Typeset in Garamond by
M Rules
Printed and bound by
Gutenberg Press Ltd, Malta

British Library Cataloguing in Publication Data
A catalogue record for this book is available from the British Library

Library of Congress Cataloging in Publication Data
A catalog record for this book has been requested

ISBN 0–415–20743–6 (hbk)
ISBN 0–415–20744–4 (pbk)

CONTENTS

INTRODUCTION

A historian's work is grounded in, and bounded by, the sources available and without them we would be authors of myth. But understanding history is not as straightforward as it might appear – for it is not just the sum of countless documents, written, visual, and oral. It involves an act of interpretation: extracting meaning from piles of paper, or ruined buildings or even the fairy tales passed from one generation to another. Every historical document has a story to tell – letters, diaries, and memoirs – even laundry lists reveal something about the time in which they were produced. But no document reveals its secrets willingly – it must be interrogated. Who wrote it? When, and why, was the document written? What was the author's perspective? An account of Henry VIII's break with the Roman Catholic church written by a committed Protestant, for example, would probably look very different from that produced by a devout Catholic. How might an author's social status, or ethnicity, or gender affect his or her views? What can the form of a particular document tell us? Down to the 1650s, for instance, the records of the common law courts in England were kept in Norman French – a language that existed only in the minds of lawyers and their clerks. Why was this so? Some would argue that this peculiarity reveals something about the conservative nature of English law. Others might claim that it reveals a self-interested determination on the part of lawyers to mystify the public, making laymen dependent upon their expertise. When the clerk of the Privy Council wrote up the minutes of its meetings, he always began with a list of those who attended, noted in strict order of rank, from the sovereign down to the untitled office holders and bureaucrats with council seats. The attendance list of a particular meeting of the council might say important things about the making of policy – who was present when a major decision was taken, for example. But the form of the document itself reveals something about the role of status and hierarchy in early modern England.

No single document ever tells the full story: it is often difficult to reconcile conflicting accounts or to fill in the blank spaces in the record. Readers must approach the sources with a critical eye as well as an understanding of the context in which those sources were produced. This collection focuses upon government and politics in early modern England – a period of rapid, and often violent, political change. During these two centuries England travelled a path – one with more than

1

a few twists and turns – towards modernity. From Henry VIII, a survivor of the Wars of the Roses, to Queen Anne, who presided over a cabinet of party politicians, a great deal had happened. Reformation, regicide, restoration, and revolution came in tumultuous succession, and sources concerned with each of those epochs are included here. But the book also includes a variety of sources that will provide readers with context – a background into which to fit the wider events of the period. The English transition to modernity took place within an institutional framework of crown, courts, and local government which shaped society's attitudes towards change, and which met – or failed to meet – the challenges change presented.

Anyone trying to select documents covering such a broad range of time and events faces a daunting task. Unlike historians of the more remote past, the editor has no shortage of documents from which to choose. Inevitably some things receive short shrift in a short volume such as this. What I hope I have done is provide a useful sample of documents illustrating the most fascinating period of English history.

Many people have contributed to the making of this volume: Tom Cogswell, Peter Lake, and Mark Kishlansky all offered suggestions for documents to include. I owe them a debt of gratitude, both for their help with this book and their past kindnesses. Librarians at the Middleton Library of Louisiana State University were always helpful in tracking down sources not in their collection, and pointing to important items that were. I am also grateful to Heather Macallum, Victoria Peters, Helen Brocklehurst, and Sunje Redies at Routledge for their encouragement and patience. Suzanne Marchand provided her usual insight and support, and my sons, Bertie and Henry, necessary distraction, for which I thank them all.

Part I

CONTEXT

1

THE COURT AND
THE CROWN

The English (British, after 1603) monarchy was one of Europe's oldest, but the role of the king and the nature of his court were under constant revision. At the end of the fifteenth century Henry Tudor seized power from the unlucky Richard III, but, like its predecessor, Henry VII's court was an intensely personal one. Influenced to some degree by the innovations of the Burgundian court on the Continent, the first Tudor was nevertheless a ruler cast in a medieval mould. Henry's successors, however, adopted and adapted their court in the light of changing circumstances – sometimes of necessity, as in the case of Elizabeth I, who was hampered by early modern notions of female inferiority.

An important theme in English history in the early modern period is the changing centrality of the court in political and social life. Its importance under the Tudors grew, if anything, as Henry VII and Henry VIII consolidated the monarchy's power over church, state, and nobility. For the earlier Stuarts, maintaining the courtly edifice built by the Tudors was a challenge, met with varying degrees of success. James I sought to shape courtly life through the exercise of his undoubted intellectual powers – but his success was inevitably undercut by his lack of interest in ceremony and ritual. Charles I redressed this balance, returning to an almost Elizabethan fascination with ritual magnificence, but without the queen's common touch. Civil war and revolution swept the court away altogether, but Cromwell himself found that governance without one was impossible. Garbed in a purple robe and sitting upon a throne, the nemesis of monarchy in England found himself engaged in the very same mysteries as his kingly predecessors. But the Civil Wars undoubtedly altered the nature of the court. Though Charles II sought to recreate the prewar institution, his efforts never could restore the court to its former centrality. Under the later Stuarts, the court dwindled in importance, even as the power wielded by the monarchy rose – William III chafed under the limits upon his powers imposed by the Revolution of 1688, yet he commanded far greater resources than any previous British monarch. As Queen Anne's example shows, the personal power wielded by a king such as Henry VIII was overshadowed by the need to manipulate a vigorous new political system, one whose centre was at Westminster rather than Whitehall.

But in every case, the personality of the monarch was a matter of crucial importance. In what follows, something of the personal qualities of individual monarchs, as perceived by their contemporaries, and the significance of those qualities for millions of subjects might be seen. Even under Anne, royal whims and quirks could make an important difference in policy.

HENRY VII: AN AMBASSADOR'S REPORT IN 1498

When Sanchez de Londoño and Johannes de Matienzo, ambassadors of Ferdinand and Isabella of Spain, arrived in London in the summer of 1498, Henry VII had worn the English crown almost thirteen years. But the first Tudor monarch never rested easy on his throne. Only a year before a major tax rebellion roiled Cornwall and Henry had faced down the latest pretender to his title, the impostor Perkin Warbeck (1474?–1499), self-styled King Richard IV. Henry's determination to assert his own place as England's legitimate king against such threats forms the background to much of his foreign policy. An alliance with Spain, sealed by the marriage of his heir Arthur, Prince of Wales, and the eldest daughter of Spain, Katherine, was a cornerstone of Henry's plans.

Along with the resident Spanish ambassador, Don Pedro de Ayala, an important part of the envoys' mission was to report back to their masters on the king's personal attributes, for fifteenth-century diplomacy was an art practised by individuals – princes, kings, and their chosen servants, rather than a bureaucratized game in which the 'national interests' of disembodied states were pursued. As a result, the Spanish did their best to weigh Henry's character as well as his policies, and their letters reflect this concern. They also cast some light on the nature of the king's inner circle, among the most influential of whom was his mother, Margaret Beaufort, Countess of Richmond.

18 July 1498 Londoño and the Sub-prior of Santa Cruz (Fray Johannes de Matienzo) to Ferdinand and Isabella

Had a very bad voyage, and did not arrive in England until the 27th of June. Travelled sixty leagues by land from their landing place, to London. Henry, on being informed of their arrival, sent two dignitaries of the Church, one of whom is his almoner, and a knight of the name of Duarte, to receive them one day's journey from London. The knight is a brother-in-law of Count Scalas, and had been knighted by Ferdinand with his own hand in the Vega of Granada. Reached London on 2nd July. Henry was staying at a palace four leagues distant from London, but came to town on Wednesday the 4th of July, and received them the next Thursday. The Bishop of London and those who had met them on their journey to London, together with a great many other gentlemen, came to accompany them to the palace. Were received by Henry with the greatest imaginable demonstrations of joy. Delivered their credentials and recommendations and communicated to the King the substance of their message. No other persons were present, except the Cardinal who is the chancellor of the kingdom, an old gentleman whom they call the treasurer, and Doctor De Puebla. After delivering their message, were asked by Henry to wait a short time, because he wanted to consult with his Council. The counsellors and many other great dignitaries of the realm were called into the room. Retired to a little distance from them. The King, surrounded by his Council, spoke to them for some time. All of them were highly gratified by what they heard. The deliberation being concluded, King Henry asked them again to come nearer, and gave a very gracious and satisfactory answer with a most cheerful countenance. The Cardinal afterwards made a speech in the presence of the King, and answered every point of their message.

Told the King that as soon as the news of disturbances in England had reached Spain, the Spanish fleet had armed and kept ready to assist him, although the truth of the tidings was doubted, because De Puebla had not mentioned them. All the Englishmen present, and especially Henry, expressed their thanks. Henry offered to serve Spain with his person and with his army. He said it in words which manifested great love and affection.

Henry expressed great satisfaction at the marriage between the Princess Katherine and Prince Arthur, and praised the Princess. The dispensation of the Pope has arrived in England.

Took leave, but were invited to stay over the next day, Sunday. Went on Sunday morning, accompanied by the Bishop of London and other great dignitaries of state, to the palace. The King and Queen heard mass in the chapel, and walked in the procession. The ladies of the Queen went in good order and were much adorned. After mass the King proceeded to dinner. Dined in the palace with the Bishop of London and others. Went after dinner to the chamber of Henry, where they found the King and the Cardinal. Henry spoke of the war in Granada.

Henry is rich, has established good order in England, and keeps the people in such subjection as has never been the case before. He is on good terms with the King of France, to whom he has sent an embassy. He is a friend of peace.

To the Italian ambassadors he answered that he liked to live on good terms with France, and that Italy is too far distant from England for an alliance. The ambassadors from Milan are expected.

The persons who have the greatest influence in England are the mother of the King, the Chancellor, Master Bray, the Bishop of Durham, Master Ludel, who is treasurer, the Bishop of London, and the Lord Chamberlain.

18 July 1498 Johannces de Martienzo to Ferdinand and Isabella

According to his instructions, spoke with Henry alone when the audience was over. Henry did not give any positive answer then, but put it off until the next Sunday.

Told Henry that there are in England and Flanders many heretics who have come from Spain, and people who have fled from the inquisition, who speak ill of Spain, and wish to excite hatred against her. Henry appreciated this advice much. He laid his hands on his breast and swore, by the 'faith of his heart', that if any one (without mentioning those cursed exiles) of his best beloved subjects should say anything against the King and Queen of Spain, he would not esteem him, or any longer treat him as his friend. He promised to punish soundly any Jew or heretic to be found in his realms. Conversed a long time on this subject.

Henry likes to speak about the Princess of Wales. He said that he would give the half of his kingdom if she were like her mother.

The Queen is a very noble woman, and much beloved. She is kept in subjection by the mother of the King. It would be a good thing to write often to her, and to show her a little love.

There is no duplicate of the bull dispensing with the consanguinity of the Prince and Princess of Wales. Send a copy. The bull dispensing with the age of the Prince and Princess has likewise arrived. The manner in which the marriage is to be performed, and the Princess to be sent to England, are all the matters that remain to be settled. He must do this, but make no haste.

25 July 1498 Don Pedro de Ayala, to Ferdinand and Isabella

The King of England is less rich than is generally said. He likes to be thought very rich, because such a belief is advantageous to him in many respects. His revenues are considerable, but the custom house revenues, as well as the land rents, diminish every day. As far as the customs are concerned, the reason of their decrease is to be sought in the decay of commerce, caused partly by the wars, but much more by the additional duties imposed by the king. There is, however, another reason for the decrease of trade, that is to say, the impoverishment of the people by the great taxes laid on them. The King himself said to me, it is his intention to keep his subjects low, because riches would only make them haughty. The rent of the domains which he has confiscated to the Crown have much diminished.

His crown is, nevertheless, undisputed, and his government is strong in all respects. He is disliked, but the Queen beloved, because she is powerless. They love the Prince as much as themselves, because he is the grandchild of his grandfather. Those who know him love him also for his own virtues. The King looks old for his years, but young for the sorrowful life he has led. One of the reasons why he leads a good life is that he has been brought up abroad. He would like to govern England in the French fashion, but he cannot. He is subject to his Council, but has already shaken off some, and got rid of some part of this subjection. Those who have received the greatest favours from him are the most discontented. He knows all that. The king has the greatest desire to employ foreigners in his service. He cannot do so; for the envy of the English is diabolical, and, I think, without equal. He likes to be much spoken of, and to be highly appreciated by the whole world. He fails in this, because he is not a great man. Although he professes many virtues, his love of money is too great.

He spends all the time he is not in public, or in his Council, in writing the accounts of his expenses with his own hand. He desires nothing more in this world than the arrival of the Princess of Wales in England. Though it is not my business to give advice, I take the liberty to say that it would be a good thing if she were to come soon, in order to accustom herself to the way of life in this country and to learn the language. On the other hand, when one sees and knows the manners and the way of life of this people in this island, one cannot deny the grave inconveniences of her coming to England before she is of age. Your Highnesses know the reasons. They are many. But the Princess can only be expected to lead the happy life through not remembering those things which would make her less enjoy what she will find here. It would, therefore, still be best to send her directly, and before she has learnt fully to appreciate our habits of life and our government.

The King is much influenced by his mother and his followers in affairs of personal interest and in others. The Queen, as is generally the case, does not like it. There are other persons who have much influence in the government, as, for instance, the Lord Privy Seal, the Bishop of Durham, the Chamberlain, and many others.

ELIZABETH I IN THE EYES OF A FOREIGN VISITOR, 1598

No less than her father and grandfather before her, Elizabeth I understood the importance of appearances at court. Even more than her male predecessors, her gender reinforced the need for a condescending but magnificent distance from her subjects. Her natural frailty as a woman – intellectual, physical, and moral – was assumed by nearly everyone, and it was important that these 'natural' disabilities were overshadowed by the commanding virtues of a prince. Her intelligence, displayed by her command of foreign languages, her piety, her desire to do justice, all attributes of a divinely appointed monarch, cast whatever sins of Eve she inherited from her mother into shadow.

Paul Hentzner, a German jurist, wrote this account of his presentation at the queen's court at its summer home in Greenwich in 1598. Elizabeth's court, the political and social centre of the realm, was open to all who cared to visit, provided they behaved properly and were decently dressed. Gentlemen and their wives from the provinces, commoners with petitions to present, great lords from home and abroad, all came and were dazzled by Elizabeth's gracious reception and the pomp with which she surrounded herself.

CONTEXT

Extracts from Paul Hentzner's travels in England, 1598

ELIZABETH, the reigning Queen of England, was born at the Royal Palace of Greenwich, and here she generally resides, particularly in summer, for the delightfulness of its situation. We were admitted by an order, which Mr. Rogers (Daniel Rogerius) had procured from the Lord Chamberlain, into the Presence-Chamber hung with rich tapestry, and the floor, after the English fashion, strewed with hay, through which the Queen commonly passes in her way to chapel. At the door stood a gentleman dressed in velvet, with a gold chain, whose office was to introduce to the queen any person of distinction that came to wait on her. It was Sunday [6 September N. S.], when there is usually the greatest attendance of nobility. In the same hall were the Archbishop of Canterbury, the Bishop of London, a great number of Counsellors of State, Officers of the Crown, and Gentlemen, who waited the Queen's coming out, which she did from her own apartment when it was time to go to prayers, attended in the following manner:

First went Gentlemen, Barons, Earls, Knights of the Garter, all richly dressed and bareheaded; next came the Lord High Chancellor of England, bearing the seals in a red silk purse, between two, one of whom carried the royal sceptre, the other the sword of state in a red scabbard, studded with golden fleur-de-lis, the point upwards; next came the Queen, in the 65th year of her age (as we were told), very majestic; her face oblong, fair but wrinkled; her eyes small, yet black and pleasant; her nose a little hooked, her lips narrow, and her teeth black, (a defect the English seem subject to from their too great use of sugar); she had in her ears two pearls with very rich drops; her hair was of an auburn colour, but false. Upon her head she had a small crown, reported to be made of some of the gold of the celebrated Luneburg table; her bosom was uncovered, as all the English ladies have it till they marry; and she had on a necklace of exceeding fine jewels; her hands were slender, her fingers rather long, and her stature neither tall nor low; her air was stately, her manner of speaking mild and obliging. That day she was dressed in white silk, bordered with pearls of the size of beans, and over it a mantle of black silk shot with silver threads; her train was very long, the end of it borne by a marchioness; instead of a chain, she had an oblong collar of gold and jewels. As she went along in all this state and magnificence, she spoke very graciously, first to one, then to another (whether foreign ministers, or those who attend for different reasons), in English, French, and Italian; for besides being well skilled in Greek, Latin, and the languages I have mentioned, she is mistress of Spanish, Scotch, and Dutch. Whoever speaks to her, it is kneeling; now and then she raises some with her hand. While we were there, William Slawata, a Bohemian baron, had letters to present to her; and she, after pulling off her glove, gave him her right hand to kiss, sparkling with rings and jewels – a mark of particular favour. Wherever she turned her face as she was going along, everybody fell down on their knees. In the ante-chapel, next

10

the hall where we were, petitions were presented to her, and she received them most graciously, which occasioned the acclamation of *God save the Queen Elizabeth*! She answered it with *I thancke you myn good peupel*. In the chapel was excellent music; as soon as it and the service were over, which scarcely exceeded half-an-hour, the Queen returned in the same state and order, and prepared to go to dinner. But while she was still at prayers, we saw her table set out with the following solemnity:

A gentleman entered the room bearing a rod, and along with him another who had a table-cloth, which after they had both knelt three times, with the utmost veneration, he spread upon the table, and after kneeling again, they both retired. Then came two others, one with the rod again, the other with a salt-cellar, a plate and bread; when they had knelt as the others had done, and placed what was brought upon the table, they too retired with the same ceremonies performed by the first. At last came an unmarried lady of extraordinary beauty (we were told that she was a countess) and along with her a married one, bearing a tasting-knife; the former was dressed in white silk, who, when she had prostrated herself three times, in the most graceful manner approached the table and rubbed the plates with bread and salt with as much awe as if the Queen had been present. When they had waited there a little while, the yeomen of the guard entered, bareheaded, clothed in scarlet, with a golden rose upon their backs, bringing in at each turn a course of twenty-four dishes, served in silver most of it gilt; these dishes were received by a gentleman in the same order as they were brought and placed upon the table, while the lady-taster gave to each of the guard a mouthful to eat of the particular dish he had brought, for fear of any poison. During the time that this guard, which consists of the tallest and stoutest men that can be found in all England, 100 in number, being carefully selected for this service, were bringing dinner, twelve trumpets and two kettle-drums made the hall ring for half-an-hour together. At the end of all this ceremonial, a number of unmarried ladies appeared, who with particular solemnity lifted the meat off the table, and conveyed it into the Queen's inner and more private chamber, where after she had chosen for herself, the rest goes to the ladies of the Court. The Queen dines and sups alone with very few attendants; and it is very seldom that any body, foreigner or native, is admitted at that time, and then only at the intercession of some distinguished personage.

A COURTIER ON QUEEN ELIZABETH'S PERSONALITY

A rather different view of the queen emerges in Sir Robert Naunton's (1566–1635) *Fragmenta Regalia*. Probably written in the 1630s, long after the passing of the queen and most of the major figures at her court, this is an account from inside. Naunton, who rose to become a Privy Councillor and Secretary of State under

James I, was in the 1590s a young man in search of preferment, busily forging connections with the great court patrons of the day. He served the earl of Essex (1567–1601) for a while, as the earl's career blossomed thanks to Elizabeth's uncommon favour for a handsome young man. But before Essex had made the fatal mistake of assuming that the queen's affection would override her political sense, Naunton had already transferred his allegiance to Sir Robert Cecil (1563–1612), the queen's hunchbacked, indefatigable, secretary. Essex went to the block. The more adroit Naunton embarked upon a long and prosperous career in the royal service.

Although he was never an intimate at Elizabeth's court, Naunton did know something about the queen and her political style. In this selection from the *Fragmenta*, he discusses some of her strengths as well as weaknesses as a monarch.

Fragmenta Regalia

To take her in the original, she was the daughter of King Henry the 8th by Ann Bullen the second of 6 wives which he had, and one of the maids of honour to the divorced Queen Katherine of Austria, (or as the now styled Infanta of Spain) and from thence taken to the Royal bed.

If we search further into her intellect and abilities; the whole course of her government deciphers them to the admiration of posterity, for it was full of magnanimity, tempered with justice, piety, and pity, and to speak truth, noted but with one act of stain, or taint;* all her deprivations, either of life or liberty, being legal, and necessitated. She was learned, her sex and time considered, beyond common belief.

Queen Elizabeth

The principal note of her reign will be, that she ruled much by faction, and parties which she her self both made, upheld and weakened, as her own great judgement advised, for I do dissent from the common, and received opinion, that my Lord of Leicester, was absolute and alone in her grace; and though I come somewhat short of the knowledge of these times, yet that I may not err nor shoot at random, I know it from assured intelligence that it was not so . . . I conclude that she was absolute and sovereign mistress of her graces, and that all those to whom she distributed her favours, were never more than tenants at will, and stood on no better terms then her princely pleasure, and their good behaviour.

Her rewards chiefly consisted in grants, and leases of offices, and places of judicature, but for ready money, and in great sums, she was very sparing;

* Naunton refers here to the execution of Mary, Queen of Scots in 1587.

which we may partly conceive, was a virtue rather drawn out of necessity, then her nature; for she had many layings out, and as her wars were lasting, so their charge increased to the last period.

We are naturally prone to applaud the times behind us, and to vilify the present, for the concurrent of her fame carries it to this day how royally and victoriously she lived and died without the grudge and grievance of her people, yet the truth may appear without retraction from the honour of so great a princess. It is manifest she left more debts unpaid taken upon credit of her privy-seales then her progenitors did or could have taken up that were an 100 years before her . . . I believe no prince living, that was so tender of honour, and so exactly stood for the preservation of sovereignty was so great a courtier of the people, yea of the Commons, and that stooped and declined low in presenting her person to the public view as she passed in her progress and perambulations, and in her ejaculations of her prayers on the people.

'THE BEST MASTER': SIR EDWARD HYDE ON CHARLES I

Sir Edward Hyde, later first Earl of Clarendon (1609–74), was a first-hand observer of affairs in Britain for nearly all of his adult life, rising from the place of an anonymous Member of Parliament to the office of Lord Chancellor. A lawyer with a gift for argument, he was an important recruit to the Royalist cause in 1641. Initially sympathetic to reform, he became alarmed at what he regarded as the extremism of the opposition, especially their hostility to the established church. He placed his pen at Charles I's disposal, and was responsible for many of the statements appealing to the sentiments of moderate conservatives, so important in creating a Royalist party in the build-up to civil war.

After fighting began, the king named Hyde Chancellor of the Exchequer, and he became one of the most influential voices in the Royalist inner circle. Hyde was charged with the care of the young Prince of Wales, and then embarked upon a career in the service of that prince which would carry him into exile, high office, and, ironically, a second, final, exile, in 1667. He wrote his massive history of the 'Great Rebellion' as he called it, while in his second exile.

Hyde's picture of Charles I is of course biased; he compares the king's execution to the martyrdom of Christ. But he does not offer a completely adulatory character. Charles has flaws, even if they are presented only reluctantly. There have been many appraisals of Charles I's character, most of them contradictory, but few have ever rivalled Hyde's in their sensitivity.

Character of the King

But it will not be unnecessary to add a short character of his person, that posterity may know the inestimable loss which the nation then underwent, in being deprived of a prince, whose example would have had a greater influence upon the manners and piety of the nation, than the most strict laws can have. To speak first of his private qualifications as a man, before the mention of his princely and royal virtues; he was, if ever any, the most worthy of the title of an honest man; so great a lover of justice, that no temptation could dispose him to a wrongful action, except it was so disguised to him that he believed it to be just. He had a tenderness and compassion of nature, which restrained him from ever doing a hardhearted thing: and therefore he was so apt to grant pardon to malefactors, that the judges of the land represented to him the damage and insecurity to the public, that flowed from such his indulgence; and then he restrained himself from pardoning either murders or highway robberies, and quickly discerned the fruits of his severity by a wonderful reformation of those enormities. He was very punctual and regular in his devotions; he was never known to enter upon his recreations or sports, though never so early in the morning, before he had been at public prayers; so that on hunting days his chaplains were bound to a very early attendance. He was likewise very strict in observing the hours of his private cabinet devotions; and was so severe an exactor of gravity and reverence in all mention of religion, that he could never endure any light or profane word, with what sharpness of wit soever it was covered: and though he was well pleased and delighted with reading verses made upon any occasion, no man durst bring before him any thing that was profane or unclean. That kind of wit had never any countenance then. He was so great an example of conjugal affection, that they who did not imitate him in that particular did not brag of their liberty: and he did not only permit, but direct his bishops to prosecute those scandalous vices, in the ecclesiastical courts, against persons of eminence, and near relation to his service.

His kingly virtues had some mixture and allay, that hindered them from shining in full lustre, and from producing those fruits they should have been attended with. He was not in his nature very bountiful, though he gave very much. This appeared more after the duke of Buckingham's death, after which those showers fell very rarely; and he paused too long in giving, which made those, to whom he gave, less sensible of the benefit. He kept state to the full, which made his Court very orderly; no man presuming to be seen in a place where he had no presence to be. He saw and observed men long, before he received them about his person; and did not love strangers; nor very confident men. He was a patient hearer of causes; which he frequently accustomed himself to at the Council board; and judged very well, and was dexterous in the mediating part: so that he often put an end to causes by persuasion, which the stubbornness of men's humours made dilatory in courts of justice.

He was very fearless in his person, but not very enterprising. He had an excellent understanding, but was not confident enough of it; which made him oftentimes change his own opinion for a worse, and follow the advice of men that did not judge so well as himself. This made him more irresolute than the conjuncture of his affairs would admit: if he had been of a rougher and more imperious nature he would have found more respect and duty. And his not applying some severe cures to approaching evils proceeded from the lenity of his nature, and the tenderness of his conscience, which, in all cases of blood, made him choose the softer way, and not hearken to severe counsels, how reasonably soever urged . . . To conclude, he was the worthiest gentleman, the best master, the best friend, the best husband, the best father, and the best Christian, that the age in which he lived produced. And if he were not the best King, if he were without some parts and qualities which have made some kings great and happy, no other prince was ever unhappy who was possessed of half his virtues and endowments, and so much without any kind of vice.

THE COURT MASQUE: WILLIAM DAVENANT'S
SALMACIDA SPOLIA OF 1640

The quintessential reflection of the Caroline court was the masque. A curious hybrid of *tableau vivant* and opera, it reflects the ratified court culture that emerged under the wintry personality of Charles I. Performed privately, courtiers painstakingly memorized their lines and even members of the Royal Family took their turns in the theatrics. But a masque was not simply a parlour game. It represented an artistic and cultural style peculiar to the court, and in some ways at odds with the world beyond the gates of Whitehall. A proper understanding of Sir William Davenant's (1606–68) *Salmacida Spolia* depended upon the possession of a stock of classical knowledge beyond the capacity of most people, even though its message, the wisdom of kings and the giddy instability of the mob, was clear to everyone. With sets designed by Inigo Jones and music by Lewis Richard, the masque, performed at court on 21 January 1640, allowed the king and his wife, who both performed in it along with an illustrious band of peers and noble ladies, the opportunity to ignore the rapid collapse of their world, now spinning towards catastrophe. In this drama, if in no other, the king would be able to impose a happy ending, banishing discord from his realm.

The Subject of The Masque

Discord, a malicious fury, appears in a storm, and by the invocation of malignant spirits, proper to her evil use, having already put most of the world into disorder, endeavours to disturb these parts, envying the blessings and tranquility we have long enjoyed.

These incantations are expressed by those spirits in an Antimasque: who on a sudden are surprised, and stops in their motion by a secret power, whose wisdom they tremble at, and depart as foreknowing that Wisdom Will change all their malicious hope of these disorders into a sudden calm, which after their departure is prepared by a disperst harmony of music.

This secret Wisdom, in the person of the king attended by his nobles, and under the name of Philogenes or Lover of his people, hath his appearance prepared by a Chorus, representing the beloved people, and is instantly discovered, environed with those nobles in the throne of Honour.

Then the Queen personating the chief heroine, with her martial ladies, is sent down from Heaven by Pallas as a reward of his prudence, for reducing the threatening storm into the following calm.

A curtain flying up, a horrid scene appeared of storm and tempest; no glimpse of the sun was seen, as if darkness, confusion, and deformity had possessed the world, and driven light to heaven the trees bending, as forced by a gust of wind their branches Rent from their trunks, and some torn up by the roots: afar off was a dark wrought sea, with rolling billows, breaking against the rocks, with rain, lightning and thunder: in the midst was a globe of the earth, which at an instant falling on fire, was turned into a Fury, her hair upright, mixed with snakes, her body lean, wrinkled, and of a swarthy colour, her breasts hung bagging down to her waist, to which with a knot of serpents was girt red bases, and under it tawny skirts down to her feet: in her hand she brandishes a sable torch, and looking askance with hollow envious eyes, came down into the room.

FURY

> Blow winds! until you raise the seas so high,
> That waves may hang like leaves in the Sun's eye,
> That we, when in vast cataracts they fall,
> May think he weeps at Nature's funeral.
> Blow winds! and from the troubled womb of earth,
> Where you receive your undiscover'd birth
> Break out in wild disorders, till you make
> Atlas beneath his shaking load to shake.
> How am I griev'd, the world should every where
> Be vext into a storm, save only here?
> Thou over-lucky too much happy isle,
> Grow more desirous of this flattering style!
> For thy long health can never alter'd be,
> But by thy surfeits on Felicity:
> And I to stir the humours that increase
> In thy full body, over-grown with peace,
> Will call those Furies hither; who incense
> The guilty, and disorder innocence,
> Ascend! ascend! you horrid sullen brood
> Of evil spirits, and displace the good!
> The great make only wiser, to suspect

16

Whom they have wrong'd by falshood, or neglect;
The rich, make full' of avarice as pride,
Like graves, or swallowing seas, unsatisfied;
Busy to help the State, when needy grown,
From poor men's fortunes, never from their own.
The poor, ambitious make, apt to obey
The false in hope to rule whom they betray:
And make religion to become their vice,
Nam'd, to disguise ambitious avarice.

This antimasque being past, the scene changed into a calm, the sky serene, afar off Zephyrus appeared breathing a gentle gale: in the landscape were corn fields and pleasant trees, sustaining vines fraught with grapes, and in some of the furthest parts villages, with all such things as might express a country in peace, rich, and fruitful. There came breaking out of the heavens a silver chariot in which sat two persons, the one a woman . . . representing Concord: somewhat below her sat the good Genius of Great Britain, a young man in a carnation garment embroidered all with flowers, an antique sword hung in a scarf, a garland on his head . . .

1 SONG

Good Genius of Great Britain, CONCORD.
CONCORD.
Why should I hasten hither, since the good
I bring to men is slowly understood?
GENIUS.
I know it is the people's vice
To lay too mean, too cheap a price
on ev'ry blessing they possess,
Th' enjoying makes them think so less.
CONCORD.
If then, the need of what is good,
Doth make it lev'd,* or understood,
Or 'tis by absence better known,
I shall be valued, when I'm gone.
GENIUS.
Yet stay! O stay! if but to please
The great and wise Philogenes.
CONCORD.
Shall dews not fall, the sun forbear

* Believed.

His course, or I my visits here?
Alike from these defects would cease
The power and hope of all encrease.
GENIUS.
Stay then! O stay! If but to ease
The cares of wise Philogenes.
CONCORD.
I will! and much I grieve, that though the best
Of kingly science harbours in his breast,

Yet 'tis his fate to rule in adverse times,
When wisdom must awhile give place to crimes.

Being arrived at the earth, and descended from the chariot, they sing this short dialogue, and then departed several ways to incite the beloved people to honest pleasures and recreations, which have ever been peculiar to this nation.

BOTH

O who but he could thus endure
To live, and govern in a sullen age,
When it is harder far to cure,
The People's folly than resist their rage?

The song ended they return up to the stage, and divide themselves on each side; then the further part of the scene disappear'd, and the King's Majesty and the rest of the Masquers were discovered, sitting in the throne of Honour, his Majesty highest in a seat of gold, and the rest of the Lords about him. This throne was adorned with palm trees, between which stood statues of the ancient heroes; in the under parts on each side lay captives bound in several postures, lying on trophies of armours, shields, and antique weapons, all his throne being feigned of Goldsmith work.

III SONG

'To the King, when he appears with his Lords in the Throne of Honour.
1.
Those quar'ling winds, that deafned unto death
The living, and did wake men dead before,
Seem now to pant small gusts, as out of breath,
And fly to reconcile themselves on shore.

2.
If it be kingly patience to out last
Those storms the people's giddy fury raise,

Till like fantastic winds themselves they waste
The wisdom of that patience is thy praise . . .

Whilst the Chorus sung this song, there came softly from the upper part of the heavens, a huge cloud of various colours, but pleasant to the sight, which descending to the midst of the scene open'd, and within it was a transparent brightness of thin exhalations, such as the gods are feigned to descend in: in the most eminent place of which her Majesty sat, representing the chief heroine, environed with her martial ladies . . .

The Queen's Majesty and her ladies were in Amazonian habits of carnation, embroidered with silver, with plumed helms, baudrickes with antique swords hanging by their sides, all as rich as might be but the strangeness of the habits was most admired.

When this heavenly seat touched the earth, the King's Majesty took out the Queen, and the lords the ladies, and came down into the room and danc't their entry . . .

The second dance ended, and their Majesties being seated under the State, the scene was changed into magnificent buildings composed of several selected pieces of architecture: in the farthest part was a bridge over a river, where many people, coaches, horses, and such like were seen to pass to and fro: beyond this, on the shore were buildings in prospective, which shooting far from the eye showed as the suburbs of a great city.

From the highest part of the heavens came forth a cloud far in the scene, in which were eight persons richly attired representing the spheres; this, joining with two other clouds which appear'd at that instant full of music, covered all the upper part of the scene, and, at that instant beyond all these, a heaven opened full of deities, which celestial prospect with the Chorus below filled all the whole scene with apparitions and harmony.

VI SONG

To the King and Queen, by a Chorus of all.
So musical as to all ears
Doth seem the music of the spheres,
Are you unto each other still;
Tuning your thoughts to eithers' will.
All that are harsh, all that are rude,
Are by your harmony subdu'd;
Yet so into obedience wrought.
As if not forc'd to it, but taught.
Live still, the pleasure of our sight!
Both our examples and delight,
So long until you find the good success
Of all your virtues, in one happiness.

Till we so kind, so wise, and careful be,
In the behalf of our posterity,
That we may wish your sceptres' ruling here,
Lov'd even by those, who should your justice fear,
When we are gone, when to our last remove
We are dispatch'd to sing your praise above.

After this song the spheres passed through the air, and all the deities ascended, and so concluded this Masque: which was generally approved of, especially by all strangers that were present, to be the noblest and most ingenious that hath been done here in that kind.

TOUCHING FOR THE KING'S EVIL, 1662

The execution of Charles I, the overthrow of the traditional constitution of government by King, Lords, and Commons, and the social and religious upheavals of the Interregnum presented the restored Charles II (1630–85) with many difficulties. Not least of these were fundamental questions of legitimacy; if a people could declare their king a traitor, what would insure the survival of monarchy? From the start, Charles and his advisors hoped to avoid such hard questions by recreating the world as it was – or as they thought it was – before the cataclysm of civil war. An element of this policy was the revival of the practice of touching for the King's Evil.

One powerful piece of evidence for the divinely inspired nature of monarchy was the king's ability to heal his subjects. The efficacy of the royal touch had been a part of the mystique of monarchy for generations, and in the case of English kings, the power to heal diseases of the skin, 'the King's Evil' was well known. People afflicted with a wide range of disorders, many so severe as to make them objects of revulsion at home, clamoured for relief. Although it was an unpleasant chore at the best of times, as the long line of pitiful, diseased subjects shuffled forward for a gentle stroke by the (gloved) royal hand, Charles II bore his responsibility with grace. The numbers of individuals healed will never be known, but the ceremony's importance in the 1660s lay in its reassertion of an old order, an assurance that despite almost twenty years of experiment and chaos, God and the king had restored the natural order. English monarchs continued to perform this disagreeable duty into the eighteenth century, when the more fastidious German prince George I finally balked and refused to continue the tradition.

By the King.
A proclamation for the better ordering of those who repair to
the Court for their Cure of the Disease called the King-Evil.
Charles R.

Whereas by the grace and blessing of God, the Kings and Queens of this Realm by many ages past, have had the happiness by their Sacred Touch, and Invocation of the Name of God, to cure those who are afflicted with the Disease called the King-Evil; and this now most excellent Majesty in no less measure than any of His Royal Predecessors hath had good success herein, and in his most gracious and pious Disposition is as ready and willing as any King or Queen of this Realm ever was in any thing, to relieve the distresses and necessities of his good subjects; yet in his princely wisdom foreseeing that in this (as in all other things) order is to be observed, and fit times are necessary to be appointed for the performing of this great work of Charity, his most excellent Majesty doth hereby publicly and declare his Royal will and pleasure to be: That whereas heretofore the usual times of presenting such reasons for this purpose, have been prefixed by his Royal Predecessors; that from henceforth the times shall be from the feast of All Saints, commonly called Alhallowtide, to a week before Christmas, and in the month before Easter, being times more convenient both for the temperature of the realm, and in respect of any contagion which may happen in this near access to His Majesty's Sacred Person.

And his Majesty doth accordingly will and command, that from the time of publishing this proclamation, none presume to repair to his Majesties court to be healed of that Disease, but only at, or within the times for that purpose hereby appointed as aforesaid. And his Majesty doth further will and command, that all such as hereafter shall come, or repair to the Court for this purpose, shall bring with them Certificates under the hands of the parson, Vicar, or Minister, and Church-Wardens of those several parishes where they dwell, and from whence they come, certifying according to the truth, that they have not any time before been Touched by the King, to the intent to be healed of that Disease. And his Majesty doth straightly charge all justices of the peace, constables, and other officers, that they do not suffer any to pass, but such as have such certificates, upon pain of his Majesties displeasure: and to the end that all his loving subjects may the better take knowledge of this his Majesties pleasure and command, his will is, that this proclamation be published and affixed in some open place in every Market town of this Realm.

Given at Our Court of Hampton-Court, the Fourth day of July, 1662, in the Fourteenth year of Our Reign.

God save the King.

THE MONARCH AS POLITICIAN:
QUEEN ANNE IN 1706

The stifling boredom of the court under Anne (1665–1714) contrasted sharply with the struggles that shook the political world beyond the palace in the early eighteenth century. The Revolution of 1688 had fixed the character of politics for a generation, exalting Parliament at the expense of the Crown, and enshrining the Whig and Tory parties as the arbiters of policy. The kingdom was now governed by a radically different set of rules than the ones Elizabeth I or James I had known. Every political player, the monarch not least, had to learn – even if reluctantly – to cope with changed circumstances. The queen, determined to avoid becoming the captive of either party, struggled to avoid the extremes of both sides – passionate Tories such as her uncle, the earl of Rochester (1642–1711), and violent Whigs, among whom was the earl of Sunderland (1674–1722). In 1706 Anne relied upon a talented pair of politicians to steer her away from the rocks of party: Sidney, Lord Godolphin (1645–1712), her Lord Treasurer, and John, Duke of Marlborough (1650–1722). Marlborough was her Captain General, England's most successful commander since the glory days of Henry V, and had been Anne's friend since she was a girl. But Marlborough and Godolphin both knew the realities of the post-Revolutionary political world: government policy could not be enacted without the assent of Parliament, and Parliament was a partisan body. In these letters they attempt to persuade the queen of that reality, while she valiantly resists their arguments. The ministers contend that only appointing Sunderland Secretary of State will insure a smooth parliamentary session. Anne refused to consider sacking loyal servants such as Sir Charles Hedges (d. 1714), then Secretary, merely because they were Tories. She sought compromise: a powerless office for Sunderland as a sop. The letters reveal something of Anne's personality: a curious combination of diffidence and obstinacy, leavened by common sense, which belies her reputation as something of a dolt. But in the end the combined pleading of her ministers forced her to capitulate. Sunderland was duly appointed, and nearly every prominent Tory officer in her government was removed. The queen had become the prisoner of a party system she dreaded. Ironically, she would remain a Whig captive for only a brief period, for having seen the light, she began to play the political game herself, finding a skilful party politician in Robert Harley (1661–1724), who would in due course send the hated Sunderland and his allies packing. The Revolution had transformed the monarch from God's anointed to the most powerful party politician in the land, the former omnipotent in theory, but the latter extraordinarily influential in practice.

Queen Anne to Lord Godolphin. *August 30 1706.* I think one should always speak one's mind freely to one's friend on every occasion, but sometimes one is apt to hope things may not come to that extremity, as to make it necessary to trouble them, and therefore it is very natural to defer doing so as long as one possibly can. The difficulties I labour under at this time are so great, and so uneasy to me, that they will not suffer me any longer to keep my thoughts to myself; and I choose this way of explaining them to you, rather than endeavour to begin to speak, and not to be able to go on. I have been considering the business we have so often spoke about, ever since I saw you, and cannot but continue of the same mind, that it is a great hardship to persuade any body to part with a place they are in possession of, in hope of another that is not yet vacant. Besides, I must own freely to you, I am of the opinion, that making a party man secretary of state, when there are so many of their friends in employment of all kinds already, is throwing myself into the hands of a party, which is a thing I have been desirous to avoid. May be some may think I would be willing to be in the hands of the Tories; but whatever people may say of me, I do assure you I am not inclined, nor ever will be, to employ any of those violent persons, that have behaved themselves so ill towards me. All I desire is, my liberty in encouraging and employing all those that concur faithfully in my service, whether they are called Whigs or Tories, not to be tied to one, nor the other; for if I should be so unfortunate as to fall into the hands of either, I shall not imagine myself, though I have the name of queen, to be in reality but their slave, which as it will be my personal ruin, so it will be the destroying of all government; for instead of putting an end to faction, it will lay a lasting foundation for it. You press the bringing Lord Sunderland into business, that there may be one of that party in a place of trust, to help carry on the business this winter; and you think if this is not complied with, they will not be hearty in pursuing my service in the parliament. But is it not very hard that men of sense and honour will not promote the good of their country, because every thing in the world is not done that they desire, when they may be assured Lord Sunderland shall come into employment as soon as it is possible. Why, for God's sake, must I, who have no interest, no end, no thought but for the good of my country, be made so miserable, as to be brought into the power of one set of men? And why may not I be trusted, since I mean nothing but what is equally for the good of all my subjects? There is another apprehension I have of Lord Sunderland being secretary, which I think is a natural one, which proceeds from what I have heard of his temper. I am afraid he and I should not agree long together, finding by experience my humour and those that are of a warmer will often have misunderstandings between one another. I could say a great deal more on this subject, but fear I have been too tedious already. Therefore I shall conclude, begging you to consider how to bring me out of my difficulties, and never leave my service, for Jesus Christ's sake, for besides the reasons I give you in another letter, this is a blow I cannot bear.*

---

* From a copy by the duchess of Marlborough.

Godolphin to Anne. *Saturday Morning, at nine.* I come this moment from opening and reading the letter which your majesty gave yourself the trouble to write to me last night. It gives me all the grief and despair imaginable, to find that your majesty shows inclination to have me continue in your service, and yet will make it impossible for me to do so. I shall not therefore trouble your majesty with fruitless repetitions of reasons and arguments. I cannot struggle against the difficulties of your majesty's business, and yourself at the same time; but I can keep my word your majesty.

I have no house in the world to go to but my house at Newmarket, which I must own is not at this time like to be a place of much retirement, but I have no other. I have worn out my health, and almost my life, in the service of the crown. I have served your majesty faithfully to the best of my understanding, without any advantage to myself, except the honour of doing so, or without expecting any other favour than to end the small remainder of my days in liberty and quiet.*

Godolphin to Anne. *Oct. 7. 1706.* As I am persuaded that the safety of your government, and the quiet of your life, depend very much upon the resolution you shall take at this time, I think myself bound in gratitude, duty, and conscience to let you know my mind freely; and that you may not suspect me of being partial, I take leave to assure you, in the presence of God, that I am not for your putting yourself into the hands of either party. But the behaviour of Lord Rochester, and all the hot heads of that party, is so extravagant, that there is no doubt to be made of their exposing you and the liberties of England to the rage of France, rather than not be revenged, as they call it. This being the case, there is a necessity, as well as justice in your following your inclinations in supporting [your] lord treasurer, or all must go to confusion. As the humour is at present, he can't be supported but by the Whigs, for the others seek his destruction, which in effect is yours. Now, pray consider, if he can, by placing some few about you, gain such a confidence as shall make your business and himself safe, will not this be the sure way of making him so strong that he may hinder your being forced into a party? I beg you will believe I have no other motive to say what I do, but my zeal for your person, and friendship for a man whom I know to be honest, and zealously faithful to you.

Anne to Godolphin. *Sep. 21. 1706.* I have read your letter over and over and considered it very well before I have answered it; but I cannot but remain of the same mind I was when I wrote last concerning Sir Charles Hedges, thinking that he did once desire the place you have now a mind to get for him; yet it is a hard thing for me to remove him, and I can never look upon it otherwise. As to my other difficulties concerning Lord Sunderland, I do

* Draught in the hand of Lord Godolphin.

fear, for the reasons I have told you, we shall never agree long together; and the making him secretary I can't help thinking, is throwing myself into the hands of a party. They desire this thing to be done, because else they say they can't answer that all their friends will go along with them this winter. If this be complied with, you will then in a little time, find they must be gratified in something else, or they will not go on heartily in my business. You say yourself, they will need my authority to assist them, which I take to be the bringing more of their friends into employment, and shall I not then be in their hands? If this is not being in the hands of a party, what is? I am as sensible as any body can be of the services Lord Sunderland and all his friends have done me, and am very willing to show I am so, by doing any thing they desire that is reasonable. Let me, therefore, beg of you once more to consider of the expedient I proposed, of bringing Lord Sunderland into the cabinet council with a pension, till some vacancy happens. When I mentioned this before, I remember your objection against it was, that so young a man taken into the cabinet council, without having any post, might look more like an imposition upon me than a desire of my own. May be some people may find this fault; but I confess I can but think if he were made secretary others would say *that* was also an imposition upon me. One of these things would make me very easy, the other quite contrary, and why, for God's sake, may I not be gratified as well as other people? I cannot but think my Lord Sunderland, who has so much zeal and concern for my interest, and believes I have nothing so much at my heart as the good and happiness of my own subjects, and the quiet of all Europe, will act heartily upon this principle, however station he is in, and have patience till it is in my power to put him in some post. And if all his friends have this opinion of me that you say he has, they can't sure, for their own and their country's sake, but concur in my service, especially when they see, as they will, by my taking Lord Sunderland into the cabinet council, that I am willing to employ them in any thing I can. By this he will he brought into business, and be able both to assist you and have it in his power to do good offices to his friends. If they are not satisfied with so reasonable a thing as this it is very plain, in my poor opinion, nothing will satisfy them but having one entirely in their power. This is a thing I have so much at my heart and upon which the quiet of my life depends, that I must beg you, for Christ Jesus' sake, to endeavour to bring it about. I know very well that you do not serve for advantage or ambition but with entire duty and affection, which makes me that I cannot bear the thought of parting with you; and I hope, after what the Duke of Marlborough has said to you, you will not think of it again; for, to use his words, 'you cannot answer it either to God nor man, but are obliged both in conscience and honour to do it.' Let his words plead for her, who will be lost and undone if you pursue this cruel intention, and begs that you would neither think of it nor mention it any more to one, that is so affectionately and sincerely your humble servant.

Further reading

David Bevington and Peter Holbrook, eds, *The Politics of the Stuart Court Masque* (Cambridge, 1998).

David Loades, *The Tudor Court* (revised edn, Bangor, Wales, 1992).

Graham Parry, *The Golden Age Restor'd: The Culture of the Stuart Court* (New York, 1981).

R. Malcolm Smuts, *Court Culture and the Origins of a Royalist Tradition in Early Stuart England* (Philadelphia, 1999).

David Starkey, ed., *The English Court* (New York, 1987).

Simon Thurley, T*he Royal Palaces of Tudor England: Architecture and Court Life. 1460–1547* (New Haven, CT, 1993).

2

CENTRAL GOVERNMENT

England's central government – until 1707 Scotland maintained its own, while the Irish government remained subject to London throughout the early modern period – was a complex, even arcane, set of institutions. Having evolved over centuries in response to particular needs, reducing it to tidy charts illustrating lines of authority is a near impossibility, for even at the end of the period, the personal continued to play a crucial role in the organization and function of central government. The ability and industry of a single individual could permanently alter the status of the king's government, as Thomas Cromwell did when he consolidated power in the hands of Henry VIII's secretariat in the 1530s.

Broadly speaking, central government's tasks revolved around the raising and spending of money, and the maintenance of order. Throughout the early modern period, the most important part of the central state (apart from the legal system, to be treated separately below) was the Privy Council. The Council put the monarch's wishes into action – or at least attempted to, for, as the documents in this section show, royal wishes were not always effected. Subordinate to the Council was a panoply of other offices, ranging from the Treasury, an institution far older than the Council, and one which, by 1714, threatened to overshadow it entirely, to the Board of Green Cloth, whose job it was to provision the royal household. Change in the institutions of central government was evolutionary, but there were periods – the Interregnum being an obvious example – when change was rapid and far reaching. War, and the demand for revenue wars created, was the most important factor driving change under the Tudors and Stuarts. Henry VIII's wars forced the creation of more efficient institutions, such as the Court of Augmentations, which administered the monastic windfall of the Reformation. Charles I's wars impelled the further consolidation of power in the hands of the Privy Council (the outcome of which, be it said, was not a happy one for either the king or his subjects). William III's wars consolidated the growing power of the Treasury, as expenditures on campaigns soared beyond anything the Tudors could have imagined.

The growth of central government's power from 1485 to 1714 was steady, as bureaucracy flourished and revenue rose. But Britain was by no means 'overgoverned'. Even by Anne's day the number of office holders was relatively small; certainly smaller than in many other European states, such as France. The state's growth was permanently hampered by the difficulty of raising money. No monarch from Henry VIII forward could boast about his financial stability; even when revenues exceeded spending, insolvency was never far away. Moreover, central government's authority could be tenuous beyond the capital. Enforcement of the royal will depended upon local officers, magistrates, constables, and others, who were not invariably obedient. The Council frequently found itself reiterating, over and over, commands, and feigning incredulity that its orders were taken so lightly. The following chapter illustrates some of the concerns and difficulties involved in governing the realm.

HENRY VIII AND HIS SERVANTS

Early Tudor government was personal government. Distinction between public and private service was never clear; the king's servants were his, not the state's, though they might perform the duties of a bureaucrat. These letters give some idea of the nature of the king's government in the reign of Henry VIII. Gaining a foothold in the royal service depended upon the cultivation of personal ties. Patrons found posts for clients, who in turn magnified the importance of their benefactors, giving them eyes and ears in the bureaucracy. Henry VIII, though at times a conscientious monarch, was neither willing nor able to carry out every function of his government, and he usually relied upon 'men of business' to shoulder much of the administrative burden. These men survived thanks to their political skill, ambition, and efficiency, but they all began their careers as a servant to a great patron. Thomas Wolsey (c.1475–1530), eventually a cardinal and the richest man in England after the king himself, started out as chaplain to an archbishop. Thomas Cromwell (1485?–1540), who succeeded Wolsey in the king's favour, began his rise as Wolsey's personal secretary. In both cases they fell spectacularly from grace – Cromwell ended his days on the block – but finding a patron, and cultivating him (for it was almost always a man) remained the only way to rise in the king's service for those born outside the charmed circle of the peerage. Cromwell's letter to his old master on behalf of his client Dr Carbot is typical of the approach that might start a career in government.

Having found a place for himself in the king's government, the ambitious bureaucrat faced a bewildering array of challenges. For Tudor government was not neatly compartmentalized, with areas of responsibility specifically marked out for each officer. Orders came from the king or his closest servants, and were issued when and to whom they pleased. Routines there certainly were, and no royal servant could hope to succeed if he did not come to master the intricacies of the Exchequer or Privy Seal office, and a host of other arcane purlieus of state. Different offices poached upon rival territory, struggling to prove to the final judge in such matters, the king himself, their worth. All of the central government's servants faced some intractable problems, among which was transforming the royal will into action. Enforcing the king's command could be difficult, as Henry's letter to the Lord Mayor of London shows. Powerful as a Tudor monarch was, corporate privileges such as those of the City of London were long standing and ferociously defended. William Blakenhale's desire to fill the office of Meter of Linen Cloth and Canvas probably had nothing to do with a love of measures or service to the merchant community. It was a reward for other services, and for the king, a way to reward the faithful at someone else's expense – in this case, City merchants. In the absence of suitable salaries, royal servants depended upon such back-door payments, and lacking reliable revenue, it suited the Crown to shift its responsibilities to others. Finally, Cromwell's letter to the Lord President of the Welsh Marches is another example of the problem of enforcement. Gypsies had already been banished from the kingdom – and now it was being done all over again. It was neither the first nor the last time that central authorities would 'marvel' as they often put it, at the failure of their underlings to carry out their orders.

Cromwell to Cardinal Wolsey, in recommendation of his kinsman, Dr Carbot

After my most humble recommendations, with my daily service and continual prayer, may it please your Grace to call to your good and most gracious remembrance how that I being with your Grace in your gallery at the Charterhouse at Shene most humbly applied unto the same for the acceptance of this bearer, Mr Doctor Carbot, my kinsman, unto your service. At which time it pleased your Grace benignly to grant me to accept him promising both unto him and me that ye would be his good and gracious lord; upon the which he hath tarried here in these parts continually to his great cost, supposing that I should have repaired with him unto your Grace, by means whereof he thought the better to be esteemed. But forasmuch as he now perceives that for divers causes I may not, he hath desired me to write unto your Grace in his favor, most humbly and effectually beseeching your Grace to receive him into your House and service, whom I trust your Grace shall find apt, meet, discrete, diligent, and honest, and such a one that willingly, lovingly, and obediently shall and will be glad to serve your Grace in any thing that your pleasure shall be to command him: trusting firmly that by experience ye shall right well like him, eftsoones most humbly and effectually beseeching your Grace to be his good and gracious Lord for my sake, and at this my poor and most humble suit and contemplation to take him without rejection. And thus the holy Trinity preserve your Grace in long life and good health. At London, the 24th day of July.

Your most humble servant and bedesman
THOMAS CROMWELL.
To my Lord's Grace.

King Henry the Eighth to the Mayor and Aldermen of London, respecting the Office of Metership of Linen Cloth and Canvas in London

By the King.

HENRY R.

Right trusty and well beloved We greet you well. And whereas our trusty and well beloved servant William Blakenhale, chief clerk of our Spicery was in possession of the office of metershipp of linen cloth and canvas within our City of London and suburbs of the same, as ye now being Mayor know and can testify, till of late, without cause or desert, both contrary to the gift to him made, and also against justice and equity, you have evicted him of the possession of the same, and also have taken the profits to him appertaining to your own use. We therefore marveling not a little of your ingratitude to us and to our servant in that case exhibited, by these our Letters require you, and nevertheless command you that you not only put our said servant in full possession of the said office immediately upon the sight hereof, according to the gift to him given, but also to restore him to all such profits and sums of money as you have received by reason of the said office; failing not thereof as you tender our pleasure. Given at our manor of Westminster, the 16th day of May the 28th year of our Reign [1537].

To our trusty and right well beloved Councillor Sir John Allen knight Mayor of our City of London, and to the Aldermen of the same.

Thomas Lord Cromwell to the Earl of Chester, for the extirpation of Gypsies

After my right hearty commendations. Whereas the King's Majesty, about a twelve month past, gave a pardon to a company of lewd persons within this realm calling themselves Egyptians [Gypsies], for a most shameful and detestable murder committed amongst them, with a special proviso inserted by their own consent, that unless they should all avoyde* this his Grace's realm by a certain day long since expired, it should lie lawful to all his Graces officers to hang them in all places of his realm, where they might be apprehended, without any further examination or trial after form of the law, as in their letter patents of the said pardon is expressed. His Grace, hearing tell that they do yet linger here within his realm, not avoyding the same according to his commandment and their own promise, and that albeit his poor subjects be daily spoiled, robbed, and deceived by them, yet his Highness' officers and Ministers little regarding their duties towards his Majesty, do permit them to linger and loiter in all parts, and to exercise all their falsehoods, felonies, and treasons unpunished, hath

* Leave.

commanded me to signify unto you, and the Shires next adjoining, whether any of the said persons calling themselves Egyptians, or that hath heretofore called themselves Egyptians, shall fortune to enter or travail in the same. And in case you shall hear or know of any such, be they men or women, that ye shall compel them to depart to the next port of the Sea to the place where they shall be taken, and either without delay upon the first wind that may convey them into any part off beyond the Seas, to take shipping and to pass in to outward parts, or if they shall in any wise break that commandment, without any tract* see them executed according to the King's Highness said Letters patents remaining of Record in his Chancery which, with these, shall be your discharge in that behalf: not failing to accomplish the tenor hereof with all effect and diligence, without sparing upon any Commission, Licence, or Placards that they may show or allege for themselves to the contrary, as ye tender his Grace's pleasure which also is that you shall give notice to all the Justices of Peace in that County where you reside, and the Shires adjoining, that they may accomplish the tenor hereof accordingly. Thus fare ye heartily well; From the Neate the 5th day of December the 29th year of his Majesty's most noble Reign

Your loving friend

Thomas Cromwell.

To my very good Lord my Lord of Chester President of the Marches of Wales.

THE ELIZABETHAN PRIVY COUNCIL

The Privy Council was in its infancy during the reign of Henry VIII, but by the 1570s, during the reign of his daughter Elizabeth I, the Council had become an essential part of central government. The passage of a generation provided it with clerks, messengers, carefully preserved records, and the royal confidence. Growing out of the medieval royal council, under Elizabeth it was the closest thing to an executive authority there was in England. It continued to play this crucial role down to the Revolution of 1688, after which the rise of a new institution, the Cabinet, reduced its importance. The queen appointed the Council's members, and they served at her pleasure. A mixture of peers, officers of state, lawyers, and royal confidants, the Council was compact enough to facilitate decision-making, but broad enough to present a wide range of opinion to the Crown. This was a crucial part of the Council's job, for it did not make policy, only carried out the queen's will. No monarch need accept the Council's advice, as when Elizabeth refused its repeated pleas to marry.

Though at times, as when acting the pander for the obstinate Elizabeth, the Council could be troublesome to the Crown, it remained important because it

* Hesitation.

worked. The range of business councillors transacted was astonishing, as these extracts from their Register shows. Judicial matters – murders, political crimes, even accusations of incest, fell within its ambit. Broader concerns, such as the state of the food supply, frequently came up at the Board's twice- or thrice-weekly meetings, usually held wherever the court happened to be. The monarch did not always attend the Council's meetings, unless the matters under discussion were of special importance. Most meetings dealt with a list of items that seem trivial by today's standards, but early modern government's priorities were often different from the bureaucratized modern state with its armies of public servants and bottomless treasuries. Preserving order was the heart of the Council's business; thus their seeming obsession with the grain markets, as well as the perennial question of gypsies. Even so apparently trivial a matter as the upbringing of an infant Irish boy occupied their Lordships – for his father, the earl of Desmond, was a powerful man in Ireland, and having his son as the queen's ward – hostage, really – was a matter of importance. For sixteenth- and seventeenth-century people, tumult was the natural state of the world, and the Privy Council strove – with some success – to be a bulwark against disorder, intervening whenever and wherever it thought necessary. And its powers were commensurate with its ambitions, as the rack standing in the Tower grimly testified.

At The Exchequer Chamber at Westminster, the first of April, 1573

The Lord Treasurer. Mr. Secretary.
The Lord Admiral. Mr. Mildmay.
The Lord Chamberlain.

The rack in the Tower.
A letter to the Knight Marshall to deliver unto the Lieutenant of the Tower George Browne, to be further ordered as he shall receive from the Lords of the Council.

A letter to the Master of the Rolls, Justice Southcote and Justice Manwoode, or any two of them, to examine George Browne and all others suspected to be contrivers of the murder of Saunders, upon such instructions as shall be given them by the brethren and friends of the said Saunders, to put Browne to torture if they find cause, to commit such to prison as they shall find touched with the facts, and to admit the brethren and friends of Saunders to be present at the examination, and to minister interrogatories if they find cause.

At Greenwich, the 13th of June, 1573

The Lord Treasurer.	The Earl of Leicester.
The Lord Chamberlain.	Mr. Treasurer.
The Earl of Bedford.	Mr. Secretary.

The President of Munster.
A letter to the Judge of the admiralty to send a particular certificate of all such complaints as have been made unto him against Sir John Perrot, knight, President of Munster in Ireland, &c.

An Irish pension.
A letter to the Lord Deputy of Ireland to continue a pension of eight Irish pounds to Captain Portasse, in consideration of his old years and long service, notwithstanding the former restraints to the contrary, and by some means to give order for the defence of his house without any new charge to the Queen.

The Bath waters.
A letter to the Mayor, &c., of the City of Bath to cause certain orders, heretofore by good advice made for the ordering of the baths, to be more strictly kept hereafter.

The High Commissioners.
A letter to the Lord President of the North and the archbishop of York, with a Supplication of Anthony Hudleson of Cumberland, esquire, that where he was convented before the High Commissioners of that Province for suspicion of incest and adultery, and thereupon was bound in recognizance not to depart home, which hath been almost two years, they would proceed without further delay to some final trial and determination of the matter, and to advertise their Lordships what they have done therein.

Lord Desmond's son.
A letter to the Mayor of Bristol that where the Earl of Desmond desireth to have his son, late born in that City, to remain in this realm and be brought up as her Majesty shall thinks good, and her Highness had not resolved where he should be bestowed, but would have him well and carefully looked unto in the mean time; to require him to give order that in some Alderman's house of that City the said child and his nurse might be placed; and for the charges, upon knowledge from him what they do amount unto, their Lordships will see it discharged.

The corn trade.
A letter to the Lord Chandos, Sir Giles Poole, Sir Nicholas Arnold, knights, Thomas Throgmerton, John Pates, Gabriell Blike, esquires, or to any two of them, that notwithstanding the General Restraint of carrying of corn out,

which was only meant for strangers, they would suffer William Burley, Rice ap Redd and Richard Swanley to buy so much as might be spared for the relief of the county of Carmarthen in Wales.

Gypsies.
A letter to the Justices of Assizes of the County of Hereford that where their Lordships be advertised of certain assemblies and companies of lewd persons calling them selfs Egyptians in that county, they would try and execute according to law the principal heads and ringleaders for terror and example; and, for the rest, proceed against them as rogues and send them home into their countries, or use such moderation as they shall think good.

At Hampton Court, the 21st of February, 1573

The Lord Treasurer.	The Earl of Leicester.
The Lord Admiral.	Sir Treasurer.
The Lord Chamberlain.	Sir Secretary Smyth.
The Earl of Warwick.	Mr. Secretary Walsingham.

The observance of Lent.
Twenty nine letters into divers shires and places of the realm for the observation of keeping of Lent and forbearing of eating and killing of flesh, &c., according to an old minute of the same effect remaining in the Council Chest.

The corn trade.
Three letters to the Justices of Peace and Sheriffs of the counties of Berkshire, Bedford and Hertford at their next Sessions to call in all licenses granted to badgers* who inordinately, by procuring hands from one Justice of Peace to another, bought up corn to sell it dearer again; and there to admit only so many and such as they should think convenient, and in the shire town to set up their names that it might be known who were admitted, and for how long; and generally to have good regard that neither by forestalling, regrating or other deceitful and corrupt dealings the price of corn be enhanced; with a postscript to communicate these with the Justices of Assizes and to take their advice therein.

Aliens in London.
A letter to the Lord Mayor and other her Majesties officers within the Liberties adjoining to the City of London, that whereas upon a view of strangers remaining thereabout their Lordships were informed that there were 1500, which being repaired under colour of religion were of no church nor registered in any

---

* Corn merchants.

book; her Majesty's pleasure is they should be commanded to depart the realm within a time to be by them prescribed; and in case any upon notice hereof would associate himself to any church, for that it could not be thought but that this proceeded rather of collusion then otherwise, he should not be admitted, but commanded to depart; and for the execution of the promises they should confer together and with the Lord Bishop [of London].

THE 'SINEWS OF POWER': THE TREASURY IN 1705

The growth and complexity of government gathered pace following the Revolution of 1688. The single most important factor in the burgeoning of central government between 1688 and 1714 was war. William III's (1650–1702) War of the League of Augsburg began in 1689 and ended in 1697, to be followed by an even greater struggle, the War of the Spanish Succession (1702–13), under his successor, Queen Anne. Fought across the globe at sea and on land, these wars were the biggest England had ever engaged in, involving hundreds of thousands of soldiers and sailors. They were also the most expensive conflicts ever. The government poured millions of pounds into fielding its armed forces – and it also subsidized the armies of its allies at great expense. Such vast expenditures required sophisticated management, and the Crown's servants came more and more to resemble the civil servants of modern states. There were many more tax collectors, clerks, inspectors, and others employed to collect these funds than ever before, increasing the efficiency – and expense – of government.

At the head of this vast body of royal servants was the Lord Treasurer and his colleague the Chancellor of the Exchequer. In 1705 the former was Queen Anne's trusted advisor Sidney, Lord Godolphin, and the latter Sir Charles Hedges. Either or both of them met Treasury officers several times a week to conduct the complicated business of raising and spending money. As the following minutes of their meetings show, a vital part of England's success in meeting the challenge of constant war was a reliable system of credit; Godolphin spent a great deal of time cajoling lenders to part with their money. This was far easier after the Revolution, when loans were secured on the proceeds of parliamentary taxation, but it was nevertheless often a struggle to marshal the huge amounts of money every season's campaign required. But despite the overwhelming cares of modern war, this is still not quite a 'modern' institution, as the queen demonstrates when doling out pensions and grants to petitioners such as the poverty-stricken seventh Lord Eure. There remained, in spite of the immense pressure of a world war, a reluctance on the part of the queen to abandon an older, more personal style of government.

Treasury Minutes

1705
April 3, forenoon, at my Lord Treasurer's house.
Present: Lord Treasurer.
Ordered that Sir Thomas Littleton [Treasurer of the Navy] do take up 52,000*l.*
at an interest of 5 per cent. on the Land Tax tallies *anno* 1705 in his hands; the
said interest to commence from the time he receives [borrows] the money: and
my Lord will endorse the orders [for interest] accordingly: out of which sum
there is to be applied as follows:

	£	s.	d.
to the Victualling, for bills of exchange, Necessary and Extra-necessary Money to pursers, short allowance to seamen and contingencies, according to a memorial of the Victuallers of March 28 last	20000	0	0
to be paid over to Walter Whitfeild, Pay-master of the Marines, on account of subsistence from Feb. 24 last for such of the marines as are still on shore	4000	0	0
to Walter Whitfeild for offreckonings to several Companies [of Marines] according to the Establishment and muster rolls as in [his] memorials of March 15 last (18,886*l.* 9*s.* 10*d.*) and March 30 last (1888*l.* 4*s.* 0*d.*)	20774	13	10
to same upon account of recruits at the rate of 100*l.* a Company to each Company of the 6 Marine Regiments, according to said Whitfeild's memorial of the 30th last, to enable them to recruit forthwith: being part of the savings by respits	7200	0	0
	£51974	13	10

The residue of 25*l.* 6*s.* 2*d.* is to remain in the Navy Treasurer's hands
for uses to be directed.

A memorial of Charles Fox [Paymaster of the Forces Abroad] dated March
30 last is read [and my Lord Treasurer-thereupon] ordered that a sum of
34,601*l.* 8*s.* 8½*d.* be issued to him upon the proper orders in that behalf: out
of loans to be made by [Fox] himself on the Land Tax *anno* 1705: and to be
applied to the following uses mentioned in his memorial:

on the order for the 40,000 men

	£	s.	d.
for carriages for 18 English Battalions of Foot at 200*l.* each which they are to provide themselves with before they can take the field	3600	0	0
for one half of 12,659*l.* 15*s.* 0*d.* allowed by Parliament to the General Officers and Regiments for Forage Money	6329	17	6
for a quarter of the sum allowed for pay of the General Officers	4075	12	8 ½
for a quarter of the sum allowed for Contingencies	2500	0	0

on the order for Subsidies

	£	s.	d.
for a quarter's subsidy to the King of Denmark to June 24 next by way of advance	9375	0	0
for half a year's subsidy to June 24 next to the Landgrave of Hesse Cassel, to be also reckoned by way of advance	5813	19	0
for half a year to the Elector of Treves to June 24 next	2906	19	6
	£34601	8	8 ½

May 3, forenoon.
Present: Lord Treasurer, Chancellor of the Exchequer.
The [gentlemen of the] Bank of England [are] called [in]. My Lord acquaints them that the pressing occasions of setting out the Fleet requires a considerable supply and therefore hopes they will be ready to give their assistance by lending 100,000*l.* upon the Land Tax [*anno* 1705]. They say they will call a Court on purpose and give his Lordship their answer in a few days.

June 6, forenoon.
Present: [Attendance not stated.]
[My Lord directs] 1000*l.* to the hands of Mr. Van Huls for the Earl of Albemarle [as royal] bounty: out of secret service money.
    Likewise 200*l.* to Mrs. O'Brien as royal bounty: out of same.
    Likewise 2000*l.* to the Cofferer of the Household, for the servants attending the Queen at Windsor: [out of Civil List moneys].
    Likewise 2806*l.* 15*s.* 0*d.* to the Treasurer of the Chamber, to wit 1500*l.* for

servants [below stairs] attending at Windsor and 1306*l*. 15*s*. 0*d*. for travelling charges to the Gentlemen of the Chapel Royal in the three last years.

Likewise 2000*l*. [to William Lowndes] for secret service.

Likewise 1000*l*. to the Paymaster of the Works: to be paid over to Mr. Wise as in part of 3323*l*. 1*s*. 0*d*. resting due on bills passed by the officers of the works, being for works in her Majesty's Gardens at Kensington, Windsor, etc.

Prepare the state of a case for the Attorney General's opinion whether the 6472*l*. 1*s*. 0*d*. in the Exchequer [arising out] of [pirate] Kid's* effects may be issued for the service of the Hospital at Greenwich:

And another state of a case for his opinion whether the remainder of 6000*l*. in the Exchequer of the 61,102*l*. 14*s*. 2½*d*. allowed by Parliament for arrears to Sick and Wounded in the late war (after so much is reserved as will discharge all claims that can justly be made for such arrears) may not be applied to the service of the Sick and Wounded during the present war.

June 19, Windsor Castle, afternoon.
Present: the Queen: Lord Treasurer, Chancellor of the Exchequer. The inhabitants of Drury Lane in the parish of St. Martin's in the Fields [their petition is read setting forth] that there is a building, late Mr. Burgesse's Meeting House situate in Russell Court, which being convenient for a chapel of ease for the use of the said inhabitants who are very remote from their parochial church, they have taken and fitted up for that use: but now finding the charge thereof to amount to about 650*l*. they are unable to raise the same, being for the most part small retailing traders: therefore praying the Queen's benevolence towards the said charge. *Her Majesty is inclined to give* 100*l*. *but see first whether the works be completed by the inhabitants.*

The Lord Eure [his petition is read] praying to be recommended to her Majesty for her bounty and promises never to give her Majesty any further trouble. [The Queen orders him] 100*l*. [out of] *Secret Service*.

Peter Wentworth Esq. [his petition is read] setting forth that Etienne Cambolive, a French alien, is dead intestate and without heirs; that he has left to the value of about 500*l*. which belongs to your Majesty: therefore prays a grant of same pursuant to a gracious promise lately made him (as he alleges) by your Majesty. *The Queen did not make him any promise, but doth grant it.*

The inhabitants of Westminster [their petition is read] praying leave to make a door out of Queen's Square into St. James's Park: *granted*.

Susanna Arnold [her petition is read] setting forth her father's services to the Government in the last reign, for which he was detained a prisoner in France: in consideration whereof a pension of 100*l*. per an. was settled on her mother who died about 12 months since leaving petitioner in a miserable

---

* Captain William Kidd, tried and hanged for piracy in 1701.

and perishing condition: therefore praying relief. [*The Queen orders*] 30*l. a year to be paid to Mrs. N. Arnold for her* [*Susanna's*] *maintenance and education*: [*to be paid*] *by Mr. Nicholas*.

Seignor Verrio [his petition is read] setting forth that it is now four months since he finished [painting] the Great Drawing Room at Hampton Court; that having applied to the Queen to begin to paint some other room her Majesty was pleased to say though there was no haste of any more painting, yet her Majesty would take care of him: that this being the most seasonable time for painting and the petitioner wanting wherewithal to support himself he prays leave to put her Majesty in mind of her gracious promise. [*Her Majesty's decision is*] *give him a pension but no more charge for painting*: 200*l. a year*.

Further reading

Gerald Aylmer, *The King's Servants: The Civil Service of Charles I, 1625–1642* (revised edn, London, 1974).

F.C. Dietz, *English Public Finance, 1485–1641* (2nd edn, New York, 1964).

G.R. Elton, *Studies in Tudor and Stuart Government and Politics* (4 vols, Cambridge, 1974–92).

John Guy, *The Tudor Privy Council* (New York, 2001).

Steve Hindle, *The State and Social Change in Early Modern England* (New York, 2000).

T.A. Morris, *Tudor Government* (London, 1999).

Henry Roseveare, *The Treasury 1660–1870: The Foundations of Control* (London, 1973).

3

THE LAW

'First thing we do, let's kill all the lawyers', says Dick the Butcher in Shakespeare's *Henry VI, Part II*. The sentiment was all but universal in the early modern period: 'pettifoggers and vipers of the commonwealth' was another popular description of members of the legal profession. And yet had England's lawyers magically disappeared overnight, the kingdom would certainly have felt the loss: for the English were addicted to the law. Virtually everyone would at one time or another find themselves concerned in a legal action: as a juror, witness, plaintiff, or defendant. More than a few people, especially amongst the gentry, were embroiled in lawsuits every day of their lives. Access to the legal system was surprisingly broad, for while attorneys at the Inns of Court charged hefty fees, poor neighbours could, and often did, club together, contributing a few pennies or shillings to fund a lawsuit, even against powerful adversaries.

The ubiquity of the law required an elaborate regime of courts and procedures to support it. The king's courts included the Star Chamber, founded upon the royal prerogative and endowed with sweeping powers; Chancery, whose task it was to apply the rules of equity, modifying the rigour of the common law as it was administered in King's (or Queen's) Bench and the Court of Common Pleas. The Court of Exchequer dealt with matters involving the king's revenue. Most of their business was civil, and revolved around the perennial bones of contention: land, inheritance, and contract. Criminal matters also came before the central courts, but most of the case-load involving serious crimes came before the justices when they rode circuit to the Assizes, held regularly throughout the provinces.

The legal system was formidably complex. There were other courts beyond the king's: some privileged individuals held special judicial powers from the Crown; the bishop of Durham, for example, enjoyed a virtually independent jurisdiction. In Scotland judicial authority was hereditary in many places. The church had its own system of courts, dealing primarily with theological, moral, and marital causes: cases of, for example, heresy, fornication, and separations. There were admiralty courts, dealing in matters concerning wrecks, prizes, and piracy. Operating under the Roman-inspired rules of the civil law, the church and admiralty courts were deeply unpopular with those who practised the common law. Common lawyers, indeed, resented any competing jurisdiction – including Star Chamber and

Chancery. There was also an elaborate system of manorial courts, controlled by manor lords, performing many of the routine legal chores of daily life: regulating tenancies, confirming leases and inheritances, and enforcing local by-laws.

The delays and pitfalls inherent in such a complicated legal system deterred very few people from trying their cases at law. In fact the arcane nature of the courts and their procedures worked to the advantage of lawyers, experts in their manipulation, and also of many litigants, who might defend themselves – or assault their enemies – with a nearly inexhaustible fund of legal tricks. For all of the complaints about delays and expense from litigants, pressure for reform built very slowly. Sometimes generations passed before disputes were finally resolved – but this litigiousness indicates the fundamental commitment to the rule of law that permeated society. Confidence in the law had the effect of limiting recourse to violence.

The criminal law shows a commitment to stability and order, if necessary, at the expense of the accused. The system was biased against defendants but it worked with the understanding that sometimes order required leniency. Although the law might appear to be rigid, in fact judges and juries exercised a surprising amount of flexibility. Overall, even with its many flaws, the early modern legal system appears to have retained society's confidence and was an important force for social stability.

STAR CHAMBER UNDER HENRY VII

Star Chamber was the premier prerogative court. Its powers derived from the king's responsibility to provide order and justice for his subjects, and, unlike the common law courts, no precedents bound it. It evolved from the medieval council, which had always had a judicial function, but by the late fifteenth-century the court began to take on a separate existence. A 1487 Act of Parliament gave form to the new court, granting it subpoena powers and reinforcing its jurisdiction over a variety of causes, most importantly offences connected with disorder: riot and affray. Common targets of these charges were peers, bishops, and their hangers-on, whose dominance in the provinces Henry VII sought to break. The monarch determined membership in the court, which was considered a committee of the royal council. Judges and royal councillors did most of the work, although on rare occasions the monarch might attend personally. By the mid-sixteenth century, Star Chamber had established itself as an important part of the kingdom's legal structure. Useful for the Crown as a means to rein in overmighty subjects, the court was, until the seventeenth century, quite popular with ordinary litigants. They valued the court's straightforward procedure, whose forms lacked the complexity of the traditional common law or equity courts. Moreover, Star Chamber tended to act with far more dispatch than the other mechanisms available to litigants. These thrived upon delay and obfuscation, qualities the Star Chamber strove to minimize.

As the court's popularity increased, so did its jurisdiction as suitors invented 'riots' and 'affrays' merely to come within its scope. Disputes over inheritances or legal rights found their way to Star Chamber – even though they should probably have been heard in another court. The growth of Star Chamber's business led inevitably to hostility from common lawyers, whose livelihood it threatened, and its reputation fell further in the seventeenth century when James I and Charles I turned to it to silence critics of their policies, particularly Puritans. A reforming Parliament abolished it in 1641.

What follows are records of two cases from Star Chamber's early days: a complaint about injustices committed by a great man, and a 'riot', which concealed a local dispute over privilege.

Idele v. Abbot of Saint Bennettes Holme

To the king our sovereign lord & the lords of his most honorable Counsel spiritual & temporal.

1495 Sheweth & grievously complaineth unto your most noble grace your true & faithful subject Thomas Idele, How that where as he upon saint Peters even last past [28 June] rode to the house of Saint Bennet's of Holme in Norfolk to the intent to deliver unto the Abbot of the same house your gracious letters under your privy Seal which your said Oratour had purchased before upon certain great Injuries by the said Abbot of his great might & power to the wife of the said Thomas committed & done contrary to all right reason & good conscience, lacking power to secure his remedy therein after the course of your common law, It is so gracious lord, that at the deliverance of your said letters to the said Abbot in the presence of five or [blank] of his brethren monks of the same house he received it without reverence by putting off his bonnet or otherwise and when he had it, threw it from him into a window in great anger and before he opened it or read it, he entreated your said Oratour to have taken it home with him again, and offered him a Noble* so to have done; Which to do your said Oratour utterly refused and for the bringing thither of your said letters & for no other cause, your said Oratour was right sore & fearfully menaced & threatened by one of his Monks to beat kill & slay to the intent to make others to beware of bringing thither any privy Seals hereafter saying that the best knight in the Shire durst not have done such a deed unto them. And so your said Oratour departed thence in great fear & jeopardy of his life, beseeching your grace to take such way & direction therein for the misbehaviour of the said Abbot & of his said Monk as by your highness shall be thought consonant to reason & good conscience. At the reverence of God & in way of charity.

---

* Gold coin worth ten shillings.

Walterkyn v. Lettice

To the King our sovereign lord.

In most humble wise sheweth unto your highness your poor humble Oratour and daily Bedeman Thomas Walterkyn hermit of Saint Michael besides Highgate in the parish of Harnesey, Where one Sir Robert Lettice Vicar of the parish of Saint Pancras in the field called Kentishtown, William Chadwyk of the same parish yeoman John Hosteler yeoman and Richard Taylour with other divers, and many Rioters and evil disposed persons to the number of 40 persons and more upon Tuesday last past the 23rd day of this present month of May in riotous wise and in manner of war that is to say with bills* and staffs and other weapons defensible came into the house and hermitage† of your said Oratour in the parish of Harnesey aforesaid, your said Oratour then being in his garden and his servant with him in peaceable manner there laboring, And then and there riotously with divers menacing and threatening words broke and hewed down as well the pale of the orchard of your said Oratour as the pale of his garden and unlawfully entered into the same. And without cause or occasion given by your said Oratour the said William Chadwyk struck your said Oratour upon the arm with a bill and would have murdered him Except he had escaped from the said William and his company into the Steeple of his said hermitage, wherein he continued by all the time of their being there. And furthermore your said Oratour saith that the said Rioters entered into the dwelling house of your said Oratour and some of them took away two Altar cloths, a Surplice and a book called a grail†† with other stuff besides other hurts and harms to him done in his said orchard and garden. And as yet your said Oratour dare not presume to go home to his said hermitage, unless your gracious succour to him be shewed in that behalf. Please it therefore your said gracious highness the premises tenderly considered grant your gracious letters of privy Seal to be directed to the said sir Thomas [sic] William Chadwyk John Hostel and Richard Tailour or a servant of Arms or some other commandment them and every of them straitly commanding by the same to appear before your said highness and the lords of your most honourable council at a certain day and under a certain pain to them and to every of them to be limited by the same. And your said oratour shall daily pray to God for the preservation of your most noble and Royal estate.

---

* A weapon similar to a halberd.
† A hermitage was a chapel.
†† A liturgical song book.

The answer of sir Robert Lettice Clerk Vicar of Saint Pancras, William Chadwyk, John Hosteler and Richard Tayllour to the bill of complaint of Thomas Walterkyn of Saint Michael by Highgate

The said vicar and the other seven that the said bill is not certain nor sufficient to be answered unto but of great malice untruly feigned and imagined only to slander vex and trouble the said vicar and the others. And the matter therein contained determinable at the common law and not in this Court, whereto they pray to be remitted, and the advantage thereof to them saved for declaration of truth and answer. They say that the said vicar and the other before named with the whole parish of Kentish Town the said 23rd day of May in the bill of the said Hermit specified, which was in the Rogation week according to the laudable Custom of England, went in procession about their said parish in their prayers as they and their predecessors have used to do out of time of mind in God's peace and the king's till they came to the Hermitage of the said Hermit at Highgate, which Hermit and his predecessors stopped the procession way of your said vicar and of his parishioners by means of making of pales and dikes and would not suffer them to pass with their procession as they were wont to do. Albeit the said Hermit was courteously entreated by the said Chadwyk and others to suffer them peaceably to pass with their procession. And then the said Hermit having a great Club by him in his garden & two others with him with Clubs also. Richard Yerdeley and Thomas Marshall suddenly took the said Clubs and Struck at the said Chadwyk over the pale with the violence of which stroke the said Hermit broke divers of his pales. And afterward divers of the said parish pulled down certain pales for the said parish to pass with their procession and so departed peaceably that way with their procession without any occasion giving or quarrel making to the said Hermit or to any other. And as to the entering into the dwelling House of the said Hermit and taking away of certain books thence they say that they be not thereof guilty but they say that the said Hermit is a man of ill conversation and rule for they say that the said Hermit hath laid to pledge* one of the books that he supposeth should be stolen that is to say A Grail and other stuff to one John Phelippe for a certain sum of money which the said Phelippe will avow and testify, which he [Walterkyn] would now colorably and untruly lay to the charge of divers of the said parishioners. Without that that the said vicar and the other before named came riotously into the house and hermitage of the said Hermit in the parish of Harnesy in manner and form as by the said bill is supposed, and without that that they be guilty of breaking or hewing any pale otherwise but as before doth appear and without that that the said William Chadwyke is guilty of striking the said Hermit with a bill or otherwise in

---

* 'Laid to pledge', that is, pawned.

manner and form as by the said bill is also supposed and without that that the said vicar and the other aforesaid be guilty of any Riot or were of any such misdemeanour in manner and form as by the bill of the said Hermit is supposed. ALL WHICH matters the said vicar and the others are ready to prove and make good as this Court will award and pray to be dismissed with their reasonable costs and charges for their wrongful vexation and trouble sustained in this behalf.

This is the Replication of Thomas Walterkyn hermit of Saint Michael besides Highgate to the Answer of Sir Robert vicar of Saint Pancras, William Chadwyk & others

The said hermit saith that his bill of complaint is true in every thing and sufficient to be answered and he saith that the said vicar and others be guilty of the said riot & misbehaving in manner and form as in the said bill is supposed and moreover he saith that the said hermitage is in the parish of Harnesy out of the parish of Saint Pancras and he saith that divers persons as well of the said parish as of other places of their devotion have used to enter in to the Chapel of the said hermitage to hear divine service & to honour God there at times convenient. Without that the said Vicar or any of the said parish of Saint Pancras have or ought to have any procession way there or any other colour or title of entry into the said hermitage or any part thereof other than as he hath before rehearsed, and without that the said hermit nor any other with him had any club or staff at the time of the said riot & forcible entry committed by the said vicar and others. And without that the said hermit is a man of misrule or that he pledged any stuff belonging to the said hermitage as the said vicar and others in their answer have supposed. All which matters he is ready to prove as this court will award and prayeth as in his bill &c.

THE MANOR COURT

Although the ordinary person's contact with the courts would have been fairly broad, the realms of Star Chamber and the King's Bench were well beyond most people. Even the Assizes, where serious crimes were usually judged, was largely the preserve of the gentry and the more substantial yeomen who served as jurors. But nearly everyone outside of the largest towns would have known something of the work of the manorial courts, or courts baron. Held at various times depending on local custom (often annually, sometimes more frequently), these courts dealt with some of the most important legal matters affecting the common villager. They regulated the customs of the manor: determining who inherited customary tenures such as copyhold, who was entitled to the all-important rights of common, and determining minor debts and disputes among neighbours. Usually presided over by the lord's steward, they drew local communities together, and although their work was hardly glamorous, it was nevertheless vital. Where steward and lord were conscientious and fair, they could preserve the local peace through their mediation; where oppressive they could easily rend the social fabric of the manor. As the grip of the market economy tightened in England during the seventeenth century, the courts baron were at times seen as a means to maximize a landlord's income, but in many places they continued to perform their stabilizing function well into the eighteenth century.

What follows are excerpts from *The Court-Keeper's Guide*, a manual for landlords and their servants in need of guidance in their responsibilities. That such books were as common as they were – and this is one example among many – is evidence of social change. Such 'how-to' books had circulated for centuries to print and manuscript, but their numbers grew considerably in the early modern period as newly minted gentlemen sought to establish themselves. Here is a sample charge, or instructions, to be delivered by the steward to the court before it begins its work.

The Foreman's Oath

You shall swear that you as Foreman of this Homage [jury] with the rest of your fellows shall duly inquire, and true Presentment make of all such Articles and things as shall be given [and] spare no man, for love, favour or affection, nor Present any man for malice, hatred or envy, but according as things here Presentable, shall or may come to your knowledge, by information or otherwise: so shall you make thereof true Presentment, without concealment: *So help you God*.

Then call the rest of the Homage, and swear them by four of a time thus:

The same Oath that A. B. your Foreman hath taken before you on his part; you and every one of you shall observe and keep of your parts: *So help you God*.

Then let the Bailiff call them by name, and bid them stand near, and hear their Charge.

Then give them their Charge to this effect:

You good men that are sworn; Our work is short, and we cannot be long about it.

Our meeting is to keep a Manor Court, or Court Baron; we shall not stand to show you the Antiquity; or Original of this Court, but in a word or two by opening the nature, use and end of the Court. It is called a Court Baron, for that it is a Court incident to every Manor, which anciently, or originally were the Courts and Manors of Barons. For the King, having all the Demesne Lands, with liberty to parcel it out, and reserve what Services they thought fit, and to keep Courts within their precincts, granted great quantities of Land to the Barons and great Men; and they granted away part of this some to one, and some to another, to hold of them by such Services as they thought fit, and kept the rest in their hands: And hereof Manors were made which consist of Demesnes and Services, and they exercised that power of keeping Courts within these Manors, which hath been continued as now we find it: So that these Courts notwithstanding at this day they are kept by prescription and custom by the King's grant of them, the Fountain of Justice, who can erect and make Courts. And he gave to these Lords in their Courts. The jurisdiction they now have to redress misdemeanors within their precincts, punish offences committed by their Tenants, and decide controversies within the Jurisdiction.

This Jurisdiction is double, the one part is for the trial of the Title of the Lands, for the taking and passing of estates, surrenders of estates, admittances and grants: and herein the Lord or his Steward, as the custom of the place is, is Judge. And the other is for the trial of Actions under forty shillings, and herein the Freeholders are Judges: and one of these may continue though the other be gone. So that the main end of the Institution of this Court was for administration of Justice . . . In order to which end, you are put upon this office and duty being bound by your Tenure to it, and engaged by a solemn and strict Oath to be faithful in it. Your Office lies in your Oath, and your Oath contains your Office; which is to inquire of, and Present the things which shall be given you in Charge, which are such things only which concern the profit and advantage of the Lord and Tenants of the Manor. In all which according to the conditions of an Oath rightly taken you are to do in Truth & to present what you know to be true, and perform what you have promised and undertaken, (and to take heed of perjury) in Judgement, with due consideration of your calling to, engagement and duty in this work; and in righteousness, to do Justice impartially between Lord and Tenant, and Tenant and tenant, and give to every one his own without respect of persons, or any partiality: the which in this work of Justice, you must carefully shun. And so we shall hold you no longer in the Porch, but lead you into the House, and show you your work contained in the Articles of your Charge, which follow.

First, you are to inquire of such things which concern the Lords benefits; as of suitors to this court, and for this you are to know that all that owe suit to the Court, be they Copyholders, or customary Tenants, where ere they dwell, or what age soever they be, are to attend here or be Amerced.*

Item, if any of the Lord's Land, Custom, Rents, Services, Franchises, Royalties, Services or Evidences be concealed, or withheld from him, or Heriots,† Wards, and the like without his consent, by whom and what it is, and how long it hath been withheld.

Item, if any encroachment be made upon the Lord's Land, or upon the Common, without license of the Lord.

Item, if any Tenant take away his Hawks, Woods, Fish, Fowl, or take any

* Fined.
† Heriots were customary payments – often the 'best beast' due upon the inheritance of a tenancy.

47

swarms of Bees, Swan's eggs, Partridge or Pheasants eggs, Hawk or Hunt in his manor, or do him other trespass in his Manor, without leave of the Lord.

If any Tenant ought to grind at the Lord's Mill, and do not.

Item, if any of the Lord's Tenants, Freeholders, or others be dead, whose death is not yet presented, and by what tenure he held his land, in Knight service or in Socage or by Copy, and what is come to the Lord thereby, and who is his next Heir, of what age he is, and in whose custody, that it may be known what is due to the Lord; whether Wardship, Relief, Escheat,* Heriot, or other profit hereby: If any Tenant be dead without heir general or special, or if any Bastard purchase land and die without heir of his body: For in these Cases the Lord is to have the Land by Escheat.

Item, If any Tenant have Aliened [sold] their Lands, when, what, and to whom, and what is due to the Lord thereby, by the custom; for the Lord must know who is his Tenant, that he may know of whom to expect his Service.

Item, If any Tenant have committed any forfeiture, Freeholders may forfeit by committing Felony, in which Case after the King hath his year and day, the Lord is to have the Land.

Copyholders may forfeit by doing waste, letting houses fall, or be very ruinous by want of repair, or if he have two Copyholds, and impair one to amend the other; by doing Felony, by cutting down or marring Timber contrary to custom. By passing or letting their Land by Charter and Deed, for it must be by surrender. By letting for longer then a year and a day according to the custom. Or be a Recusant,† and the Lord no Recusant. By not paying his rent, or performing his Services, as suit of Court and the like, especially if he deny and refuse it. Or if any Copyholder have surrendered into the hands of the Bailiff or Tenants to the use of another according to the custom, and the Bailiff or Tenant do not Present at the next Court:

This is a forfeiture if the custom be not against it. If any rescue or pound breach be made of a distress taken by the Lord or his Bailiff within the Manor, for any rent or Service due to the Lord.†† If any remove the ancient bounds between Lord and Tenant, or one Lord and another, or between Tenant and Tenant. And many other ways he may forfeit his Copyhold.

Next we shall speak of the things which concerns the benefit of the Tenants: For this you are to inquire, if any take Common [rights to pasture] that hath none, or having Common keep more than his number, or the quantity of his Land, or Chase and rechase between two Farms in two Parishes, or put in

* Reversion for lack of legitimate heirs.
† One who refuses to attend the Church of England; usually a Roman Catholic.
†† Recovering property lawfully seized by the lord for some infraction.

Cattle not Commonable, or enclose, dig, build upon, or otherwise abuse and oppress the Common without License of the Lord. Or any Tenant enclose the Land which ought to be Common.

And lastly, you shall inquire of all other things by me omitted, which you know to appertain to your Charge; and of all these and the rest, make and return in to me a true Presentment by four of the clock in the afternoon.

Then let the Bailiff make an Oyez, and adjourn the Court till after dinner . . . And then: after dinner if any Surrenders or Admittances be to be made, or Actions to be tried, those things must be done: Otherwise call the Jury; take their Presentments, and swear two or more assurers, and then discharge the Court.

CRIME AT THE ASSIZES

Four times a year the king's judges went on circuit through the provinces, hearing criminal cases at the Assizes. They were solemn occasions where royal power was displayed to the local community assembled to see justice done. The judges led a procession into town, presided over feasts attended by the local gentry, and were edified by sermons delivered by local clerics. Most of the cases before them were criminal: those accused of felonies such as murder, robbery, or rape. Decided by juries chosen from the more prosperous men of the area, the Assizes often determined dozens of cases in only a few days. Early modern criminal law had one overriding goal: maintaining order. Justice for the individual was less important than the safety of the community, and as a result the law was skewed against the accused. They were not allowed counsel (though few defendants could afford a lawyer in any case); they could not compel witnesses to testify; they could not force their witnesses to swear to the truth of their testimony. If convicted, the range of punishment was narrow: whipping, mutilation, or death. Only towards the end of the period did transportation become a possibility. There were no penitentiaries, only gaols where the accused were held between their arrest and trial, and where they awaited final punishment. Acquittals did happen – even when jurors thought the accused guilty. First offenders, or those who could claim mitigating circumstances, sometimes persuaded a jury to declare the guilty innocent. Many of those convicted could claim benefit of clergy, a right formerly available only to clerics, but by the sixteenth century to all literate men, and later extended to literate women, and by 1705 to everyone. Benefit of clergy spared first offenders full punishment, usually requiring branding – sometimes even with a 'cold iron', a purely symbolic punishment.

Crime fascinated people in the early modern period as much as it does today, and every Assize generated a stream of pamphlets describing the offences tried. What follows is a typical pamphlet printed in 1680 following the Assizes held at Maidstone in Kent. The crimes it describes were typical of the day: murder, manslaughter, theft, and burglary.

Justice in its Annual progress seldom misses to revenge Affronts imposed upon its Integrity, and loudmouthed crimes still hurry a deserved punishment on such offending Miscreants as dare by vile offences to transgress the best of Laws, as may in the sequel of this dread result be shown.

The first that was called to the *Bar* was *James Wattle*, of the Town of Maidstone Grocer, who was Arraigned and tried, for murdering his Apprentice, a Youth of about eighteen years of Age; the manner thus. The deceased being his Cousin, or some near akin, to him, was by his indulgent Parents committed to his Care and tuition, not doubting [expecting] such barbarous usage as followed from a Friend and by reason of their distant living could not easily be informed, but as it is commonly seen, a stranger is more kind than a perfidious friend, so in this; for the youth had not lived long with him, before he began to use him at a gross rate that made him complain he was weary of his Life, and all the neighbours took no little notice of the same; but as to the Murder for which the Prisoner was tried, he coming home late, the 10th of February last, knocked at the Door, but the Youth as it is supposed, being drowsy by reason of his tedious watching, did not quickly hear to let him in, the which so enraged his fury that no longer was he admitted, but with his unlawful Cudgel he having shut the door fell upon him so unmercifully, that he cried out murder, and begged of him for Heaven's sake to forbear, but this not at all appeased his violence, but continued beating of him till he was tired out of breath, giving him so many mortal blows as cannot well be numbered and so left him weltering in his Gore, who was afterwards by some kind hand conveyed to Bed; but in some few days after died, complaining of his Master's cruelty. After his death the aforesaid *Wattle* was apprehended, and bound to answer at this Assizes, where he pleaded that it was not in the least his design to murder him, but to correct him for his negligence, and that he was sorry for those unfortunate blows that had brought the youth to his end, yet upon all circumstances, the Jury brought it in Manslaughter, and he was burned in the hand.

Richard Field had two Indictments brought against him, for stealing a Horse and a Mare, out of a Farmer's grounds near *Maidstone*, he being taken on the back of one of them, his plea was that he bought them but could not produce the man he named that sold them, nor bring any proof that he had bought the same and having been formerly a man of ill repute, and one that had sold many horses to several in that place, but could give no account how he came by them, the witness against him being plain and positive, the Jury brought him in Guilty, and he according to Law, received Sentence of Death.

George Baker and *William Beston* were indicted the former for stealing of Sheep, the latter for stealing pewter and Linen to a considerable value, all which being proved against them, they were brought in Guilty, and were both burned in the hand.

The next was one *Bridges* who was tried [for] Murdering (after an inhumane manner, seldom heard of) a little Girl about three years old, the circumstances as follows. This murder was committed about eighteen years since, yet to see how Divine Vengeance finds those out that dye their cruel hands in Blood of innocents, the Girl aforesaid being as we are credibly informed his Brother's Daughter, was by her Parents deceasing left with a considerable Competency of Monies, if not lands or houses, left and bequeathed to him, with all the endearments of her departing Friends to be brought up by him, the which he most willingly undertook, but had not long ere the Devil, that grand promoter of all dire Designs, prompted him on to make her away, and get the possession of what she had to his own proper interest his hellish suggestion prevailed so far with him that he thought fit to put it in practise, and so cunning in contriving, as the better to evade if a discovery should be made of Violence done to the Child, that might appear upon search, he tied her up in a thin Sack and hanging it up in the Chimney made a fire with wet straw and other combustible matter, which made a noisome smoke and so smothered her. Not at all regarding the distressed infant's crying and entreating her to take her down till she were dead, and finding none observed it but those that himself thought fit to make privy to it viz. one Dux a servant Maid, he caused [her] to be buried, and gave out that he had sent the Child to London to be educated there, and so stopped the mouths of those that were inquisitive in that particular, but about eighteen years being expired, his Maid fell sick and thinking death was near at hand, her Guilty Conscience started up this most inhumane and barbarous Crime, so that it long lying heavy on her she at last divulged it in its horrid circumstances as before recited, but recovering of that sickness, her Master was apprehended upon those words, she had confessed, and being committed, received now this Trial, his plea was that she was light headed when she spoke those words, but he not being able to make out what became of the Child, and there being no other Witness but her Confession the best the Jury could make of this barbarous Act was Man-slaughter.

Robert Morgan was Indicted for Felony and Burglary for breaking open the house of one Mr. *Wincomb* a Victualer, and taking away divers Pots, and Flagons, two Pewter Basins, and several parcels of Linen, with 20s [*shillings*] in money, all which amounted to 8 or 9 pounds but being taken with the Goods, he was Committed, yet they could not prove the door to be broken open, so that only the Felony was materially proved, for which he was convicted and burned in the hand.

Mary Willis and *Thomas Ward*, for stealing several pieces of Linen from the Hedges near Maidstone, were found Guilty to the value of ten pence, and ordered to be scourged for remembrance.

There were in all five burned in the hand, one condemned to die, and two to be whipped.

Further reading

John H. Baker, *An Introduction to English Legal History* (3rd edn, London, 1990).

Christopher Brooks, *Pettyfoggers and Vipers of the Commonwealth: The Lower Branch of the Legal Profession in Early Modern England* (Cambridge, 1986).

Christopher Brooks, *Lawyers, Litigation, and English Society since 1450* (London, 1998).

J.S. Cockburn, *A History of English Assizes 1558–1714* (Cambridge, 1972).

D.R. Hainsworth, *Stewards, Lords, and People* (Cambridge, 1992).

Cynthia Herrup, *The Common Peace* (Cambridge, 1988).

E.W. Ives, *Common Lawyers of Pre-Reformation England* (Cambridge, 1986).

David Lemmings, *Gentlemen and Barristers: The Inns of Court and the English Bar, 1680–1730* (Oxford, 1990).

4

LOCAL AUTHORITY

Village, parish, hundred, borough, and county: these were some of the myriad institutions through which government exercised its authority. For most people, local government was the only government they knew. Responsible to the king and council, yet endowed with considerable autonomy, these institutions played the most important part in maintaining the order early modern society craved.

Forms and customs varied from place to place; administrative subdivisions might be hundreds in the Midlands or wapentakes in Yorkshire. But local authority was fundamentally the same throughout England. Every county had magistrates who directed the labours of lower officers, by whatever title they went: constables, tythingmen, or borseholders. All of them had chartered boroughs – ranging from villages with little more than a dirty street and market cross to substantial cities like Norwich and York, cathedral towns with long-standing traditions of self-government.

Participation in local government was broad, but at the top were the gentlemen who served as Justices of the Peace. The elite of county society, members of the bench wielded great power. The sheriff, formerly the shire's premier officer, remained a significant figure, but his day was past, as central government came to rely more and more upon the JPs to carry out its policies. Beneath the gentlemen who formed the magistracy, however, there was a much broader group, which had its own role to play in local affairs – substantial farmers and tradesmen, yeomen and husbandmen, and freeholders of even modestly sized properties. These men formed the backbone of local government, serving as constables, churchwardens, overseers of the poor, and as jurors in the courts. Government could not have functioned without such a deep pool of experience from which to draw. Although central authorities routinely lambasted local governors for their shortcomings, in fact most local government worked reasonably well, where the ravages of famine, crime, and social disorder were largely tamed thanks to the work of a legion of unpaid officers. Even during the disruptions of civil war in the mid-seventeenth century, local authority remained functional, relieving the poor and maintaining order.

URBAN GOVERNMENT UNDER HENRY VII

The kingdom's corporate boroughs were, thanks to their royal charters, islands of privileged self-governance. The precise forms varied widely from town to town, but most were dominated by a self-selecting group of merchants. The corporations kept tight control over the 'freedom' of a borough – the right to participate in trade and government – limiting it to inheritance or on occasion, purchase. In every case, corporations were jealous of their privileges, and often had to defend them against the encroachments of rivals: local gentlemen, the Crown, or merchant strangers.

Mostly dependant upon trade for their livelihood, the oligarchs who ruled most boroughs took great care to protect themselves against outsiders. Towns fined burgesses who traded with outsiders, seized the goods of interlopers, and kept a watchful eye on local markets to insure that prices and quality met traditional standards. Much of the work of the corporation involved such economic matters, but every town had a wide range of other responsibilities. Setting night watches, insuring at least a rudimentary level of sanitation, and suppressing public nuisances all fell within its purview. More broadly, the oligarchs – like all other governors – sought to maintain stability, for disorder threatened society. Laws and ordinances no less than civic rituals such as mayoral processions on holidays sought to allay conflict and keep the fragile peace.

The port town of Southampton was typical of many corporate boroughs; its privileges were ancient, and were first guaranteed by a twelfth-century charter. By 1447 the city gained county status, an important right freeing it from the jurisdiction of the surrounding shire. The Oak Book, from which excerpts follow, offers a good sample of the nature of government in corporate boroughs. This selection is taken from the laws and customs of the town, and reflects some of the main concerns of its governors.

Certain old, ancient, and laudable ordinances, touching the Burgesses and their Duties of and within Southampton, here ensueth and followeth

The Assembly Days for the Burgesses, for their attendance upon the Mayor

No Burgess dwelling within this Town shall be absent at any assembly days, upon pain of two shillings without the licence of the Mayor, or some other reasonable cause. And the days of assembly are these, viz.: – The Friday before St Mathew's day, Michaelmas day, the Friday after Michaelmas day, and Saturday following, Christmas day, Easter day, Trinity Eve, the Quarter Sessions, Gaol delivery, and at the coming and departure of the King.

When any Burgess dies, the rest that be within the Town to be at his burial

If any Burgess of the town dies or be departed out of this world, all those that be Burgesses, and at home, and in health, shall attend Mr. Mayor and his brethren to bring the corpse of the said Burgess towards his sepulture, upon pain of two shillings a piece, to every one that shall be absent.

The Burgess son to have his father's place

When any Burgess dies, his eldest son, being of full age [and of] good behaviour, ought to have his father's place, without paying any [thing]; but if his father be alive, he shall pay ten shillings, But no [husband], by means of his wife, may have any place of a Burgess, [by reason of] his Predecessors without he agree and pay therefore; neither [any Burgess] may give or sell his burgesship to any other.

If any Burgess smite another, {he is} to lose his freedom

If any Burgess smite another, with his fists, and thereof be attainted, by confession or other good sufficient proof, before the Mayor and his Brethren, he shall lose his Burgesship, until such time he hath bought it again, and hath paid ten shillings to the use of the Town; and ought to pay it for new entry. And if any Burgess smite another with a staff, knife, or other weapon, what ever it be, he shall lose his Burgesship and shall be taken for a stranger, until such time he be reconciled by the Governours of the town, and agreed with him to whom he hath trespassed; and shall be amerced [fined] twenty shillings to the use of the Town, and not to be pardoned.

If any of the Guild revile another, how he shall be punished

If any of the Guild revile another, and that proved or confessed, he ought to be amerced and pay twenty shillings to the use of the Town; and if he be not able to pay it, then to lose his privilege and Burgesship.

How none ought to buy any thing within the town, except it be a burgess

No man ought to buy any thing in the Town of Southampton, or liberties thereof, to sell it yet again in the said town or liberties, if he be not a free Burgess or of the franchise, for his retail; if any so do, and thereof be attainted before the mayor and his brethren, all that he hath bought in such manner shall be forfeit to the town.

How a Burgess fallen into poverty shall be relieved, and how no burgess
colour or aver any Stranger's goods

If any Burgess shall fall into poverty, and have not whereof to live . . . [he is] to have, towards his or their relief in such extremity, thirteen shillings four pence, by the discretion of Mr. Mayor and his Brethren. And also, that no Burgess, nor any of the franchise, aver any other man's goods or things under colour of his own, where through the custom of the King or the Town might be embezzled; and if any so do, and be attainted, he shall lose his Burgesship and franchise, and also the merchandise so averred shall be forfeited to the Town.

No Butcher nor seller of victual shall sell, but what is
good and wholesome

No butcher, nor other seller of victual, shall sell to any man any victual, but if it be wholly clean, well ordered and wholesome; who so doth the contrary shall lose for his trespass, to the use of the Town, two shillings besides the penalty contained in the statutes.

No butcher, nor cook leave no filth, neither cast any foul thing
in the streets

No butcher, nor Cook shall leave no filth, neither cast any foul thing into the streets, whereby the town, or streets, be corrupt and unclean; and if any so do, and thereof be attainted, he shall pay twelve pence for his amercement,* as oft times as he shall trespass in manner aforesaid.

How no man shall have dunghills before his door, neither hogs
going in the streets

No man shall have any hog or pig going in the streets, neither upon any of the keys [quays], upon pain of twelve pence for every hog or pig; neither shall have dung or dunghills before his street or back door, passing two nights; if any so do, he shall pay, for every of his offences, two shillings to the use of the poor.

How, if any contention or strife rise between Burgesses, it
shall be reformed

If any contention or strife happen and befall within the Town, betwixt Burgesses of the said Town, they are anon to be sent for by Mr. Mayor and his

* Fine.

Brethren, and he or they that shall trespass, or be Trespassed, shall make amends for his or their trespass, so that tranquility, rest, good peace, and unity may daily be had among them. And if any will be willful and not be ruled, then he shall have a fine set upon him of twenty shillings, which must be paid, which, if he or they refuse, he shall be committed to the Hall, until he have paid it, and shall make amends to the party, at the discretion of Mr. Mayor and his Brethren shall think good.

For mastiff dogs or bitches kept within the town

Whosoever doth or shall keep any manner [of] mastiff dogs or mastiff bitches, within the town and county of Southampton, and do suffer any of the said dogs or bitches to go abroad in the streets], but shall keep them tied, upon pain of forfeiture, to every one that shall be f[ound] to let such dogs or bitches to go about the streets, two shillings for every time they shall be so found to go about the streets; and if they shall happen to do any harm or damage to any person, to make recompense to the party grieved.

THE 1630 BOOK OF ORDERS

1630 was a year of bad harvests and economic hardship, conditions that hit the village poor especially hard. Unemployment was high and food prices soared. There were sporadic outbreaks of rioting, often directed against grain merchants, whose high prices put the necessities of life out of reach for many. Such episodes of disorder alarmed the central government, and the result was the Book of Orders.

A product of the reforming zeal of Charles I, the book attempted to reinvigorate local authority. Both Elizabeth I and James I had also issued similar injunctions: the book did not offer any radical new solutions to the problem of poverty, but strove to increase the efficiency of traditional methods. There already existed a large body of law dealing with the poor and subsistence crises – fixing wages and regulating prices, as did the Statute of Labourers and the Assize of Bread. The king believed that these laws failed in 1630 because of the laxity of local officials, especially Justices of the Peace. The Book was meant to stir activity on the part of magistrates and their assistants. It imposed a more systematic regime on them, requiring monthly meetings and written reports. For a time, in the midst of the crisis, the king's orders worked reasonably well. But as conditions improved, compliance declined. Some justices resented what they saw as an unwarranted interference in local affairs; some disliked the expense involved in setting up houses of correction, and others were simply too lazy to deal with the extra work of monthly meetings and reports. Magistrates, who served for no pay, did not see themselves as minions of the Privy Council, nor could the Council force these gentlemen to act. The lackadaisical conservatism of the JPs stifled the Book of Orders well before they became established administrative practice. Like Charles I's reforms, the Book was a well meaning, but irritating, scheme that alienated more people than it helped.

Orders

I

That the Justices of Peace of every shire within the Realm do divide themselves, and allot amongst themselves what justices of the Peace, and what Hundreds shall attend monthly at some certain places of the Shire. And at this day and place, the High Constables, Petty-Constables, and Churchwardens, and Overseers for the Poor of those Hundreds, shall attend the said Justices. And there inquiry shall be made, and Information taken by the Justices, how every of these Officers in their several places have done their duties in Execution of the Laws mentioned in the Commission annexed, and what persons have offended against any of the said Laws.

II

Where neglect or defect is found in any of the said Officers, in making the Presentments, condign punishment to be inflicted upon them by the Justices according to Law . . .

V

For encouragement to men that do inform and prosecute others for offending against these Laws or any of them, liberty to be left to the Justices of Peace that do meet to reward the Informer or Prosecutor, out of part of the money levied upon his, or their Presentments, or Information.

Though the Statute do not prescribe this, yet this is not against the Law that gives the penalty to the Poor, which penalty nor no part thereof would else come unto the poor but by this means.

VI

That the several Justices of Peace of every Shire, do once every three months certify an account in Writing to the high Sheriff of the County, of their proceedings in this way, whom they have punished, what they have levied, and how they have employed it.

Directions

I

That the Lords of Manors and Towns, take care that their Tenants, and the Parishioners of every Town may be relieved by work, or otherwise at home, and not suffered to straggle, and beg up and down in their Parishes.

II

That Stewards to Lords and Gentlemen, in keeping their Leets* twice a year, do specially enquire upon those Articles that tend to the reformation, or punishment of common offences and abuses: As of Bakers and Brewers, for breaking of Assizes: Of Forestallers, and Regraters:† Against Tradesman of all sorts, for selling with under weight, or at excessive prices, or things unwholesome, or things made in deceit: Of people, breakers of houses, common thieves, and their Receivers; haunters of Taverns, or Alehouses; those that go in good clothes, and fare well; and none knows whereof they live; those that be night-walkers; builders of Cottages, and takers in of inmates; offences of Victuallers, Artificers, Workmen and Labourers.

III

That the poor children in every Parish be put forth Apprentices to husbandry, and other handy crafts, and money to be raised in the Parishes for placing them, according to the Law; and if any party shall refuse to take the said Apprentice, being put out according to the Law; such party shall refuse to take the said Apprentice, to be bound over to the next quarter Sessions, or Assizes, and there to be bound to his good behaviour, or otherwise ordered, as shall be found fit.

IIII

That the Statute of Labourers, for retaining of Servants, and ordering of Wages, betwixt the Servant and the Master be not deluded by private Contracts, before they come to the Statutes, and the common fashion of Essoining many absent,†† not to be allowed of course, as is used . . .

---

* Manor courts; courts baron.
† Those who hoard food or otherwise manipulate markets for profit.
†† An 'essoin' was an excused absence from court.

59

V

That the weekly taxations for relief of the Poor, and other purposes mentioned in the Statute of 43. Eliz. be in these times of scarcity raised to higher Rates in every Parish, then in times heretofore were used. And Contributions had from other Parishes, to help the weaker Parishes, especially from those places where depopulations have been, some good Contribution to come, by help of other Parishes. And where any money or Stock hath been, or shall be given to the relief of the Poor in any parish, such Gift to be no occasion of lessening the Rates of the Parish.

VI

That the petty Constables in all Parishes, be chosen of the abler sort of Parishioners, and the office not to be put upon the poorer sort, if it may be.

VII

Watches in the night, and Warding by day, and to be appointed in every Town and Village for apprehension of Rogues and vagabonds, and for safety and good order.

VIII

And because it is found by daily experience, that the remissness and negligence of petty Constables are a great cause of the swarming of Rogues and beggars, therefore the high Constables in their several Divisions are specially to be charged to look unto the petty Constables, that they use diligence in their Offices, and the High-Constables to present to the Justices of Peace, the defaults of the petty Constables, for not punishing the Rogues, or not preventing those that are Relievers of the Rogues and Beggars, the Law inflicting a Penalty upon the Constable for not punishing them, and upon such party as shall relieve them.

IX

If in any Parish there be found any persons that live out of Service, or that live idly and will not work for reasonable wages, or live to spend all they have at the Alehouse, those persons to be brought by the High Constables, and petty Constables to the Justices at their meetings, there to be ordered and punished as shall be found fit.

X

That the Correction houses in all Counties may be made adjoining to the common Prisons, and the Gaoler to be made Governour of them, that so he may employ to work Prisoners committed for small causes, and so they may learn honestly by labour, and not live idly and miserably long in prison, whereby they are made worse when they come out then they were when they went in, and where many houses of Correction are in one Country, one of them at least to be near the Gaol.

XI

That no man harbour Rogues in their Barns, or Out buildings. And the wandering persons with women and children, to give account to the Constable or Justice of Peace, where they were married, and where their children were Christened; for these people live like Savages, neither marry nor bury nor Christen, which licentious liberty makes so many delight to be Rogues and wanderers.

Further reading

Thomas Cogswell, *Home Divisions: Aristocracy, the State, and Provincial Conflict* (Stanford, 1998).

Andrew Coleby, *Central Government and the Localities: Hampshire, 1649–89* (Cambridge, 1987).

Anthony Fletcher, *Reform in the Provinces* (New Haven, 1986).

John H. Gleason, *The Justices of the Peace in England, 1558–1640* (Oxford, 1969).

Steve Hindle, *The State and Social Change in Early Modern England* (New York, 2000).

Joan Kent, *The English Village Constable* (Oxford, 1986).

J.R. Lander, *English Justices of the Peace 1461–1509* (Stroud, Gloucs., 1997).

Catherine Patterson, *Urban Patronage in Early Modern England* (Stanford, 1999).

5

PARLIAMENT

When Henry VII seized the English throne in 1485 he could have had no inkling of the importance Parliament would come to have in the future. Yet he made a small contribution to the growth of its importance himself, when he prudently arranged for his first Parliament to recognize his right to the crown in one of its first acts. Nevertheless, the process by which parliament, an irregularly held meeting of the estates of the realm, became Parliament, sovereign over Britain, was a tortured one. Every monarch from the first Tudor to the last Stuart found them to be difficult to deal with, fractious, often obstructive, and, in the case of Charles I, downright treasonable. And yet kings and queens were almost touchingly optimistic about the value of these troublesome bodies. In a crisis, even kings whose experience might have taught them otherwise – like Charles I in 1640 – called them together in hopes of a solution to the realm's problems. The people were no less convinced of their value; looking to them for reform, and hoping that a new meeting of the kingdom's representatives would restore social harmony.

Parliaments rarely lived up to the expectations of kings or subjects. The fraught nature of relations between the Stuarts – and, be it said, the Stuart's nemesis, Cromwell – and Parliament demonstrates this conclusively. And yet they continued, because they were important, and they were valuable for both Crown and subject. Parliament provided welcome cover for monarchs engaged in momentous acts: Henry VIII received a great deal of aid and comfort from the Reformation Parliament (1529–36); Elizabeth I's conflict with Spain was immeasurably strengthened by parliamentary support, as was William III's struggle with Louis XIV a century later. For subjects, Parliament represented a forum for the expression of grievances, and a place where vital local interests could be pursued. Bridges, markets, fairs, highways; all of these boons might be obtained there, and no session passed without many hours spent on 'the people's business'.

Inevitably the general confidence in Parliament's value led to an increase in its own self-estimation. Broad claims for Parliament's constitutional powers were not new in the early modern period; medieval kings had also struggled with ambitious lawmakers. But the social and economic pressures exerted upon society in the early modern period, combined with the skyrocketing cost of maintaining the state, led to increased tension. The Tudors kept them in hand with difficulty, and in no small measure because the windfall from the church eased some of the fiscal pressure they faced. The Stuarts had no such luck. James I relied upon keeping the peace to avoid bankruptcy, though he came perilously near insolvency at times in any event. Moreover, as a foreigner in England, and one with exalted ideas of his prerogative, James inadvertently raised the temperature of political discourse. It was left to his son, Charles I, no less convinced of his divinely ordained powers, to achieve a fundamental break with Parliament. The Civil War that broke out in 1642 forced a reluctant Parliament to assume responsibilities of both the executive and the legislative, and even after the Restoration in 1660, all of the efforts of Charles's successors to force the spirit of political change back in the box were for naught. An increasingly self-confident Parliament, impelled by fear of Roman Catholicism and James II's potential as an absolute monarch, led to the Revolution of 1688. Questions that had grown more and more insistent since the days of Elizabeth – about the nature of royal authority and the balance of the constitution – fudged in 1660, were now answered. Parliament was sovereign, and though neither William III nor Anne ever completely accepted the Crown's new place in the constitution, both were fighting a rearguard action.

The English Parliament – British after 1707, with the admission of Scottish members and peers – was not the only Parliament in Britain in the period, but it was by far the most important. The Scots Parliament was weaker than its southern counterpart, dominated by royal control over its agenda. The Irish Parliament was also under the English thumb, its acts subject to review by the Privy Council in London. For this reason we focus here on the Westminster Parliament. The early modern period saw a variety of significant changes in Parliament's organization and structure. The Lords remained the dominant House throughout the period, but the Reformation changed the balance of the house. Mitred abbots disappeared, to be replaced by a new crop of secular peers, many of whom had waxed rich from monastic spoils. Even the bishops found themselves forced out of the House in the 1640s, victims of the excesses of the Laudian church. The upper House itself was abolished in 1649, although this expedient ultimately failed. Cromwell experimented with a nominated 'other House', and the Restoration brought the peers back in all of their prewar glory. But the House of Commons underwent changes as well. By 1714 it was substantially larger than it had been under the Tudors, growing to over 500 members. Both Tudor and Stuart monarchs granted a variety of English boroughs Parliamentary representation; Newark was the last, enfranchised by James II in 1685. The Union with Scotland brought an additional 45 members in 1707.

Parliamentary business grew in volume in the Stuart century, especially after the Restoration, and committees became a common way to handle the pressure. The Committee of Privileges gradually usurped the right to determine membership in the Commons, once the undoubted right of the monarch. The Lords too exercised a veto over its membership, as when it denied the earl of Banbury his seat in the 1660s, based upon a legally dubious declaration of his illegitimacy. Committees subtly consolidated parliamentary power, especially in matters of revenue. Beginning in the 1660s parliamentary supervision of the royal revenue grew, as did its ability to tap the resources of the nation, through new forms of taxation and loans.

But nothing altered the nature of Parliament more than the arrival of party politics during the Restoration. The emergence of Whigs and Tories undermined one of the last and most important fictions of the pre-modern political world: the necessity of consensus for stable government. Political conflict in the age of party profoundly affected British culture. While it undoubtedly raised tensions and sparked conflict, it was nevertheless an important step in the sublimation of political violence. For though Tories hated Whigs as anti-monarchical religious fanatics, and Whigs denounced Tories as boot-licking absolutist crypto-papists, the threat of civil war receded into the distance after 1700, as the parties learned how to conduct their struggle through the political process. Parliament's permanent presence after the Revolution facilitated this, giving the political conflicts of the day a focus.

QUEEN AND COMMONS:
A PRIVY COUNCILLOR'S SPEECH

One of the unintended – and ironic – consequences of Henry VIII's Reformation was the central role Parliament played in his plans. For while it remained unequivocally a tool of the Crown, the Reformation was nevertheless made through statute. Moreover, the international complications that followed – especially the enmity of the papacy and its faithful supporter, Spain, insured that demands upon the Crown would grow. War, declared and undeclared, consumed vast amounts of money, much of which was provided by Parliament. Coaxing ever-larger sums out of reluctant members required increased attention from the monarch and her ministers. Elizabeth I never accepted the principle that Parliament should have a role in determining her policy, and she jealously guarded her prerogatives. Inevitably, however, debates over the queen's need of supply sometimes drifted into waters she considered peculiarly her own. Parliament never advanced anything like a serious challenge to Elizabeth's prerogative, but by the 1580s it had moved closer to the centre of affairs, dependent though it remained upon the royal will.

What follows is a speech made on 25 January 1580 to the House of Commons by Sir Walter Mildmay (1520?–89), a member of the Privy Council. Mildmay's urgings reflect the concerns of the day, particularly the fear and hatred of Catholics, at home and abroad, which led to the passage of ever-more brutal laws aimed at recusants. Here, however, Mildmay's main subject is the need for supply. While there is no hint in his words that the queen's policies are anything but her own, the need for such eloquence demonstrates that the members of the lower House, at any rate, could not be taken wholly for granted.

The principal cause of our Assembly here being to consult of matters that do concern the Realm, I have thought good with your patience to remember you of such things as for the weight and necessity of them I take to be worthy of your considerations. Wherein I mean to note unto you what I have conceived first of the present state we be in, next of the dangers we may justly be made in time to prevent or resist them. These showed as briefly as the matters will suffer, I leave them to your Judgments to proceed further as you shall find it expedient.

That our most Gracious Queen did at her first Entry loosen us from the Yoke of *Rome*, and did restore unto this Realm the most pure and holy Religion of the Gospel, which for a time was over shadowed with Popery, is known of all the World, and felt of us to our singular Comforts. But from hence as from the Root hath sprung that implacable malice of the Pope and his Confederates against her, whereby they have and do seek not only to trouble, but if they could to bring the Realm again into a Thralldom; the rather for that they hold this as a firm and settled Opinion, that *England* is the only settled Monarchy that most doth maintain and countenance Religion, being the Chief Sanctuary for the afflicted Members of the Church that fly thither from the Tyrant of *Rome*, as men being in danger of Shipwreck do from a raging and tempestuous Sea to a calm and quiet Haven. This being so, what hath not the Pope assayed to annoy the Queen and her State, thereby as he thinks to remove this great obstacle that stands between him and the over-flowing of the World again with Popery? For the proof whereof these may suffice:

The Northern Rebellion [1569] stirred up by the Pope, and the quarrel for Popery.

The maintenance since of these Rebels and other Fugitives.

The publishing of a most impudent, blasphemous and malicious Bull against our most Rightful Queen. [*Regnans in excelsis,* 1570, excommunicating her and declaring her to be an unlawful queen.]

The Invasion into *Ireland* by *James Fitz Morrice,* with the assistance of some English Rebels.

The rising of a dangerous Rebellion in *Ireland* by the Earl of *Desmond* and others, intending thereby to make a general Revolt of all the whole Realm.

The late Invasion of Strangers into *Ireland,* and their fortifying it.

The Pope turned thus the venom of his Curses and the Pens of his malicious Parasites into men of War and Weapons, to win that by Force, which otherwise he could not do. And though all these are said to be done by the Pope, and in his name, yet who sees not that they be maintained under-hand by some Princes his Confederates? And if any man be in doubt of that, let him but note from whence the last Invasion into *Ireland* came, of what Country the Ships, and of what Nation the most part of the Soldiers were, and by direction of whose Ministers they received their Victual and Furniture.

For the Pope of himself at this present is far unable to make War upon any Prince of that Estate which her Majesty is of, having lost as you know many years by the Preaching of the Gospel those infinite Revenues which he was wont to have out of *England, Scotland, Germany, Switzerland, Denmark* and others, and now out of *France* and the Low Countries; so as we are to think that his name only is used, and all or the most part of the charge born by others.

The Queen nevertheless by the Almighty Power of God stands fast, maugre* the Pope and all his Friends; having hitherto resisted all attempts against her, to her great honor and their great shame.

The Rebellion in the North suppressed without effusion of Blood, wherein her Majesty may say as Caesar did, *veni, vidi, vici*; so expeditious and so honourable was the Victory that God did give her by the diligence and valour of those noble men that had the conducting thereof.

The Enterprise of *James Fitz Morrice* defeated, and himself slain.

The *Italians* pulled out by the ears at *Smerwick* in *Ireland*, and cut in pieces by the notable Service of a noble Captain and Valiant Soldiers.

Neither these nor any other threats or fears of danger hath or doth make her to stagger or relent in the Cause of Religion, but like a constant Christian Princess she still holds fast the profession of the Gospel that hath so long upheld her, and made us to live in Peace twenty two Years and more under her most Gracious Government, free from those troubles that our Neighbours have felt; so as is now seems to be our present State, a blessed, peaceable and happy time, for the which we are most bound to God and to pray unto him for the continuance thereof.

But yet notwithstanding, seeing our Enemies sleep not, it behooves us not to be careless, as though all were past; but rather to think, that there is but a piece of the storm over, and that the greater part of the Tempest remains behind, and is like to fall upon us by the malice of the Pope, the most Capital Enemy of the Queen and this State, the determinations of the Council of *Trent*, and the Combination of the Pope with other Monarchies and Princes devoted unto *Rome*, assuring ourselves that if their Powers be answerable to their Wills, this Realm shall find at their hands all the Miseries and Extremities that they can bring upon it. And though by the late good Success which God hath given in *Ireland*, these lewd and malicious Enterprises seem for a time to be as it were at a stand; yet let us be assured that neither their attempts upon *Ireland*, neither the mischiefs intended against *England* will cease thus; but if they find us negligent they will be ready with greater Forces than have been yet seen. The certain determination which the Pope and his Combined Friends have to root out the Religion of the Gospel in all places, and to begin here as

* Despite.

66

their greatest impediment, is cause sufficient to make us the more vigilant, and to have a wary eye to their doings and proceedings, how smoothly soever they speak or dissemble their Friendships for the time: for let us think surely, that they have joined hands together against us, and if they can, they will procure the Sparks of the Flames that have been so terrible in other Countries, to fly over into *England*, and to kindle as great a Fire here. And as the Pope by open Hostility, as you see, hath shown himself against her Majesty; so the better to Answer in time the purpose that he hath set down in the mean season till they may come to ripeness, he hath and doth by secret practices within this Realm leave nothing unproved, emboldening many undutiful Subjects to stand fast in their disobedience to her Majesty and her Laws, For albeit the pure Religion of the Gospel hath had a free course, and hath been freely Preached now many years within this Realm by the Protection of her Majesty's most Christian Government; yet such have been the practices of the Pope and his secret Ministers, as the obstinate and stiffnecked Papist is so far from being reformed, as he hath gotten Stomach to go backward, and to show his disobedience not only in arrogant words but also in contemptuous Deeds.

To confirm them herein and to increase their number you see how the Pope hath and doth comfort their hollow hearts with Absolutions, Dispensations, Reconciliations, and such other things of *Rome*. You see how lately he hath sent hither a sort of Hypocrites, naming themselves Jesuits, a rabble of Vagrant Friars newly sprung up and running through the World to trouble the Church of God, whose principal Errand is by creeping into the Houses of men of behaviour and reputation, not only to corrupt the Realm with false Doctrines but also under that pretence to stir up Sedition, to the peril of her Majesty and her good Subjects.

How these practices of the Pope have wrought in the disobedient Subjects of this Land is both evident and lamentable to consider. For such impression hath the estimation of the Pope's Authority made in them, as not only those which from the beginning have refused to obey, but many, yea very many of those which divers years together did yield and conform themselves in their open Actions, since the Decrees of that unholy Council of *Trent*, and since the publishing and denouncing of that blasphemous Bull against her Majesty, and since those secret Absolutions and Reconciliations, and the swarming hither of a number of Popish Priests and Monkish Jesuits, have and do utterly refuse to be [of] our Church, or to resort unto Preaching and Prayers. The sequel whereof must needs prove dangerous to the whole State of the Commonwealth.

By this you see what cause we have justly to doubt great mischief threatened to this Realm; therewith you may easily see also how for the preventing and withstanding of the same it behooves her Majesty not only to provide in time sufficient Laws for the continuing of the peaceable Government, but to be ready with Forces to repress all attempts that may be enterprised either by Enemies abroad, or by evil Subjects at home.

What difference there is between the Popes persecuting Church and this mild Church of the Gospel, hath been seen in all Ages, and especially in the late government compared with the merciful time of her Majesty's Reign; the continuance of which Clemency is also to be wished so far as may stand with God's Honour and the Safety of the Realm: but when by long proof we find that this favourable and gentle manner of dealing with the Disobeyers and Contemners of Religion to win them by fair means if it were possible, hath done no good, but hath bred in them a more arrogant and contemptuous Spirit, so as they have not only presumed to disobey the Laws and Orders of the Realm, but also to accept from *Rome* secret Absolutions, Reconciliations and such like; and that by the hands of lewd Renegades, priests and Jesuits, harbouring and entertaining them even in their Houses, thereby showing an Obedience to the Pope, by their direction also nourishing and training up their Children and Kinfolks, not only at home but also abroad in the Seminaries of Popery; now I say it is time for us to look more narrowly and strictly to them, lest as they corrupt, so they prove dangerous members to many born within the entrails of our Commonwealth.

And seeing that the Lenity of the time and the mildness of the Laws heretofore made, are no small cause of their arrogant disobedience, it is necessary that we make a provision of Laws more strict and more severe to constrain them to yield their open Obedience, at the least, to her Majesty in causes of religion, and not to live as they list to the perilous Example of others, and to the encouraging of their own evil affected minds: but if they will needs submit themselves to the Benediction of the Pope, they may feel how little his Curses can hurt us, and how little his Blessings can save them from that punishment which we are able to lay upon them; letting them also find how dangerous it shall be for them to deal with the Pope or any thing of his, or with those Romish Priests and Jesuits, and therewith also how perilous it shall be for those seditious Renegades to enter into the Land, to draw away from her Majesty that Obedience which by the Laws of God and Man are due unto her.

This then is one of the Provisions which we ought to take care of in Council, whereby we may both enjoy still that happy Peace we live in, and the Pope take the less boldness to trouble us by any favour he shall find here.

The next is Provision of Forces sufficient to Answer any violence that may be offered either here or abroad; for the which you know it is requisite that her Majesty do make Preparation both by Sea and by Land.

God hath placed this Kingdom in an Island environed with the Sea as with a natural and strong Wall, whereby we are not subject to those sudden Invasions which other Frontier Countries be. One of our greatest defences standing by Sea, the number of good Ships is of the most importance for us. What the Queen's Navy is, how many notable Ships, and how far behind the Navy of any other Prince, is known to all men, and therewith also it may easily considered how great Charges be incident to the same.

Necessary also it is that her Majesty has Forces by Land sufficient to chastise the Rebels in Ireland, and to repress any Foreign attempts either there or here. For which Services either by Land or by Sea her majesty needs not, as other Princes are fain to do, to entertain necessary Soldiers of Foreign Countries hardly gotten, costly and dangerously kept, and in the end little or no service done them; but may bring sufficient Forces of her own natural Subjects, ready and easy to be levied, that carry with them willing, valiant and faithful minds, such as few Nations may easily compare with. But these Forces with their Furniture and Munitions, can neither be prepared nor maintained to have continuance without provision of Treasure sufficient to bear the Charge.

This belongs to us to consider and that in time there be not lack of the Sinews that must hold together the strength of our Body. And because through the malice of our Enemies her Majesty is driven to keep great Forces in Ireland for the better suppressing of that Rebellion to her exceeding Charge, and for that also it is uncertain how sudden and how great other attempts may be; therefore in reason, our supply of that maintenance ought to be the more, especially the Wars being at this day so costly as every man in his private expence may easily judge. But lest that peradventure some may judge that the Contribution granted by us now five Years past both frankly and dutifully, might suffice for many years without any new; I dare assure you for the acquaintance I have (though I be unworthy) with those her Majesty's Affairs, that the same hath not been sufficient to Answer the extraordinary Charges happened since then, especially those of Ireland, by the one half; but her Majesty hath supplied the rest out of her own Revenues, sparing from her self to serve the necessity of the Realm, and shunning thereby Loans upon interest as a most pestilent Cancer that is able to devour even the States of Princes. Which being so, as it is most true, we are not to think upon the charge that is past, but the good we have received by it, being by that provision well and honourably defended against the malice of our Enemies. And therefore considering the great benefit we have received by the last payment being easily taxed and easily borne, whereby we have kept all the rest in Peace; let us as provident Counsellors of this State prepare again in time that which may be able to withstand the mischiefs intended against us. To do this willingly and liberally, our duty to our Queen and Country, and our Safety move us. The love and duty that we owe to our most Gracious Queen, by whose Ministry God hath done so great things for us, even such as be wonderful in the Eyes of the World, ought to make us more careful for her preservation and security than for our own. A Princess known by long experience to be a principal Patron of the Gospel, virtuous, wise, faithful, just, unspotted in word and deed, merciful, temperate, a maintainer of Peace and Justice amongst her People without respect to Persons; a Queen besides of this noble Realm, our Native Country, renowned of the World, which our Enemies daily gape to over-run, if by force or sleight they could do it; For such a Queen and such a Country, and for the defence of the Honour and

Safety of them both, nothing ought to be dear unto us, that with most willing hearts we should not spend and adventure freely.

The same love and duty that we owe to our Gracious Sovereign, and to this our Native Country, ought to make us all to think upon the Realm of *Ireland* as upon a principal Member of this Crown, having continued so this four hundred Years or more. To lose that Land or any part thereof, which the Enemies seek, would not only bring with it dishonour, but also prove a thing most dangerous to *England* considering the nearness of that Realm to this, and the goodness of so many notable Havens as be there. Again to reform that Nation by planting there of Religion and Justice, which the Enemies labour to interrupt, is most godly and necessary; the neglecting whereof hath and will continue that People in all Irreligion and Disorder, to the great offence of God, and to the infinite Charge of this Realm.

Finally let us be mindful also of our safety, thereby to avoid so great dangers, not seen afar off, but imminent over our heads.

The quietness that we have by the Peaceable Government of her Majesty, doth make us to enjoy all that is ours in more freedom than any Nation under the Sun at this day: but let not that breed in us a careless Security, as though this clear Sun-light could never be darkened; but let us think certainly that the Pope and his Favourers do both envy our Felicity, and leave no practice unsought to over-throw the same. And if any man be so dull (as I trust there be none here) that he cannot conceive the blessedness of this our golden Peace, except he felt the lack of it; let him but cast his Eyes over the Seas, into our Neighbour's Countries, and there behold what trouble the Pope and his Ministers have stirred against such as profess the same Religion of Jesus Christ as we do: there he may find Depopulations and Devastations of whole Provinces and Countries, over-throwing, spoiling and sacking of Cities and Towns, Imprisoning, ransoming and murdering of all kind of People; besides other infinite Calamities which the insolence of War doth usually bring with it.

From these God in his Mercy hath delivered us; but this nevertheless is the State and condition that our Enemies would see us in, if by any device they could bring it to pass; and to that end be then assured they will spare for no cost, nor leave any means untried.

Therefore to conclude seeing the malice of the Pope and his Confederates are so notorious unto us, and seeing the dangers be so great, so evident and so imminent, and seeing that Preparations to withstand them cannot be made without support of the Realm; and seeing that our Duties to God, our Queen and Country, and the necessity that hangs upon our own Safeguards, be reason sufficient to persuade us, let us think upon these matters the weight of them deserves, and so provide in time both by Law to restrain and correct the evil affected Subjects, and by provision of that which shall be requisite for the maintenance of Forces, as our Enemies finding our minds so willing, and our hands so ready to keep in Order our Country, and to furnish her Majesty with all that shall be necessary, may either be discouraged to attempt any thing against us, or if they do, they may find such resistance, as shall bring confusion to themselves, honour to our most Gracious Queen and Safety to all of us.

THE RULES OF THE HOUSE

Parliamentary procedure evolved over generations, and by the mid-seventeenth century had been elaborated in considerable detail. Both Houses followed much the same course in their business. Avoiding acrimonious debate was an important goal of Parliament's procedure, for among men extremely sensitive to questions of honour, a sharp debate might precipitate violence. Circumlocution was a necessary feature of parliamentary speech, where courtesy was a matter upon which lives might depend; thus no member was allowed under any circumstance to brand another a liar – even when it was plain to any who listened that untruths were sometimes presented to the House. When possible, the Speaker determined votes based upon his judgment of preponderant voices, avoiding marking individuals as being 'for' or 'against' a question. For more intractable matters, the carefully contrived method of determining majorities segregated opponents through division, reducing the chance of heated personal exchanges in the House.

Henry Elsynge was the clerk of Parliament, and his 1658 work describes the day-to-day practices of the House of Commons. Using precedents from Elizabethan and Stuart Parliaments, Elsynge presents a detailed picture of the work of members. Most of the procedures he describes remain in force in Parliament to this day. Excerpts presented here deal with decorum in the chamber and voting on bills.

Decorum to be observed in the House

When the Speaker is set in his Chair, every Member is to sit [in] his place with his Head covered.

No Member in coming into the House, or in removing from his place, is to pass between the Speaker and any Member then speaking; nor may cross or go over-thwart the House, or pass from one side to the other while the House is sitting.

No Member is to come into the House with his Head covered, nor to remove from one place to another with his Hat on, nor is to put on his Hat in coming in or removing, until he be sat down in his place.

While the House is sitting, no man ought to speak or whisper to another, to the end the House may not be interrupted when any are speaking; but every one is to attend unto what is spoken: In which case, Penalties have been imposed; as 4 *December* 1640 and at other times.

When any Member intends to speak, he is to stand up in his place uncovered, and address himself to the Speaker, who officially calls such person by his name, that the House may take notice who it is that speaks.

If more then one stand up at once, the speaker is to determine who was first up; and he is to speak, and the other sit down, unless he who was first up sit down again, and give way to the other, or that some other Member stand up and acquaint the House, that another was up before him, whom the Speaker calls, and the House judge it so.

While one is speaking, none else is to stand up or interrupt him until he have done speaking and be sat down, and then any other may rise up and speak, observing the Rules.

Rules and Method of Debate in the House

When a Motion has been made, the same may not be put to the Question until it be debated, or at least have been seconded and prosecuted by one or more persons standing up in their places as aforesaid, and then the same may be put to the Question, if the Question be called for by the House, or their general sense be known, which the Speaker is to demand, unless any Member stand so to speak.

When a Motion has been made, that Matter must receive a determination by a question, or be laid aside by the general sense of [the] House before another be entertained.

If the Matter moved do receive a Debate *pro & contra*, in that Debate none may speak more then once to the Matter: And after some time spent in the Debate, the Speaker collecting the sense of the House upon the Debate, is to reduce the same into a Question, which he is to propound to the end, the House in their Debate afterwards may be kept to the Matter of that Question, if the same be approved by the House to contain the substance of the former Debate.

Every Question is to be put first in the Affirmative: viz: *As many as are of opinion that* (repeating the words of the Question) *say, Yea*. And then the Negative thus: *As many as are of another opinion say, No*. To which Question every Member ought to give his Vote one way or other, and the Speaker is to declare his opinion, whether the *Yea's* or the *No's* have it, which is to stand as the Judgement of the House. But if any Member before any new Motion made, shall stand up and Declare, That he doth believe the *Yea's*, or *No's* (as the case shall be) have it, contrary to the Speakers opinion, then the Speaker is to give direction for the House to divide, declaring whether the *Yes's* or the *No's* are to go forth.

Upon dividing the House, the Speaker is to nominate two of those that are in the Affirmative, and two of the Negatives to count the House; which four (each of them having a Staff in his hand) are to count the number of the Persons who remain sitting in the House, and then to stand within the Door, two on the one side and two on the other, and to count the Number of them who went forth as they come in.

While the House is thus divided or dividing, no Member may Speak, nor (unless it to be to go forth upon the Division) remove out of his place.

When the House is thus told, those two of the Tellers who are of the number of those who have the major Votes, standing on the right hand, and the two others on the left at the Bar, (the rest being set in their places) are to come from thence up to the Table together, (making the usual Obeisance to the House three times; once at the Bar, again in the middle of the House, and again when they're come to the Table) And that person who stands on the right hand, is to declare to the Speaker the number of the *Yea's* (who set or went out as the Case is) and of the *No's*: and then with like reverence to depart into their places; after which, Mr Speaker is to report the same to the House.

If the Affirmatives have the major Votes by the judgement of the Speaker or (in case of division) upon the division, the Clerk is to enter the Vote, *Resolved*. If the Negatives, then he is to enter it thus; The Question being put (setting down the Words of the Question) It passed in the Negative.

Upon the division, if the Members appear to be equal, then the Speaker is to declare his Vote, whether he be a *Yea* or *No*, which in this Case is the casting Voice; but in other Cases, the Speaker gives no Vote.

WHIGS AND TORIES

Although the Civil War did not permanently establish Parliament as sovereign, the Revolution of 1688 did. Having deposed James II and bestowed the crown upon his Protestant daughter and son-in-law, Mary II and William III, many of the questions about authority and the constitution that had generated controversy for a century or more were at last settled. But controversy remained; in fact the post-Revolutionary constitution enshrined controversy at the heart of politics. The political parties, emerging first during the debates over the succession under Charles II, had, by the turn of the century, grown and matured. Politics became partisan in a way no one could have imagined a century before. Whig and Tory struggled bitterly over office, the battle sharpened by frequent elections and the near-constant presence of a Parliament in Westminster. That party rivalries did not degenerate into outright civil war testifies to remarkable changes in the political climate: divisions as deep led to bloodshed in 1642. But those involved in the battle never suspected that the stakes were any less high than in the fateful year of '42, and so it was easier to demonize the opposition who threatened (depending upon one's perspective) monarchical tyranny and slavery or parliamentary tyranny and slavery.

Partisans carried on the war of words both on the hustings and in the streets, during carefully organized demonstrations and less-carefully organized, but nevertheless terrifying, riots. More startling was the explosion of printed political literature. By the 1690s both sides had practically abandoned traditional attempts at censorship, and embraced a free-for-all of political speech. Here are samples of the genre, one venomously anti-Tory, the other, anti-Whig. Both reproduce the sorts of arguments marshalled for the public: it was not sophisticated, but it was effective. The first was published anonymously, the second came from the pen of Charles Davenant, a Tory playwright and propagandist.

A Smith and Cutler's Plain Dialogue about
WHIG and TORY

S.   Good morrow Neighbour, what news have we this morning?

C.   There is a great noise of the *French* baffling our Fleet, which differently affects as come to buy Swords at my shop.

S.   I find the same, with persons that come to buy Arms from me. If you note your men, you'll find the countenance of the Tory well pleased; but the Whig incensed. The Tory obstructs our preparations by subtle Tricks, the Whig is intent to remove the Reproach and prevent our danger. He fears nothing as the Treachery of Tory, and therefore is more forward to act separate from him, than in conjunction with him.

C.   The difference between these Whigs and Tories is too great in every thing as if they were neither of one Religion Country, or Nativity.

S.   I hear a confused Talk of Whig and Tory, I could wish I well understood what is intended by these Names and how I may know the men.

C.   The whole Kingdom is divided into Whigs and Tory, and ever was; and will be distinguished by that which these later names do signify it concerns us to understand them, that we undo our selves by following the wrong side in our Votes or otherwise; for our Nation's safety or ruin depends on this: whether the Whigs or Tory do prevail.

S.   I have been made to believe that all the Church of *England* are Tories, and only the Dissenters are the Whigs.

C.   What can be plainer mistake? For the Heads and chief Body of the Whigs are in the Church of *England*, and Dissenters are only Helpers to the Church Whigs, as the Papists do assist the Tory. Observe in all Elections, are they not generally constant Churchmen whom the Dissenters vote for, look into late Convention and Parliament, you'll not find there Twenty Dissenters, though it was called a Whiggish Parliament.

S.   I see it's a cheat that Dissenters are the only Whigs. But others tell me that all such are Tories who are for Monarchy, and all the Whigs for a Commonwealth.

C.   That's false as the other. The Whigs are for an *English* Monarchy, though not a *French* one. The Whig is for the Commonweal, that is for the general good of the Nation, but he is not against Kingly Government; yea he is zealous for K. W. and Q. M. whereas the Tory would enslave the

Nation under the Name of Monarchy, and destroy Parliament and Liberty under the name of Commonwealth.

S. It seems then that civil Rights divide the Whigs and Tory, the Whig is concerned to preserve them, the Tory to destroy them.

C. You have the true notion, especially if you add, that a safe design of enriching himself on the Ruins of public Liberty is the Heart of Toryism, the very Tory himself would not be Slave, but that he may be able to enslave others that are below him.

S. Can you tell me, what are the principles of a Tory?

C. It's hard to resolve you because a Tory's Principles are suited to all new occasions, and they never govern him further then a selfish end can be served, yet they have any principles, with most they are these: to scruple nothing so it may serve a present turn, to set up the will of a prince above all Laws so that the prince will gratify him, to anoint the succession with a *Jus divinum* if it serve the Tory interest; to give Bribes for Places, that he may cheat the Public; to cry up Nonresistance when he hath all the Power, and bear nothing when stripped of all chief Employments; to hector bravely rather than fight; to make a tearing noise, when he cannot answer reason; to insult over all below him and basely all in power. To cry up the Church, or such popular terms for destroying that Government they cannot bewitch. To oppose by all arts the employment of a Whig, and grossly belie every honest Candidate in any election. To buy Fool's Votes in all Elections, that he may sell their Birthright, and get back his tribe in a large Pension, for an oppressive Tax. To do no Man right, unless he purchase it and sell his Country to his utmost influence, where he can gain a little by the bargain. In short, if you tell me the instincts of an abject selfish Spirit in all occasions, those be a Tory's Principles.

S. God deliver me and mine from the power of a party acting by such rules. But what are the Principles of a Whig?

C. They are the common Sentiments of every Soul that's virtuous, brave and manly, to love his Country, to . . . uphold its civil liberties, to expect no more than Law and justice allows him, and to expect all that. To defend his Birthright and Laws, if fundamentally invaded; and yet be at hardships in his own concerns, so the nation prosper: To deserve an employment, and not buy it: To manage his office by rules of Justice and Humanity. To resent an injury from his Superior and to treat his Foes with equity, yea, to pity even a Tory in distress; to fight rather than huff; to satisfy his Judgment in every vote, whoever is offended; to enrich his Family by diligence, and not by the Spoils of others; to quit the best employment rather than to bury his Country: to have all power regulated by the Laws; to have Kingship and Parliament conform to our English constitution, which is adopted to the common good: To scorn a base action, perjury, falsehood and little Tricks.

The true picture of a modern Whig, &c.
Whiglove and Double

Wh. Sir I am glad to meet you at *Garraways* [a famous London Whig coffee house]. I was coming to your House.

Do. And I came hither on purpose to find you: 'Tis very early, and there is no Body upon the exchange, when you have drunk your Tea, if you please let us take a Turn there. Pray when do you think of going into the Country?

Wh. In three days at farthest; but I was resolved not to stir till I had received your particular Directions how I shall behave my self in my Progress.

Do. What Circuit have our noble Friends allotted you?

Wh. I am ordered for *Kent* and *Sussex*; my Cousin *Rattlehead* went yesterday for *Essex*, Suffolk and *Norfolk*; Mr *Selfish* and *Mr. Project* have all the North committed to their Care; besides the common Concern, they have Business of their own, they are gone to look upon some Estates that are to be sold, and have a great deal of Money to lay out.

Do. Indeed they have made a fine Hand of these Times, you and I knew 'em both ten Years ago not worth a Groat [fourpence], and now each of 'em has his threescore thousand Pounds ready for a Purchase.

Wh. And the Wonder is, they have got all this in little sneaking Employments, which heretofore did not afford a Man a Bottle of Claret at Night.

Do. Well much good may do their Hearts, for though they have notoriously cheated the King and Kingdom, they are very honest and hearty to us. There is no Lie ever so gross they are not willing to spread abroad to carry on our Designs. They disperse news, Rail at some, and Cry up others, just as they are directed; and, to speak Truth; there are not two men in *England* that do more Service to the Party.

Do. I have good store of Money in my Pocket; and he who has that shall be esteemed and courted, let his Birth be never so mean, or his Life never so infamous.

Wh. This has been a happy Revolution to you, *Mr. Double*, for if I am not mis-informed, Matters are well mended with you of late Years.

Do. They are So, Thanks to my Industry. I am now worth Fifty thousand Pound, and 14 years ago I had not Shoes to my Feet.

Wh. This is a strange and sudden Rise.

Do. Alas 'tis nothing, I can name you fifty of our Friends who have got much better Fortunes since the Revolution, and from as poor Beginnings.

Wh. It would serve as a good Instruction if you would please to let me know how you did rise in the World. I am a Gentleman born to some Fortune and have good Relations, yet I can do nothing, and rather grow worse than better in my Estate, notwithstanding that all along I have been as hearty a Whig as the best of you.

Do. That's true, but you have been always a Whig out of Principle, and we have no regard for such People at all, they are Volunteers that will serve us for nothing; we value none but those who are Whigs out of Interest, and who . . . are ready to do any thing, Good, Bad, Indifferent, that may promote our Designs. I'll lay a Guinea you think I was always a Whig.

Wh. Truly, Sir, I ever took you for an Original staunch Whig, and for one who had despised the Church, and disliked Kingly Government from your very Cradle.

Do. Alas you are utterly mistaken, and if you can make any Profit from Example, I will give you a short Narrative of my whole Life. I was first bound to a Shoemaker in *London*, and being an impudent young Rogue, I got into the Gang of Loyal Apprentices that Addressed to King Charles II* and I was one of those who were Treated with *Hyde-Park* Venison at the *Wonder* Tavern. My Grandmother, who sold Barley-broth and Furmenty by *Fleet-ditch*, died and left me three hundred Pound, with which I set up for a Gentleman and a Spark; and I was so remarkable a *Tory*, that I got a Place in the Customs of about a hundred Pounds a year. But in King James's time, the Commissioners of the Customs detected me in a notorious Fraud, and turned me out, upon which I became a Malcontent . . . From the time I lost my Office, I became a furious Whig, and as long as my Money lasted, I went to all the discontented Clubs in Town where we drank Confusion to the Government, and talked Treason Dagger out of Sheath. But I was still so wise to set down in Writing when I came home, what had passed among us.

Wh. Why did you that?

Do. To be safe; for with those Materials I was prepared to be a Witness in case any one of us had been taken up, and to have saved my self, I was ready to hang all my Companions.

Wh. 'Twas indeed a piece of Caution our Party has always observed, nor have they been afterwards a lot the worse thought on for it.

Do. My Grandmother's Legacy was soon spent, and at last I was reduced to that necessity, that I was forced to be a Corrector of private Press in a Garret, for three Shillings a Week; and in this miserable Condition did I languish for near three Years; but at last Fortune vouchsafed to give me a favourable Smile, and it was just the Week after the King† landed at *Torbay*. I had eaten nothing all day, and had not a farthing in my Pocket, but knew an Ale-house where I could have Credit for a black

---

* These loyal addresses, organized by Tories, denounced those who supported the exclusion of James, Duke of York, from the throne.
† William III.

Pudding and a Pot of Ale; thither I stole about six at Night, and found sitting at the Kitchen-Fire, Smoking his Pipe, an *Essex* Gentleman, who was formerly used to haunt *Richard's* Coffee House: He was Half Seas over, and I perceived had been drinking the Prince of *Orange's* Health. With my familiar Confidence I presently accosted him; *Mr. Aletope*, said I, I am mighty glad of the Honour to meet you here. He knew me, but seeing me in such a shabby Dress; he received me somewhat coldly; upon which I drew him into a Corner of the Room and whispered him that I was now in disguise, that for two Years I had been Abroad, in *Rome*, in *Germany*, and in *Holland*, to carry on the good Work; that I was just come from *Exeter* with Letters from our Friends in the *West*. I told him I was going back tomorrow Morning with bills of Exchange for one hundred and fifty thousand Pound, and with Letters from five and forty Lords. In short, I told him above an hundred impossible Stories and Lies, all which he listened to gravely, and swallowed greedily; and when I had done, he began to think me a Person of some Importance. And when the convention was dissolved [in 1689], it came into my Head, that the best way to raise my Fortune, was to get my self chosen Parliament Man; for I was discerning enough to see what Card would turn up trump. Down therefore I went into *Cornwall* in a good Equipage, and, with store of Guineas in my Pocket.

Wh. But you did not succeed in that Undertaking.

Do. No, I was disappointed by an unlucky Chance. I had secured the Election, and bribed the Majority of the Corporation, and was huzza'd into the Borough: But, as the Devil would have it, one who had been my Fellow apprentice knew me; and as soon he saw my Calash stop, he came bawling up, took me by the Hand, and cried, Honest *Tom Double* thou art welcome, who thought to see thee in *Cornwall?* My Electors stared to see him so familiar with their Member, and began to shove him away; but he would not take it so, and growing Angry, bellowed out, What a plague you think I don't know *Tom Double!* Why he and I were Fellow apprentices with *Jack Last*, the Shoemaker in *Fleet-street*. I took upon my self to be mightily affronted, and fain would have out-faced the Man. He persisted in his Story, I to deny it; but Truth has something in it irresistible, he was believed, and I was thought an Impostor, and the Rabble began to hoot me.

Wh. What did you do then?

Do. I bore up as well as I could, and went to my Inn. But at Night the mayor came and told me there was an Uproar in the Town, and a Plot to toss me in a Blanket next day, if I did not get away as fast as I could. I gave Credit to his Intelligence, and stole out of the Borough next Morning by three a Clock.

Further reading

G.R. Elton, *The Parliament of England* (Cambridge, 1986).

Mark A. Kishlansky, *Parliamentary Selection* (Cambridge, 1988).

S.E. Lehmberg, *The Reformation Parliament, 1529–36* (Cambridge, 1970).

Jennifer Loach, *Parliament under the Tudors* (Oxford, 1991).

John S. Roskell, *Parliament and Politics in Late Medieval England* (London, 1981).

Conrad Russell, *Parliaments and English Politics, 1621–29* (Oxford, 1979).

David L. Smith, *The Stuart Parliaments 1603–89* (Oxford, 1999).

W.A. Speck, *Tory and Whig: The Struggle in the Constituencies 1701–15* (London, 1970).

6

THE BRITISH CONTEXT

English dominance of the British archipelago was always contested. Relations among the British nations under the Tudors and Stuarts ranged from being merely difficult to bloody warfare. The English quest for control in Scotland and Ireland began centuries before and continued unabated in the early modern period. Ireland probably suffered the most from English attentions. Henry VII, with reason, considered it a nursery of rebellion, and tightened English control over the island, bringing Irish government formally under English supervision with Poynings's Law (1495). His successes were limited, and the English government expended vast quantities of treasure and lives in repeated attempts to subdue Irish resistance. Major rebellions shook English rule in the 1580s, 1590s, 1640s, and 1690s. Each uprising led to increased brutality and new schemes designed to tame the Irish. Henry VIII proclaimed himself king of Ireland in 1541, and initiated a policy of 'surrender and regrant' – persuading Irish leaders to accept titles and estates on English terms. The limited success of this policy led Queen Elizabeth to begin the plantation of English settlers on seized Irish lands. Under James, English plantations were reinforced by Scottish settlements in the northern province of Ulster. The process of remaking Ireland as a Protestant, Anglo-Scots settler society gained headway. The marginalization of traditional Irish culture and leadership resulted in the massive rebellion of 1641. Ireland plunged into a welter of violence and disorder that lasted into the 1650s, when Cromwell's government imposed peace by conquest. The Interregnum authorities tried a new tactic: the forcible expulsion of all Irish from their native lands, resettling them in the wilderness of Connaught, in the far west of the island. The advent of the devoutly Catholic James II in 1685 briefly offered the Irish majority hope, but his expulsion from England prompted still more bloodshed, as the exiled king sought to rally the Irish against his rival, William of Orange. James's hopes to use Ireland as a springboard for an invasion of England were dashed at the Battle of the Boyne in July 1690.

The king fled to his permanent exile in France, and once again the English grip tightened. More Irish lands were seized and given to Protestants (both English and Dutch). More punitive laws were aimed against Catholics. By Queen Anne's death in 1714, England had erected a fairly stable – albeit fragile – order in Ireland, based upon the dominance of a small Protestant minority, legal discrimination against Catholics, and the liberal use of force.

Scotland too suffered the attentions of its ambitious neighbour, though it was for a time sheltered by the accession of its Royal Family to the English throne. James VI became James I of England in March 1603, and so began a long period of neglect – occasionally benign, but often of a less generous sort. The Stuarts tended to leave Scotland in the hands of a small group of nobles, sitting as the Scottish Privy Council. Scottish affairs rarely impinged upon the monarch's consciousness. Only in the event of crisis – as in the late 1630s – did London look north. Charles I's disastrous attempts to meddle with Scotland's beloved kirk in 1636–7 sparked a rebellion that would finally unleash war throughout Britain. Scots participated enthusiastically in the Civil Wars, and played an important role in the war in England, through their occasional interventions south of the border. Scotland's troublesome nature forced Cromwell to impose a union in 1654, but that expedient lapsed with the Restoration. Scotland's refusal to submit meekly to England under William III and Anne led to the Union of 1707. Unlike Cromwell's military coup, the new Union tempted the Scots with guarantees for the kirk, Scottish law, and offers of access to once-forbidden English markets. Even so, the Scots accepted Union only reluctantly, and their resistance would continue well into the eighteenth century (see below, Chapter 10, on the Union).

Welsh integration had gone further than either Scottish or Irish, for England's grip on the principality was of longer standing. The process had gone farthest in the south, where an Anglicized Welsh gentry dominated the countryside. But there were nevertheless parts of Wales where English power remained feeble, especially in the mountains. It was to remedy this perennial difficulty that the Tudors founded the Council of the Marches of Wales. This body was supposed to act as the Crown's eyes and ears in the province, and had extraordinary powers to maintain order. While the Council did manage to safeguard English rule – there were no major uprisings in Wales under the Tudors or Stuarts – transforming the principality into just another part of England was a process still incomplete by the end of the Stuart period.

GOVERNING TUDOR WALES

Wales occupied a special place in the mind of Tudor monarchs. The dynasty sprang from Welsh soil, and taming its turbulent population was a priority. The Crown's chosen instrument was the Council of Wales and the Marches, headquartered at Ludlow, and presided over by a peer appointed by the sovereign. The president's difficult task was to advance the Anglicization of the principality and to preserve order, goals that were not always complementary. The Council's authority covered all of Wales as well as the English counties along its borders. The president's powers were broad, based as they were in the royal prerogative, but they were also vaguely defined and at times controversial. Complicating matters was the tendency of the Privy Council to intervene in Welsh affairs, at times ignorantly. What follows is a series of entries from the Privy Council's registers dealing with Wales, in which the demands of central government for order are undercut by its meddling in individual cases.

27 September 1542

Whereas for certain slanderous words spoken [of] the Lord President of the Council in the Marches of Wales, by two lewd persons, inhabitants of the town of Ludlow, [who] were therefore committed by the said President to ward, and yet foreasmuch as the matter touched the said President he would take no further order therein, but committed the matter to the Privy Council, this day letters were sent to him from the Council with answer for that foreasmuch as the matter was not great he should do well to content himself with the said imprisonment and for the rest with a good lesson to dismiss them and set them again at large.

8 May 1546

A letter was addressed to the President and Council of Wales signifying unto them that where the King's Majesty had pardoned Lowes ap Watkyns, his Highness' servant, of the murder of Roger ap Watkyns, which notwithstanding, the wife of the said Roger did not cease to prosecute the appeal; his Majesty's pleasure was that by such good means as they could best devise they should see her pacified, and to stay the matter from preceding to any further issue, so as the woman may be contented and yet the law not seem to be impeached.

26 July 1601

A letter to the Sheriff and Justices of the Peace in the county of Stafford. We have received a letter from the Council of the Marches of Wales and therewith a petition in the name of many townships and villages presented of late unto that Council complaining of notorious disorders and outrages committed by many lewd and wicked persons usually associating themselves together at a place called Areley within the county of Stafford, where they behaving themselves (as by the petition you may perceive) little better then outlaws do escape unpunished and give cause of fears and unsafe living to her Majesty's good subjects thereabouts. In perusal of which petition as we do find very just cause of complaint and need of redress, so it seems strange unto us that any such notorious disorders and abuses in that county should be in such manner continued and pass without due remedy and punishment, for although the said place of Areley be (as we are informed) in a far remote part of the shire from the Justice of the Peace, yet we cannot think that any part of the shire is, and we are sure it should not be, so void of good government but that regard may easily be had both to the preventing and to the punishing of such offenses, and therefore we cannot but impute it for great slackness and negligence unto you or some of you, the Justices of the Peace in that county, that should cause diligent enquiry to be made and punishment to be inflicted upon such offenders, wherein it shall be your part with earnest diligence to make amends for any former slackness.

And therefore we do hereby pray and require you, the Sheriff and the Justices of the Peace or of so many of you as by the situation of your dwellings may most conveniently take care of this service to meet together and to take present order for redress of the aforesaid abuses and misdemeanours by diligent enquiry of the offenders and by the apprehension of them, and by causing such punishment to be inflicted as to every of them according to their several offences as due by the law, and furthermore by all good and lawful means to procure that the said place of Areley and the inhabitants of the country thereabouts may be cleared and freed from such fear and disturbance as is caused by those lewd assemblies of evil persons. For the better performance whereof you shall do well to give notice unto the Justices of the Peace near unto you in the counties adjoining, that if the said offenders shall betake themselves into the said counties adjoining they may use the like means for their apprehension and punishment, and to make the said Justices acquainted with this our direction. And so, &c.

GOVERNMENT AND REBELLION IN ELIZABETHAN IRELAND

Hugh O'Neill, second Earl of Tyrone (c.1540–1616), dominated the northern province of Ulster in Ireland, and when he abandoned his allegiance to the English Crown in 1595, Elizabeth's rule over the Irish was badly shaken. Tyrone defeated English forces sent against him, and in 1601 he negotiated Spanish aid for his cause. The possibility of the complete overthrow of the English regime loomed. In 1600 the Queen appointed a new Lord Deputy of Ireland, Charles Blount, Lord Mountjoy (c.1562–1606). It was Mountjoy's difficult task to prevent catastrophe for England. A professional soldier who had already fought the Spanish in the Low Countries, Mountjoy was the man for the job. A combination of skill and brutality forced the Spanish to withdraw their troops from Ireland, and Tyrone's forces were slowly ground down until he made peace with the newly arrived James VI and I in 1603. Mountjoy became a hero in England, and was raised to an earldom; Tyrone, despite the lenient terms of his surrender, ultimately fled to Europe and died in exile in Rome.

What follow are letters from Mountjoy to the Council in London that illustrate the violence and brutality of Anglo-Irish affairs in the early modern period.

19 July 1601. The Lord Deputy Mountjoy, Sir Richard Wingfield, and Sir George Bourchier, to the Privy Council

Having, since our last letters to your Lordships from the Moyerie, planted a garrison in Lecale and another at Armagh, and being able to undertake no further at that time, both for want of victuals, tools and carriages, I, the Deputy, remained in the field, thereby to cause the traitor to keep his forces the longer together, the sooner by it to weaken him, and desired the Marshal and Sir George Bourchier to repair to Dublin, the one to haste away the. . . beeves and carriages, the other tools and munitions. While I encamped some three mile[s] from the Newry, Sir Henry Davers drew from Armagh into the fastness where Brian McArt encamped, had the killing of divers of his men, took many of his horses, the spoil of much baggage, and at that time took a prey of above 300 cows from Magennis, and since (before my return to Armagh) took some chief horses from Tyrone's camp, entered into the MacCanns' country, of [*sic*] the greatest fastness of any in Ireland, and brought from thence a great prey. But being himself over-wearied with the travel of that night, and putting a strong guard of horse upon the cows while they grazed, by the negligence of the corporal and guard, that wearied with overtravel had withdrawn themselves to sleep, he lost the greatest part of the prey he had taken by Tyrone himself, who the same morning drew thither with his whole force. The country answering their rising out for the general hosting exceeding slowly and backwardly, and the Council certifying me from Dublin that neither the victuals, the most part of the munitions, nor any pick-axes, were as then arrived, and besides that the carriages and beeves appointed to be brought in were in the greatest part like to fail us, I thought fit to fall back unto Dundalk with three companies only for a few days, thrusting the rest of the army to those garrisons that fronted nearest unto the rebels' countries.

On Thursday, the 16th, whilst some were busily working at the fort, we sent out a regiment in the highway towards Dungannon, to discover what way we shall find it to be, and whether the rebels did possess it. When they came somewhat beyond Benburb, being, a greater fastness, the rebels fell into a very hot skirmish with them, which was well maintained on both sides by the space of two hours and above, Tyrone with all his horse and foot coming in, which were laid thereabout for such a purpose, and on our side other regiments being drawn from our camp for seconds, as providing for that which might and did happen. In this fight were many hurt and killed on both sides, though we verily think (and might perceive by our eyes, for our men cut off almost as many of their heads, as we had in all killed) many more of their side than of ours. For ours did many times make very good retreats, our purpose not being to go further, and then would they come on so hotly, as if they had gotten the day upon us, even upon good hard ground without their woods, though their woods were always round about them; and then would ours turn and charge them to their woods again, which makes us assure ourselves we have killed many of

84

them. The number of the hurt and slain on our side will appear unto your Lordships by the enclosed note, which we have caused truly to be collected, as we will answer it upon our credits. And yet, if we had lost many more, being Irish, as in a manner all these were, for there was but one Englishman killed, being mine own chaplain, that would needs strive to be the next man unto me, we think we have done Her Majesty almost as good service, as by killing so many of the rebels; for so those were, or would have been, upon any slight occasion. And therefore we hold it a very good piece of policy, to make them cut one another's throats, without which this kingdom will lie never in quiet.

{Postscript}

We have of new proclaimed a reward for Tyrone's head, because we hear no man durst take notice of the old proclamation, and we have caused our scouts to publish it, that the rebels cannot but hear thereof.

THE SCOTTISH PRIVY COUNCIL AT WORK, 1617

James VI's accession to the English throne as James I deprived Scotland of its king's physical presence. James wasted no time departing Edinburgh for London – indeed, some on both sides of the border thought his haste to leave unseemly. But nevertheless in the absence of its sovereign Scotland required an executive. The Scottish Privy Council undertook the job. Like its counterpart in the south, the Scottish Council was the main executive authority in the country, but with the king in distant London, its members had more freedom to act. After 1603 none of the Stuarts devoted themselves to Scottish affairs unless there was a crisis, and ordinarily the Council, composed of judges, lawyers, and peers, handled most of the routine administration. Many complained that its membership was dominated by a self-interested clique, but it must be admitted that ruling Scotland in the absence of its monarch was never easy. Poor (by comparison to the English) and often quarrelsome, the Scots gave the councillors plenty to do. The Council's business ran the gamut from murder to markets, but a persistent source of trouble was religion. What follows is the record of a session in which councillors tried to get to the bottom of an alleged riot in Edinburgh, the result of royal interference in the selection of a minister. Scots were fiercely protective of their ecclesiastical rights, and James VI and I was no less determined to protect his own. Inevitably clashes occurred. In this case the community closed ranks and denied that there had been any tumult at all.

22 January 1617

The which day William Nesbitt, Provost, James Nesbitt . . . and John Fairlie, Beillies, David Aikinheade, Deane of G[ild, and] Johnne Byris, Treasurer, with some of the Council of the burgh of Edinburgh, Mr Patrick Galloway, Mr John Hall, Mr Andrew Ramsay, Mr William Strutheris, and Mr Thomas Sydserff, ministers of Edinburgh, appeared before the Lords, and they being demanded anent [about] the form and manner of the tumultuous and mutinous coming of a number of the inhabitants of the said burgh to that meeting and assembly which was kept in the said burgh for the [nomination] and election of some persons for their ministry, it was answered by the said Provost and by the ministers that the form and order usually observed within the said burgh anent the election . . . of the ministry is to warn the whole neighbourhood of the town to convene at the time and place appointed to give their opinion and voices anent the said election, and that this warning is commonly made from the pulpit by the ministers; and that accordingly the Provost and Baillies, with the old and new Council and the old and new Session, with a number of other neighbours of the town, convened in the Little Kirk upon the seventeenth day of December last in a very peaceable, quiet, and modest manner, without any kind of appearance or show of mutiny or tumult, and that not any of them spoke any word while they were called upon and their voices and opinion craved anent the matter which was in hand; and that no man was called upon but these of the old and new Council and of the old and new Session, with some four grave and honest men of the town who had borne office and charge within the same; and that they all delivered their voices with that kind of respect and modesty that became them. And the said Provost and Baillies and ministers declare that they never saw a more calm, peaceable, and quiet meeting within the burgh of Edinburgh [than] they saw that day. And, they being demanded upon what occasion the listing of Mr Robert Balcanquell for one of their ministers was brought in question, seeing he had been once formerly and orderly [nominated], it was answered that he was once [nominated], and at the second meeting of the brethren upon the seventeenth day of December last the matter was then brought in question by a number of persons who were present, who alleged that they had the first [nomination], because they apprehended that, albeit they had nominated him, that notwithstanding the nomination and approbation of him to be their minister would be reserved to the town; and, seeing his Majesty by his most gracious letter sent to the town in favour of Mr Robert had reserved to the town their own freedom and liberty in their election, and had only recommended Mr Robert conditionally so as he was found qualified, they therefore desired that they might be heard anew; and, the same being with some difficulty granted, it then past through with plurality of votes that he should be first tried afore he was nominated. And the Provost and Baillies declared that they and the Council convened that same day in the forenoon afore the general meeting of the whole company and resolved amongst themselves to stand to their first nomination of Mr Robert.

Further reading

Brendan Bradshaw and John Morrill, eds, *The British Problem c.1534-1707* (New York, 1996).

Nicholas Canny, *Making Ireland British, 1580–1650* (Oxford, 2000).

Peter Donald, *An Uncounselled King: Charles I and the Scottish Troubles, 1637–41* (Cambridge, 1991).

R.A. Griffiths and Roger S. Thomas, *The Principality of Wales in the Later Middle Ages* (Cardiff, 1972).

Philip Jenkins, *The Making of a Ruling Class: The Glamorgan Gentry* (Cambridge, 1983).

James Lydon, *Ireland in the Later Middle Ages* (Dublin, 1973).

Roger A. Mason, *Scots and Britons: Scottish Political Thought and the Union of 1603* (Cambridge, 1994).

Ian. D. Whyte, *Scotland Before the Industrial Revolution: An Economic and Social History, c.1050–c.1750* (London, 1995).

Glanmor Williams, *Recovery, Reorientation and Reformation: Wales 1415–1642* (Oxford, 1987).

Part II

POLITICS IN ACTION

7

THE EARLY TUDORS

LAMBERT SIMNEL'S IMPOSTURE (1487)

Seized forcibly from Richard III on Bosworth Field in the summer of 1485, Henry Tudor's crown was by no means secure. Although a Parliament declared his title good, Henry knew as well as anyone that his power might not survive a challenge from an enemy. The new king's experience taught that the English throne was a perilous seat. Moreover, there was no shortage of rivals with closer ties to the blood royal than Henry's own. Although Richard III had probably murdered the two most dangerous members of the Royal Family – his nephews Richard and Edward, sons of Edward IV – there was still another potential threat alive in 1487: Edward, earl of Warwick. Son of the duke of Clarence, Edward IV's younger brother, Warwick might plausibly claim to be the true king. Henry wasted no time locking him up in the Tower, but there he remained, alive.

The uncertainty surrounding the fates of both the princes and Warwick allowed Richard Symonds (or Simons), an ambitious Oxford priest, to hatch a plot that threatened Henry's throne. A local boy, Lambert Simnel, was the key to Symond's plans. Simnel, the son of a tradesman, apparently bore some resemblance to Edward IV, and after a period of instruction in courtly manners, Symonds revealed his young protégé as Edward, Earl of Warwick. Taking him to Ireland, where he found support from disgruntled nobles there, Symonds engineered Simnel's coronation as 'Edward VI' in Dublin. In June 1487 Simnel and his manipulators invaded England leading a force of Irish troops and German mercenaries paid for by Margaret, duchess of Burgundy – Edward IV's sister. Symonds hoped to repeat Henry's own success two years earlier by drawing support from the restless English nobility, but his hopes were dashed at the Battle of Stoke (16 June 1487). Henry triumphed, killing many of his enemies and capturing Symonds and Simnel. Simnel, who Henry believed was a mere pawn, ended his life long after, having served in the royal kitchens and as the king's falconer. The account of Simnel's brief career as the king of England excerpted here is by Polydore Vergil (c.1470–1555), whose *Anglicae Historia* included Henry VII's reign. Vergil was an accomplished humanist scholar who had made a name for himself in the papal service, and who came to England in 1502. He was hardly unbiased; Henry VII appointed him archdeacon of Wells, a lucrative place in the English church, and his history, while not completely uncritical, is notably kind to its patron. In 1582 the Privy Council proclaimed his *Historia* to be required reading in English schools, and it was the source of much of the historical knowledge of generations of students, one of whom was Shakespeare, whose history plays reflect Vergil's text.

Meanwhile, from something petty and feigned there arose a major disturbance. For indeed from the time when Edward [IV] having overthrown Henry VI, arrogated to himself the kingdom of England, men were so nourished on sectionalism that they could not later desist from it, and so confounded their divine and human obligations by every conceivable means that, blinded by partisan devotion, led not by reason but by evil and distorted partiality, they were distracted into a thousand factions. This mischief, which was largely subdued by Edward after the destruction of almost all the descendants of Henry VI, was renewed by his brother Richard, who by his example suggested to others the stirring up of new factions and the embarking on other schemes whereby they might acquire for themselves power or privileges. Latest among such adventurers was a lowborn priest called Richard, whose surname was Simons, a man as cunning as he was corrupt. He evolved a villainous deed of this sort, by which he might trouble the country's tranquility. At Oxford, where he devoted himself to scholarship, he brought up a certain youth who was called Lambert Simnel. He first taught the boy courtly manners, so that if ever he should pretend the lad to be of royal descent (as he had planned to do) people would the more readily believe it and have absolute trust in the bold deceit. Some time having elapsed since Henry VII had (as soon as he had gained power) flung Edward, the only son of the duke of Clarence, into the Tower of London, and since it was popularly rumoured that Edward had been murdered in that place, the priest Richard decided that the time had arrived when he might profitably execute the villainy he had projected. He changed the boy's name and called him Edward, by which name the duke of Clarence's son was known, and forthwith departed with him to Ireland. There he secretly summoned a meeting of a considerable number of Irish nobles whom he understood by popular report to be ill-disposed to Henry. Having secured their trust, he described to them how he had saved from death the duke of Clarence's son, and how he had brought him to that land, where (so he had heard) the name and family of King Edward were always cherished. The story was readily believed by the nobles and was soon communicated to others. It was accepted without dispute to such an extent that Thomas Fitzgerald, the Irish-born chancellor of King Henry in the island, was among the first to entertain the boy as if he were of royal descent and to begin to give him all his support. Fitzgerald first called together all his own followers [and] informed them of the boy's arrival and how the kingdom of England was his by right as the only male of royal descent, and exhorted them on that account to support him in an attempt to restore the boy to the throne. He then communicated the project to other nobles who, having heard his plan, promised all the help in their power. Thus it quickly came about that the news spread to all Irish cities, which spontaneously transferred their allegiance to the youth and called him king. Then the leaders of the conspiracy sent secret messengers to those in England whom they knew had been of King Richard's party, to implore them to remain loyal and decide upon supporting the boy . . . When these things were told to Henry he was profoundly disturbed (as was indeed natural) that the deception of a mere priest should precipitate so great an attack against him. However, because he agreed with the rule that it is incumbent upon a good general to overcome the enemy by stratagem no less than by force, he proposed to try whether he could bring his subjects to their senses without armed conflict. Accordingly a council of nobles having been summoned at the Carthusians' convent at the royal palace which the king later called Richmond, the remedies appropriate to the dangerous condition were debated. As soon as they were Assembled all agreed that it would be well-advised if, before discussing anything else, a pardon were extended to any guilty of offenses, lest, were this to be delayed, Sir Thomas Broughton (who had long adhered to Francis lord Lovel, and was with him at present) and other participants in the new conspiracy should in despair of pardon have no alternative but to persist in their resolution; and, exposing themselves to greater dangers, plunge into open revolution. Accordingly the king at once by proclamation pardoned and excused from punishment all who were accused of treason or any other crimes. Secondly, after long deliberation, it seemed prudent to all that the duke of Clarence's son should be shown to the people, so that thereby the foolish notion that the boy was in Ireland would be driven from men's minds. Many ordinances were at the same time authorised dealing with improvements in public administration . . . The king, having dismissed his council, came to London and on the following Sunday ordered Edward the duke of Clarence's son to be led from the tower through the centre of the city to St. Paul's Cathedral. Here the boy (as he had been instructed) showing himself to everyone, fell to prayer and took part in worship and then spoke with many important people and especially with those of whom the king was suspicious, so that they might the more readily understand that the Irish had based their new rebellion on an empty and spurious cause. But this medicine was of no avail for diseased minds. For John earl of Lincoln, the son of John duke of Suffolk and King Edward's sister Elizabeth, together with Thomas Broughton and many more who longed for revolution, joined the conspiracy against Henry, and decided to cross over to Margaret* so that they could unite with the other originators of the rebellion. Therefore

* Edward IV's sister, widow of the duke of Burgundy, enemy of Henry VII.

as soon as the council had been dismissed by the king, the earl fled secretly to Flanders and there busied himself with Margaret and Francis lord Lovell in preparations for war.

Meanwhile King Henry, who hoped to have quieted his nobles by showing them Edward the genuine son of the duke of Clarence, was concentrating his efforts on curbing the rashness of the Irish, when suddenly he learned of the earl of Lincoln's flight. Deeply provoked by this the king resolved to prosecute his enemies openly and revenge by force the wrongs they had done him, which he perceived could not be avoided by mere prudence. He accordingly ordered levies of soldiers to be raised and himself being fearful lest the earl should in the meantime entice many nobles into the conspiracy, thoroughly traversed that part of the island nearest to Flanders since it was by that route that the earl when fleeing to Flanders had earlier made his way. When the king reached Bury St. Edmunds he was informed that Thomas marquis of Dorset was approaching. Suspecting him of being party to the plot, the king ordered him while journeying to be arrested by John earl of Oxford and put in the Tower of London. While the king delayed at Bury St. Edmunds, Richard Fox – one of his most intimate counsellors – was promoted to the see of Exeter and consecrated bishop. Moving thence, the king came to Norwich, where he celebrated Eastertide. He then came to the place called Walsingham, where he prayed devoutly before the image of the Blessed Virgin Mary, who is worshipped with especial devotion there, that he might be preserved from the wiles of his enemies. Finally, after he had thoroughly traversed the coastal area and found all quiet, the king returned to Cambridge.

Meanwhile John earl of Lincoln and Francis Lovell, having received from Margaret an army of about two thousand Germans, whose commander was that most martial man Martin Schwartz, crossed over to Ireland and in the city of Dublin crowned as king the lad Lambert, of ignoble origin and, having changed his name, called Edward, whom falsely (as they very well knew) they called the duke of Clarence's son. After this, having assembled a great number of the destitute and almost unarmed Irish under the leadership of Thomas Geraldine, they sailed to England with their new king. They landed according to plan on the west coast not far from Lancaster, putting their trust in the wealth and assistance of Thomas Broughton, who was of great authority in that part and who (as was explained above) was one of the conspirators.

King Henry indeed had anticipated what actually happened, and had a little prior to the arrival of the enemy despatched Christopher Urswick to find out whether the ports on the Lancashire coast were capable of handling large ships; so that if they proved likely to be useful to his enemies he could at once so place his soldiers as to deny them the coast. Christopher carried out these orders and, after he had learnt from the depth of the bed of the sea that the ports were deep, returned to the king. But on his way he was informed of the sudden landing of the enemy, sent ahead a messenger to tell the king of the approach of his enemies and, following on the heels of the messenger, himself gave a fuller account of the whole matter. The king was at Coventry when he received the messenger, and, abandoning all other business, he judged he must set out forthwith against the foe wherever he might betake himself, lest time should be given him for assembling greater forces. He marched to Nottingham and encamped not far from the town in a wood which is called Banrys in the vernacular. Accompanied by a great number of armed men, George Talbot earl of Shrewsbury, George lord Strange, and John Cheyney, all outstanding captains, with many others well versed in military affairs, came to him there.

The earl of Lincoln meanwhile had entered Yorkshire with the other rebels proceeding slowly and offering no harm to the local inhabitants, for he hoped some of the people would rally to his side. But when he saw his following was small he resolved none the less to try the fortunes of war, recalling that two years earlier Henry with a small number of soldiers had conquered the great army of King Richard: and although both the Germans and the Irish in the force announced they had come to restore the boy Edward, recently crowned in Ireland, to the kingdom, the earl (who, as we have shown, was the son of Edward's sister) planned to seize the throne himself in the event of victory. Thus placing his trust in the fortunes of war, the earl began to make his way out of Yorkshire towards the town called Newark, situated on the bank of the river Trent, so that, having augmented his troops there, he could march directly on the king. But before he came to this place, King Henry (on the evening of the day preceding the battle) set off to meet the enemy and came to Newark. He did not tarry there for long but marched three miles beyond the town and there encamped for the night. The earl, having learnt of the king's approach, was by no means alarmed but continued on his chosen way, until the same day he came to a village near the camp of his enemy, a place they call Stoke, where he pitched camp. The following day the king, having formed his whole force into three columns, marched to the village of Stoke, halted before the earl's camp and, on the level ground there, offered battle. Accepting the chance, the earl led forward his troops and, at a given signal, gave battle. Both sides fought with the bitterest energy. Those rugged men of the mountains, the Germans, so practiced in warfare, were in the forefront of the battle and yielded little to the English in valour; while Martin Schwartz their leader was not inferior to many in his courage and resolution. On the other hand the Irish, though they fought most spiritedly, were nevertheless (in the tradition of their country) unprotected by body armour and, more than the other troops engaged, suffered heavy casualties, their slaughter striking no little terror into the other combatants. For some time the struggle was fought with no advantage to either side, but at last the first line of the king's army (which was alone committed to the fray and sustained the struggle) charged the enemy with such vigour that it at once crushed those of the hostile leaders who were still resisting. Thereupon the remaining enemy troops turned to flight, and while fleeing were either captured or killed. Indeed it was only then, when the battle was over, that it was fully apparent how rash had been the spirit inspiring the enemy soldiers: for of their leaders John earl of Lincoln, Francis lord Lovell, Thomas Broughton, the most bold Martin Schwartz and the Irish captain Thomas Geraldine were slain in that place, which they took alive in fighting [*sic*]. Lambert the false boy king was indeed captured, with his mentor Richard: but each was granted his life – the innocent lad because he was too young to have himself committed any offense, the tutor because he was a priest. Lambert is still alive to this very day, having been promoted trainer of the king's hawks; before that for some time he was a turnspit and did other menial jobs in the royal kitchen.

The king was greatly pleased that he had overcome his enemies, thereby evading not merely the immediate danger, but also that future threat which he dreaded more. For when he had observed that his enemies' force, though much smaller in number and inferior in resources, had come against him with such good morale and had in the end given battle energetically he had suspected that there must be yet further members of the conspiracy who, at a convenient time and place, would join with the rebels. Hence, when he saw the enemy line being broken in the battle, he commanded that John earl of Lincoln should not be killed in order to learn from him more concerning the conspiracy. But it is said that the soldiers refused to spare the earl, being terrified that by chance it would happen that the sparing of one man's life would lead to the loss of the lives of many. This destruction happened in the year 1489 of human salvation, and the third of Henry's reign . . .

THE HENRICIAN REFORMATION (1529–36)

No one questioned Henry VIII's (1491–1547) commitment to the Roman Catholic church in the first two decades of his reign. His leading advisor and Lord Chancellor was Thomas Wolsey, cardinal archbishop of York (1475–1530). When the Lutheran heresy broke out in Europe Henry hastened to defend the orthodox position on the sacraments in his (ghost-written) book, *In Defence of the Seven Sacraments*. A grateful pope bestowed the title 'Defender of the Faith' upon the king, who bore it proudly, even after his break with Rome.

The origins of Henry's Reformation lay in the perennial problem of the succession to the throne. In the fifteenth century political chaos and civil war devastated England as the result of a series of disputed successions; Henry VIII was the first king of England to inherit the crown peacefully since the infant Henry VI in 1422. Henry VI's incapacity – first because of his age, and later mental instability – was an object lesson for his successors. A king's first duty was to provide for a stable succession. It was apparent by about 1525 that Henry VIII was failing in this vital area, for after sixteen years of marriage, his queen, Katherine of Aragon (1485–1536) had not borne him a son. There had been six royal pregnancies, all but one ending in miscarriage or stillbirth. The surviving child was Princess Mary, born in 1516. Although a woman might legally inherit the throne, Henry, in common with most of his contemporaries, viewed the accession of a queen regnant as potentially disastrous. Women were unfit to rule, and so Henry became increasingly concerned about the future of his realm. By 1527 the queen's age seemed to rule out any further pregnancies, and the king, advised by Wolsey, had begun to cast about for a solution to his problem.

Serious thought – and wishful thinking – led Henry to conclude that his marriage to Katherine, who had originally been his long-dead brother's wife, was invalid. It would be a simple matter to persuade Clement VII (1478–1534) that an error had been made and the marriage annulled. But the pope, pressed by the queen's powerful nephew, the Holy Roman Emperor Charles V, resisted. Katherine bitterly opposed the divorce, and when a papal legate, Lorenzo Campeggio, arrived in England to judge the case, an impasse ensued.

By 1529 Henry sought new counsels, and dismissed Wolsey. The king now proposed a radical solution: breaking with Rome altogether. Using Parliament as his tool, he pushed through a series of statutes weakening the Roman church's power in England, culminating in the 1534 Act of Supremacy. Free from the papacy, Henry divorced Katherine and soon married his second wife, Anne Boleyn (1507–36). As head of the newly founded Church of England, Henry turned next to the monastic houses – they were tempting sources of wealth as well as, in many cases, centres of resistance to the royal supremacy. Government pressure upon the abbeys began in 1534–5 and ended with their dissolution.

There are three sources excerpted here. The first, written by an anonymous Spaniard who lived in London at the time of the royal divorce, gives Katherine's perspective. While it sometimes compresses events and the author makes some mistakes, it illustrates a point of view held by many contemporaries, English and foreign. The second source are two acts of the Reformation Parliament: the 1534 Act of Supremacy, declaring Henry to be head of the church, and a follow-up statute designed to punish any who continued to assert papal authority with the penalties of praemunire – life imprisonment and the loss of all property. Finally there are two letters produced during the government's suppression of the monasteries: one from a government agent whose task it was to ferret out monastic abuses, and another from an abbot defending his house.

How the cardinal was the cause of all the evil and damage that exist in England

In the year of our Lord one thousand five hundred and thirty, Henry VIII. being King of the realm of England, and in the flower of his age, determined for his own greater tranquility, and in order to be able to take his pleasure, to give over the government of his kingdom to a Cardinal who lived there, who was Archbishop of York. This Cardinal was not a very learned person, but he was much thought of by the King. He was of very low birth, his father being a butcher, but the King gave him the Chancellor's seals, and all that he ordered in the kingdom was done, even the Lords obeying him. It came to such a pass, indeed, that the King intervened in nothing, and this Cardinal did everything.

As he rose from base beginnings he rejoiced in having wise people in his train, and amongst them there was an astrologer, who said to him one day, 'My lord, you will be Destroyed by a woman.' At the time he had so much power the sainted Queen Katharine was living, and, she grieving that so low man should have so great control, showed but little love towards him, and rather tried that the King should look after the government of his kingdom. The Cardinal knowing this, and remembering what the astrologer had said, made up his mind to invent the diabolical thing we shall tell you of in the next chapter.

How the Cardinal made the king believe he was badly married and living in mortal sin

After the devil had put it into the head of the Cardinal to do all the ill he could to the sainted Queen Katharine, and the Cardinal knowing that the King was very much enamoured of one of the Queen's ladies, called Anne Boleyn, he went to the King one day, and finding him very merry, he said, 'Sir, your Majesty must know that for many days I have wished to say something to you, but I do not dare, for fear you should be angry with me.' The King wishing to know what it was, said, 'Cardinal, say what is in your heart; you have my leave.' The mischief-maker was nothing loath, and kneeling on the ground, he said, 'Your Majesty must know that for many years you have been in mortal sin and living in adultery, for you are married to the wife of your brother, the Prince of Wales.' The King was struck with astonishment, and said 'Cardinal, you deserve heavy punishment if this be so and you have not told me before. If I really am in mortal sin, God forbid that it should go on; but if it is not so, take care what you say.'

The Cardinal repeated his assurance, and to turn his wickedness to account, he said, 'Your Majesty will see to it and undo the error.' The King, as I have said, being in love with Anne Boleyn, answered him, 'Well, but, Cardinal, in what manner can I free myself from it?' Then said the Cardinal, 'Sir, your Majesty must speak to the Queen to this effect: "My lady, you well know that you were married to my brother and lived half a year with him, so by the divine law I could not marry the widow of my brother"; and when your Majesty has spoken thus, you will see what she will say, and we will proceed accordingly.' The King liked the Cardinal's advice, and presently, on the same day, he went to the sainted Queen and said, 'Well you know, my lady, that on the command of the King my father I married you, and now it seems to me that for many years we have lived in mortal sin. I know you are holy and good; let us then undo the error of our consciences, and you shall be Princess of Wales, and we will part.' From that hour forward the King was only happy in the thought of getting rid of her.

How the King dismissed Cardinal Campeggio, and presently married Anne Boleyn

As soon as the English Cardinal [Wolsey] had gone to his diocese the King called Cardinal Campeggio, and said to him, 'Cardinal, you can go when you like, for I would have you know that from this day forward the Bishop of Rome shall have no more power in my realm.'

The good Cardinal, seeing the intention of the King, resolved to leave at once; so he went, and we will make no more mention of him here. And the King ordered a meeting of the grandees of his kingdom, both temporal and spiritual and when they were met, he made them a short speech, and told them clearly not to dare to contradict him, and then he said: 'You well know the tyranny exercised every year by the Bishop of Rome in my dominions, and the large sum of money he takes out of them: and it is my will that he shall take out no more. Therefore, I wish Parliament to be called together so that it may abolish this state of things.' They all answered with one voice that it should be done, indeed they were obliged, for he had told them beforehand not to contradict him, and some of them even told him he had done well.

Then the King commanded that within eight days all should meet at Westminster, and in the meanwhile he said he wanted to marry Anne Boleyn, and begged them all to approve. The King made this speech at a town near London, called Greenwich, the blessed lady, good Queen Katharine, staying there at the same time. The King left directly afterwards for another house of his called Richmond, and then sent for Anne Boleyn and all the ladies of the Court, very few remaining with the sainted Queen. When they arrived he sent to the Archbishop of Canterbury to say mass, who married them at once.

How Anne Boleyn was taken to the tower of London, and the manner in which she passed through London

The King had not been at Greenwich three days with his new Queen when he sent word to the Captain of the Tower of London to make ready, as he was going thither, and on Monday morning he left Greenwich in one of his barges, accompanied by the Queen. There were so many barges and boats which left with them, and so many ladies and gentlemen, that it was a thing to wonder at, for it is four English miles from London to Greenwich, and the river is quite wide, but nothing else could be seen all the way but barges and boats all draped with awnings and carpeted, which gave pleasure to behold . . . And so all that day and night the King with his Queen remained in the Tower, and the next morning very early the King went in his boat to Westminster. At ten o'clock Anne left the Tower in an open litter, so that all might see her, but before she came out all the cavalry preceded her, all in very fine order and richly bedight. Then came the gentlemen of rank, and then all the ladies and gentlemen on horseback and in cars, very brave. The Queen was dressed in a robe of crimson brocade covered with precious stones, and round her neck she wore a string of pearls larger than big chick-peas, and a jewel of diamonds of great value. On her head she bore a wreath in the fashion of a crown of immense worth, and in her hand she carried some flowers. As she passed through the city she kept turning her face from one side to the other; and here it was a very notable thing to see, that there were not, I think, ten people who greeted her with 'God save you!' as they used to when the sainted Queen passed by.

Passing through London she arrived at Westminster, where the King was awaiting her, and she was received with great sounds of trumpets and other instruments. The King took her in his arms and asked her how she liked the look of the city, to which Anne answered, 'Sir, I liked the city well enough, but I saw a great many caps on heads, and heard but few tongues.' It is a thing to note that the common people always disliked her. From Westminster Hall she was taken to the church, where the Kings and Queens are always crowned, and there she was crowned with great ceremony, and carried thence to the royal palace, where great feasts were made, lasting more than a week, with many jousts and tournaments. Here we will leave them for a time to say what the King did in Parliament.

How the King was made head of the church in his realm by the parliament

I have told how the King ordered all the grandees of his kingdom to meet in Parliament within eight days, and when they were met he made this speech to them: 'You know already how the Bishop of Rome with his false Bulls and pardons took great sums of money from this country every year, and how he has made himself esteemed. I have seen this great abuse, and my will is, and I hope all will agree with it, that I should be acknowledged head of the Church within my realm. It is necessary, therefore, that all of you, both spiritual and temporal, should take the oath to that effect. From this time forward I desire to take the revenues, and that the Pope should be called only Bishop of Rome. Whoever calls him Pope must be punished.' They all, both spiritual and temporal, cried with one voice, declaring him head of the Church in England after God.

On that day nothing else was done, but in two days' time the spiritual Lords met in the great church which they call St. Paul's, and agreed that within a month all the bishops, abbots, and prelates of the realm should come to take the oath, as well as two from every monastery in the land.

Act concerning the King's Highness to be Supreme-Head of the Church of England and to have authority to reform and redress all errors, heresies, and abuses in the same {1534}

Albeit the King's Majesty justly and rightfully is and ought to be the Supreme Head of the Church of England, and so is recognised by the clergy of this realm in their Convocations; yet nevertheless for corroboration and confirmation thereof, and for increase of virtue in Christ's religion within this realm of England, and to repress and extirpate all errors, heresies, and other enormities and abuses heretofore used in the same, Be it enacted by authority of this present Parliament that the King our Sovereign Lord, his heirs and successors kings of this realm, shall be taken, accepted, and reputed the only Supreme Head in earth of the Church of England called *Anglicans Ecclesia*, and shall have and enjoy annexed and united to the imperial Crown of this realm as well the title and style thereof, as all honours, dignities, preeminences, jurisdictions, privileges, authorities, immunities, profits, and commodities, to the said dignity of Supreme Head of the same Church belonging and appertaining: And that our said Sovereign Lord, his heirs and successors kings of this realm, shall have full power and authority from time to time to visit, repress, redress, reform, order, correct, restrain, and amend all such errors, heresies, abuses, offenses, contempts, and enormities, whatsoever they be, which by any manner spiritual authority or jurisdiction ought or may lawfully be reformed, repressed, ordered redressed, corrected, restrained, or amended, most to the pleasure of Almighty God, the increase of virtue in Christ's religion, and for the conservancy of the peace, unity, and tranquility of this realm: any usage, custom, foreign laws foreign authority, prescription or any other thing or things to the contrary hereof notwithstanding.

An Act extinguishing the authority of the Bishop of Rome {1536}

Forasmuch as notwithstanding the good and wholesome laws, ordinances, and statutes heretofore enacted, made, and established . . . for the extirpation, abolition, and extinguishment, out of this realm and other his Grace's dominions, seignories, and countries, of the pretended power and usurped authority of the Bishop of Rome, by some called the Pope, used within the same or elsewhere concerning the same realm, dominions, seignories, or countries, which did obfuscate and wrest God's holy word and testament a long season from the spiritual and true meaning thereof, to his worldly and carnal affections, as pomp, glory, avarice, ambition, and tyranny, covering and shadowing the same with his human and politic devices, traditions, and inventions, set forth to promote and establish his only dominion, both upon the souls and also the bodies and goods of all Christian people, excluding Christ out of his kingdom and rule of man his soul as much as he may, and all other temporal kings and princes out of their dominions which they ought to have by God's law upon the bodies and goods of their subjects; whereby he did not only rob the King's Majesty, being the only Supreme Head of this his realm of England immediately under God, of his honour, right, and preeminence due unto him by the law of God, but spoiled this his realm yearly of innumerable treasure, and with the loss of the same deceived the King's loving and obedient subjects, persuading to them, by his laws, bulls, and other his deceivable means, such dreams, vanities, and fantasies as by the same many of them were seduced and conveyed unto superstitious and erroneous opinions; so that the King's Majesty, the Lords spiritual and temporal, and the Commons in this realm, being overwearied and fatigued with the experience of the infinite abominations and mischiefs proceeding of his impostures and craftily colouring of his deceits, to the great damages of souls, bodies, and goods, were forced of necessity for the public weal of this realm to exclude that foreign pretended power, jurisdiction, and authority, used and usurped within this realm, and to devise such remedies for their relief in the same as doth not only redound to the honour of God, the high praise and advancement of the King's Majesty and of his realm, but also to the great and inestimable utility of the same; and notwithstanding the said wholesome laws so made and heretofore established, yet it is come to the knowledge of the King's Highness and also to divers and many his loving, faithful, and obedient subjects, how that divers seditious and contentious persons, being imps of the said Bishop of Rome and his see, and in heart members of his pretended monarchy, do in corners and elsewhere, as they dare, whisper . . . preach, and persuade, and from time to time instill into the ears and heads of the poor, simple, and unlettered people the advancement and continuance of the said Bishop's feigned and pretended authority, pretending the same to have his ground and original of God's law, whereby the opinions of many be suspended their judgments corrupted and deceived, and diversity in opinions augmented and increased, to the great displeasure of Almighty God, the high discontent of our said most dread Sovereign Lord, and the interruption of the unity, love, charity, concord, and agreement that ought to be in a Christian region and congregation: For avoiding whereof, and repression of the follies of such seditious persons as be the means and authors of such inconveniences, Be it enacted, ordained, and established . . . That if any person or persons, dwelling, demurring, inhabiting, or resident within this realm or within any other the King's dominions, seignories, or countries, or the marches of the same, or elsewhere within or under his obeisance and power, of what estate, dignity, preeminence, order, degree, or condition soever he or they be after the last day of July which shall be in the year of our Lord God 1536 shall, by writing, ciphering, printing, preaching, or teaching, deed, or act, obstinately or maliciously hold or stand with to extol, set forth, maintain, or defend the authority, jurisdiction, or power of the Bishop of Rome or of his see, heretofore used, claimed, or usurped within this realm or in any dominion or country being of, within, or under the King's power or obeisance, or by any pretence obstinately or maliciously invent anything for the extolling, advancement, setting forth, maintenance, or defence of the same or any part thereof or by any presence obstinately or maliciously attribute any manner of jurisdiction, authority, or preeminence: to the said see of Rome, or to any Bishop of the same see for the time being, within this realm or in any the King's dominions or countries, that then every such person or persons so doing or offending, their aiders, assistants, comforters, abettors, procurers, maintainers, factors, counsellors, concealers, and every or them, being thereof lawfully convicted according to the laws of this realm, for every such default and offense shall incur and run into the dangers, penalties, pains, and forfeitures ordained and provided by the Statute of Provision and Praemunire made in the sixteenth year of thy reign of the noble and valiant prince King Richard the Second against such as attempt, procure, or make provision to the see of Rome or elsewhere for any thing or things to the derogation, or contrary to the prerogative royal or jurisdiction, of the Crown and dignity of this realm.

Suppression of monasteries

John Ap Rice to Cromwell
Please it your mastership.
Please it your mastership, forasmuch as I suppose ye shall have suit made unto you touching Bury ere we return, I thought convenient to advertise you of our proceedings there, and also of the compertes [conduct] of the same. As for the abbot, we found nothing suspect as touching his living, but it was detected that he lay much forth in his granges, that he delighted much in playing at dice and cards, and therein spent much money, and in building for his pleasure. He did not preach openly. Also that he converted divers farms into copyholds, whereof poor men doth complain. Also he seems to be addict[ed] to the maintaining of such superstitious ceremonies as hath been used heretofore.

As touching the convent, we could get little or no reports among them, although we did use much diligence in our examination, and thereby, with some other arguments gathered of their examinations, I firmly believe and suppose that they had confedered [conspired] and compacted before our coming that they should disclose nothing. And yet it is confessed and proved, that there was here such frequence of women coming and resorting to this monastery as to no place more. Amongst the relics we found much vanity and superstition, as the coals that Saint Laurence was toasted withall, the paring of S. Edmund's nails, S. Thomas of Canterbury's pen knife and his boots, and divers skulls for the headache; [enough] pieces of the holy cross able to make a whole cross of; other relics for rain and certain other superstitious usages, for avoiding of weeds growing in corn, with such other.

The Abbot of Faversham to Cromwell

Right worshipful sir, after humble recommendations according to my most bounden duty, with like thanks for your benevolent mind always shown toward me and my poor house to your goodness had and used; it may please you to be advertised, that I lately received your loving letters dated the eighth day of this present month, concerning a resignation to be Had of the poor house which I under God and the king's highness my sovereign lord of long time (though unworthy such a cure) have had ministration and rule of, and that by cause of the age and debility which are reported to be in me. So it is, right worshipful sir, I trust I am not yet now so far infeebled Or decayed, Neither in body nor in remembrance, either by any extremity of age whom debility lightly for the most part always accompanies, either by any immoderate passion of any great continual infirmity, but that I may as well (high thanks be unto God thereof!) accommodate my self to the good order, rule, and governance of my poor house and monastery as ever I might since my first promotion to the same, though I may not so well perhaps ride and journey abroad as I might have done in time passed. But [I] admit the peculiar office of an abbot to consist . . . in journeying forth and surveying of the possessions of his house, in which case agility and patience of labour in journeying were much required indeed: though I myself be not so well able to take pains therein as I have been in my younger years, at which time I trust I take such pains that I need less surveying of the same at this present time, yet have I such faithful approved servants whom I have brought up in my poor house from their tender years, and those of such wit and good discretion joined with the long experience of the trade of such worldly things, that they are able to furnish and supply those places, I know right well, in all points much better then ever I my self could or than it had been expedient or decent for me to have done. Again, on that other side, if the chief office and profession of an abbot be (as I have ever taken it) to live chaste and solitarily, to be separate from the intermeddling of worldly things, to serve God quietly, to distribute his faculties in refreshing of poor indigent persons, to have a vigilant eye to the good order and rule of his house and the flock to him committed in God, I trust your favour and benevolence obtained (whereof I right humbly require you) I my self may and am as well able yet now to supply and continue those places as ever I was in all my life, as concerning the sufficiency of mine own person. Yet doubtless much more ease and quiet might it be unto me, as ye in your said letters right friendly and vehemently have persuaded, for to make resignation of my said office upon the provision of such a reasonable pension as your good mastership should think meet and convenient, wherein surely I would nothing doubt your worship and conscience, but in the same have much affiaunce [confidence], not only for the great goodness and good indifferency which I hear every where commonly reported by you, but also for the great favour and benevolence which I have always found in you. And

104

because in mine own mind I could right well be contented and fully persuaded for as myself as concerns mine own part so to do for the satisfaction
and contentment of your loving motion, for I am nothing less than ambitious;
but I do more esteem in this thing the miserable state and condition that our
poor house should stand in, if such [a] thing should come to pass, than I do
my own private office and dignity, the administration whereof though it be
somewhat more painful unto me than it hath been accustomed heretofore, yet
God forbid that it should seem unto me irksome or tedious. Moreover I
[pray] your good mastership, to whom I would all these things were as openly
and manifestly known as to my self, our said poor house and monastery by
many and occasion of diverse and many importable costs and charges which
we have sustained as well toward the king's highness as otherwise: partly by
reason of divers great sums of money which it was left indebted in, in the
time of my last predecessor there (which as it is well known in the country
was but a right slender husband to the house): partly by means of divers and
many great reparations, as well of the edifices of our church as of other hous-
ing, which were suffered to fall in great ruin and decay, insomuch that some
of them were in [a] manner likely to fall clean down to the ground, as in the
[flooding] of divers marshes belonging to our said monastery which the violent rages and surges of the implacable sea had won and occupied, being now
since my time well and sufficiently repaired and fully amended, as the thing
it self may sufficiently declare, to the inestimable losses and charges of our
poor house: partly again by the mean of the great costs, charges, and expenses
which we have had and sustained by and through the occasion of divers and
many sundry suits and actions which we have been compelled to use and
pursue against divers of our tenants for the recovery of divers rights of our said
monastery of long time unjustly detained and by the same tenants obstinately
denied; and partly also by mean of divers and many great sums of money
which we have paid and lent unto the king's highness, as well in tenths and
subsidies as otherwise, amounting in all to the sum of £2,000, and above, to
our great impoverishment, and is yet now at this present time indebted to
divers of our friends and creditors above the sum of £400 as ye shall be further instructed of the particulars thereof whenever it shall please you to
demand a further and more exact declaration therein. Which sums, if it
might please Almighty God that I might live and with your good favour continue in my said office by the space of six or seven years at the farthest, I
doubt not but I should see them well repaid and contented again. But if I
should now at this present time resign my said office (the case standing as it
does) undoubtedly our poor house, being now so far indebted already by
means of the occasions before remembered (the importunate charges of the
first fruits and tenth which would be due unto the king's highness now
immediately upon the same resignation had thereunto added and accumulated), should be clearly impoverished and utterly decayed and undone for
ever in my mind, which I am right well assured your goodness would not

covet to bring to pass. And therefore Christ forbid that ever I should so heinously offend and commit against Almighty God and the king's highness and [my] sovereign lord, that by my means or consent, so godly and ancient a foundation, built and dedicated in the honour of Saint Saviour of [by] so noble and victorious a prince and one of the king's most noble progenitours, whose very body, together with the bodies of his dear and well beloved [wife] and also the prince his son, there lie buried in honourable sepulture, and are had all there in perpetual memory with continual suffrages and commendations of prayers,* should be utterly and irrecoverably decayed and undone, as it must needs of very necessity follow if any such resignation should now be had. Wherefore, the whole premises tenderly considered and deliberately perpended, right worshipful sir, I doubt not but ye will continue your accustomed favour and benevolence which you have always borne toward our poor monastery, and so doing you shall not only please and content Almighty God our Saviour, but also bind us to be your continual bedemen and pray to God during our lives for the prosperous estate of your good mastership long to endure with much increase of honour. Dated at our poor monastery aforesaid, the sixteenth day of this present month of March, anno Domini 1535.

THE REVOLT OF THE COMMONS (1549)

The mid-sixteenth century was a time of hardship across England. Poor harvests, rapid inflation, and the dissolution of the monasteries, traditional source of charity, combined to create a spirit of dangerous unrest. The religious upheavals of Henry VIII's reign further undermined social stability, and after the king's death in 1547, the crown passed into the hands of a nine-year-old boy, Edward VI. Drift and faction fighting at court, along with high expectations for reform under a new monarch, created a volatile situation. Social problems such as poverty, vagrancy, and crime had grown quickly, but solutions seemed remote. Many blamed the spread of enclosure, in which landlords consolidated their hold on their estates and in the process deprived tenants of customary rights, as the prime culprit for society's ills. The state repeatedly forbade unlicensed enclosure, and attempted to reduce the need for enclosures by restricting the size of sheep herds. But the European demand for wool impelled landowners to build their flocks, and encouraged them to turn arable fields into pasture, reducing the need for labour and undercutting traditional agricultural methods.

Frustration with the economic and social situation led, in 1549, to sporadic outbreaks of violence across England, especially in East Anglia and the west. The aims of the rebels were often confused, but they all wanted a return to a

---

* King Stephen, his queen, Matilda, and their son Eustace earl of Boulogne, were buried in the church of Faversham Abbey.

mythical past when landlords and tenants lived in prosperous harmony. The western rebels combined this view with a highly political message: England's troubles, they believed, stemmed from the Reformation. If it were reversed, God would once again smile on the kingdom. The risings were ultimately put down by force, and many rebels were executed. But the experience led eventually to the creation of what became the most effective public system of poor relief in Europe.

Excerpted here are two documents. One are the instructions to the royal enclosure commissioners of 1548, and Chief Justice Hale's charge to them. The commission, designed to investigate and punish enclosures, backfired. Though some landlords were punished, the commissioners could hardly meet the expectations of the poor, who continued to suffer. Their disappointment led to rebellion. The second source is Thomas Cranmer's reply to the demands of the western rebels. Cranmer (1489–1556), archbishop of Canterbury, denounces the rebels in no uncertain terms, and reflects the view of authority.

Instructions to the enclosure commissioners appointed June, 1548, and Hale's charge to the juries empanelled to present enclosures

First, Ye shall enquire what towns, villages, and hamlets have been decayed and laid down by enclosures into pastures, within the shire contained in your instructions, since the fourth year of the reign of K. Henry VII.

Item, What lands were then in tillage at the time of the said enclosure, and what then in pasture.

Item, How many plows, by reason of the said enclosure, be laid down.

Item, How many manses, cottages, and dwelling houses be fallen in decay, and the inhabitants of the same departed from their habitation there, by reason of the same enclosure: and how much land belonged unto the said tenants.

Item, By whom the said enclosures were made, and how long ago; and if they were made within the same time; and of what yearly rent and profit they be.

Item, Who hath now the state of inheritance, and the profits of the same enclosure; and of whom the lands be held.

Item, How many new parks be now made since the said time.

Item, What arable land, at the time of the making the said parks, were imparked within the same.

Item, How many ploughs, houses, and inhabitations be decayed by imparking of the said ground.

Item, How many parks within the said shire be enlarged since the said time; and how much of the same ground was then arable and put in tillage.

Item, How many ploughs, houses, and inhabitations be decayed by reason of the said imparking.

Item, If any person hath or doth keep above the number of two thousand sheep, besides lambs of one years age; and whether he hath kept the same upon his own lands, or upon his farm [rented] lands, or upon both, or otherwise by . . . fraud, and how long he hath kept them.

Item, How many sheep ye think have been necessary for the only expenses of such persons household for one year.

Item, If any person hath set any lands to farm, or by copy of court-roll, reserving the sheep pasture of the same to himself, or if any person hath taken from his tenants their commons whereby they be not able to breed and keep their cattle, and maintain their husbandry, as they were in time past.

Item, If any person hath had or occupied above the number of two houses or tenements of husbandry lying in one town village, hamlet, or tithing, and how long he hath occupied the same.

Item, Whether such person hath taken the same in farm, for the term of life, years at wit, by indenture or copy of court-roll or otherwise, since the feast of the Nativity of our Lord God *mill[esi]mo quingentesimo tricesimo quinto*, [1535] and where such person dwells.

Item, If every person, body politic or corporate, that has, by gift, grant, lease, or demise, the site or precinct and demesnes of any monastery, priory, or religious house, dissolved by virtue of the act of Parliament made in the 27th year of the reign of the King that dead is [Henry VIII], do keep an honest continual house and household in the same site or precinct, and do occupy yearly as much of the same demesnes, in ploughing and tillage of husbandry, as was commonly used to be kept by the governours, abbots, or priors of the same houses, monasteries, or priories, or by their farmer or farmers [tenants]occupying the same, within the time of twenty years next before the making of the said statute.

Item, That you our said commissioners, for your better instructions, take with you the copies of all such offices as were found concerning the premises in the ninth and tenth years of the reign of our most noble father K. Henry VIII.

These be our instructions, and the articles of your charge generally; howbeit we think it very good to open it more specially. For as there be many good men that take great pains to study to devise good laws for the commonwealth; so be there a great many, that do with as great pains and study, labour to defeat them, and as the common saying is, to find gaps and starting holes. But first, to declare unto you what is meant by this word *enclosures*. It is not taken where a man doth enclose and hedge in his own proper ground, where no man hath commons. For such enclosure is very beneficial to the commonwealth; it is a cause of great increase of wood: but it is meant thereby, when any man hath taken away and enclosed any other man's commons, or hath pulled down houses of husbandry, and converted the lands from tillage to pasture. This is the meaning of this word, and so we pray you to remember it.

To defeat these statutes, as we be informed, some have not pulled down their houses, but maintain them – howbeit no person dwells therein, or if there be, it is but a shepherd or a milkmaid – and convert the lands from tillage to pasture: and some about one hundred acres of ground, or more or less, make a furrow, and sow that, and the rest they till not, but pasture with their sheep. And some take the lands from their houses, and occupy them in husbandry, but let the houses out to beggars and old poor people. Some, to colour the multitude of their sheep, father them on their children, kinfolks, and servants. All which be but only crafts and subtleties to defraud the laws; such as no good man will use, but rather abhor. For every good man will direct his study to observe the laws, rather than break them, and say to himself thus: I know the makers of these laws meant good to the commonwealth. Men be but men, they cannot see all things; they be no gods, they cannot make things perfect. Therefore, I will do that they meant, although without danger of the law I might do otherwise, and I will with all my heart do good to my country, albeit it be against my private profit, rather than hurt it. And therefore if there be any such that use these tricks, albeit they be not comprehended in the letter of the law, I pray you let us know him, and present you his name.

Thus have we declared unto you the causes of our coming and your assembly here: which is only to enquire of such things as we have been charged with. If you will do your office therein as becomes good men, that is to say, without partiality or favour, accuse and present those that are to be accused and presented for offending of these statutes and in these enormities we doubt not but you shall do God as great and as acceptable sacrifice as may be. For hereby shall his glory and the fruit of his word, which is charity and love to our neighbours, be published and set forth to the world. You shall do the King the greatest service that can be devised. For hereby his people and subjects (in the multitude of whom his honour and safety consists) shall be increased; and you shall show yourselves good members of the body and the commonwealth of the realm, that covet and desire as much the wealth and commodity of your Christian brethren and neighbours, as you do your own.

And, therefore, for God's sake, good people, do as becomes honest men, declare the truth, and nothing but the truth. And of the other side, we require you on God's behalf, command you in the King's name, and exhort you as your friends that you will not abuse this the great goodness of God, the King's Majesty, and his high Council herein offered; that is to say, that you make not this godly thing an instrument of malice, to be revenged on any man to whom ye bear displeasure: for things grounded on malice, God will never suffer to prosper. Besides, we charge you and command you all, that be present on the King's behalf, and that ye likewise charge all your neighbours that be absent, that you nor none of them go about to take upon you to be executors of the statutes to cut up men's hedges, and to put down their enclosures, or by any ways to hurt them. For this is not your office to do. You shall highly offend God, break the King's laws, and be an occasion that that good that might, and is like to follow, shall not take place, nor come to that good end that is desired. But let it appear to the world that you desire a charitable and quiet reformation by the order only of the law, whereunto we ought and be bound to be obedient. Be you not breakers of the law, while you go about to have vices reformed by the law. Accuse and present you justly those that are offenders of these statutes. For this is only our duty to will you and yours to do, and let the law work his effect, power, and office afterward.

And by this means we trust in God, that as it has pleased him to put into the King's and his Council's heads to begin this matter, so will he give them grace to finish and accomplish the same; and to do greater things to his glory, the King's honour and safety, and the universal benefit of us all. And unless we will show ourselves unkind, we cannot but honour God and give him thanks, that it has pleased him to send us such a King, such a Protector, and such a Council, that only be bent and inclined to do the people good. Doubtless, good people, where the people love and honour God, favour and embrace his word, and live accordingly, to them does God send good and gracious rulers. And on the other side, where they favour not nor love his word, to them he sends unpitiful [merciless] and hard rulers, such as only shall seek their own pleasures, benefits, and commodities, not passing on their poor subjects. And therefore, good people, let us love, favour, and embrace God's word, which thing only is the cause that this godly act is set forward: it is the general comfort of all Christian men, and specially of the poor: it forbids the rich to oppress the poor, and wills and commands him to be merciful to him: it declares us to be members of one body, and bids us to love together like brother and brother: it teaches the magistrates their offices towards their inferiors, and commands all people to be obedient to their superiors: it shows how God rewards well-doers both here and with ever-lasting felicity, and punishes malefactors both in this world and with eternal damnation.

And, therefore, good people, let us not only love and embrace God's word, but also all such as be the furtherers, preachers, and teachers thereof. Thus I make an end, and God save the King.

Archbishop Cranmer's Answers to the fifteen Articles of the Rebels. Devon, Anno 1549

When I first read your Requests, O ignorant men of *Devonshire* and *Cornwall*, straightaway came to my mind a request, which *James* and *John* made unto Christ: to whom Christ answered, you ask you know not what. Even so thought I of you as soon as ever I heard your Articles, that you were deceived by some crafty Papist, which devised those Articles for you, to make you ask you knew not what.

As for the Devisors of your Articles, if they understand them, I may not call them ignorant persons, but, as they be indeed, most rank Papists, and willful Traitors and Adversaries, both to God and our Sovereign Lord the King, and to the whole realm. But I cannot be persuaded so to think of you, that in your hearts willingly you be Papists and Traitors: but that those that by such have craftily seduced you, being simple and unlearned people, to ask you know not what.

Wherefore, my duty unto God, and the pity that I have of your ignorance, move me now at this time to open plainly and particularly your own Articles unto you, that you may understand them, and no longer be deceived.

Your first Article is this,
We will have all the General Counsels, and holy Decrees of our forefathers observed, kept and performed: and whoever shall gainsay them, we hold them as Heretics.

First to begin with the manner of your phrase. Is this the fashion of Subjects to speak unto their Prince; *We will have?* Was this manner of speech at any time used of the Subjects to their Prince, since the beginning of the world? Have not all true Subjects ever used to their Sovereign Lord this form of speaking, 'Most humbly beseech your faithful and obedient subjects.'

But now leaving your rude and unhandsome manner of speech to your most Sovereign lord, I will come to the point, and join with you in the effect of your first Article. You say, you will have all the holy Decrees observed and kept. But do you know what they be? The holy Decrees, as I told you before, are called the Bishop of *Rome's* ordinances and laws. Which how *holy* and godly soever they are called, they are indeed so wicked, so ungodly, so full of tyranny and so partial, that since the beginning of the world, were never devised or invented the like.

Your second Article is this,
We will have the Law of our Sovereign Lord King Henry VIII, concerning the six Articles, to be used again, as in his time they were.

Letting pass your rude style, nothing becoming subjects, to say, *You will have*, First, I examine you of the cause of your willful will, wherefore you will have these six Articles, which never were laws in no religion, but this: nor in this realm also, until the 31st. year of King *Henry* VIII.*

And in some things so enforced by the evil Counsel of certain Papists against the truth, and common judgment, both of Divines and Lawyers, that if the King's Majesty himself had not come personally into the Parliament house, those laws had never passed. And yet within a year or little more, the same most noble Prince was fain to temper his said laws, and moderate them in divers points. So that the statute of six Articles continued in his force little above the space of one year. Is this then so great a matter to make these uproars, and to arise against the whole realm? Will you take away the present

* The Six Articles enforced Roman Catholic doctrine in the Church of England, despite its break with the papacy.

laws of this Realm, which be and ever have been, the laws of all other Countries also, and set up new Laws, which never were, but in this Realm only, and were here in force not fully thirteen months?

The third Article is this,
We will have the Mass in Latin, as was before, and celebrated by the Priest, without any man or woman communicating with him.
Forasmuch as there is nothing with you, but *Will*, let your will be conferred with reason and God's word; and then you shall see how far your Will differs from them both: First as touching the Latin Masses, Whatsoever the Priest says in the old Masses, whether he pray and ask any thing of God, or give thanks to God, or make the true Profession of the Faith, or whatsoever he does besides, all he does in your persons and in your names; and you answer unto that which he says, sometime *Amen*, sometimes *Et cum spiritu tuo*; and sometimes other things, as the matter serves. For all the whole that is done should be the act of the people, and pertain to the people, as well as to the priest. And stands it with reason, that the Priest should speak for you, and in your names and you answer him again in your own persons; and yet you understand never a word, neither what he says, nor what you say your selves? The Priest prays to God for you, and you answer *Amen* you know not whereto. Is there any reason herein? Will you not understand what the Priest prays for you? What thanks he gives for you, What he asks for you? Will you neither understand what he says, nor let your hearts understand what your own tongues answer? Then must you needs confess your selves to be such people as Christ spoke of, When he said *These people honour me with their lips, but their hearts are far from me.*

Your fourth Article is this,
We will have the Sacrament hang over the high Altar, and there to be worshipped, as it was wont to be; and they which will not thereto consent, we will have them die like Heretics against the holy Catholic faith.
What say you, O ignorant people in things pertaining to God? Is this the holy Catholic faith, that that Sacrament should be hanged over the Altar and worshipped? And are they Heretics, that will not consent thereto? I pray you, who made this Faith? Any other, but the Bishops of *Rome*? And that after more then a thousand years after the Faith of Christ was full and perfect. *Innocent* III. about 1215 years after Christ did ordain, that the Sacrament and Chrism should be kept under lock and key. But yet no motion he made of hanging the Sacrament over the high Altar, nor of the worshiping of it. After him came *Honorius* III. and he added further, commanding that the Sacrament should be devoutly kept in a clean place, and sealed, and that the priest should often teach the people reverently to bow down to the host, when it is lifted up in the Mass time, and when the priests should carry it to the sick folks. And although this *Honorius* added the worshiping of the Sacrament, yet he made no mention of the hanging thereof over the high Altar, as your Article purports. Nor how

long after, or by what means, that came first up into this realm, I think no man can tell. And in *Italy* it is not yet used until this day. And in the beginning of the Church it was not only not used to be hanged up, but also it was utterly forbid to be kept.

Your fifth Article is this,
We will have the Sacrament of the Altar but at Easter delivered to the Lay-people; and then but in one kind.

Methinks you are like a man, that were brought up in a dark dungeon, that never saw light, nor knew nothing that is abroad in the world. And if a friend of his pitying his ignorance and state, would bring him out of his dungeon, that he might see the light and come to knowledge, he being from his youth used to darkness could not abide the light, but would willfully shut his eyes, and be offended both with the light, and with his friend also.

And that you may understand how far you be wandered from the right way in this one Article, wherein you will have the sacrament of the Altar delivered to the Lay-people but once in the year, and then but under one kind, be you assured, that there was never such law, nor such request made among christian people, until this day. What injury do you to many godly persons, who would devoutly receive it many times, and you command the priest to deliver it them but at *Easter*, All learned men and godly have exhorted christian people, (although they have not commanded them) often to receive the Communion. And in the Apostles' time, the people at *Jerusalem* received it every day, as it appears by the manifest word of the Scripture.

[. . .]

Your seventh Article is this,
We will have holy bread and holy water every Sunday, *palms and ashes at the time accustomed; Images to be set up again in every Church; and all other ancient, old Ceremonies used heretofore by our Mother holy Church.*

Oh! Superstition and Idolatry, how they prevail among you? The very true, heavenly bread of life, the food of ever lasting life, offered unto you in the Sacrament of the holy Communion, you refuse to eat, but only at *Easter*. And the Cup of the most holy blood, wherewith you were redeemed and washed from your sins, you refuse utterly to drink of at any time. And yet in the stead of there you will eat often of the unsavoury and poisoned bread of the Bishop of *Rome*, and drink of his stinking puddles, which he names Holy bread and Holy water. Consider, oh! ignorant people, the authors and intents of the makers of them both. The water of Baptism, and the holy bread and wine of the holy Communion, none other person did ordain, but Christ himself. The other that is called Holy bread, Holy water, Holy ashes, Holy Palms, and all other like ceremonies, ordained the Bishops of *Rome* adversaries to Christ, and therefore rightly called *Antichrist*. And Christ ordained his Bread and his Wine and his Water to our great comfort, to instruct us and teach us what things we

113

have only by him. But Antichrist on the other side has set up his superstitions, under the name of Holiness, to none other intent, but as the Devil seeks all means to draw as from Christ. Too, does Antichrist advance his holy Superstitions, to the intent that we should take him in the stead of Christ, and believe that we have by him such things, as we have only by Christ. That is to say, Spiritual food, Remission of our sins and Salvation.

Your eighth Article is this,
We will not receive the new Service, because it is but like a Christmas game; but we will have our old Service of Matins, mass, evensong, and procession in Latin, as it was before. And so we the Cornish *men whom certain of us understand no English, utterly refuse this new English.*

As concerning the having of the Service in the Latin tongue, is sufficiently spoken of in the answer to the third Article. But I would gladly know the reason, why the *Cornish* men refuse utterly the *New English*, as you call it, because certain of you understand it not: and yet you will have the service in Latin, which almost none of you understands. If this be a sufficient cause for *Cornwall* to refuse the English Service, because some of you understand no English, a much greater cause have they, both of *Cornwall* and *Devonshire*, to refuse utterly the late Service; for as much as fewer of them know the Latin tongue, then they of *Cornwall* the English tongue. But where you say, that you will have the old Service, because the new is *like a Christmas game*, you declare your selves what spirit you be led withal, or rather what spirit leads them that persuaded you that the Word of God is but like a Christmas game.

Your ninth Article is this,
We will have every preacher in his sermon, and every Priest at the Mass, pray especially by name for the souls in purgatory, as our forefathers said.

To reason with you by learning, who are unlearned, it were but folly; Therefore I will convince your Article with very reason. First, Tell me I pray, if you can, whether there be a Purgatory, or no: and Where or What it is. And if you cannot tell, then I may tell you, that you ask you know not what. The Scripture makes mention of two places, where the Dead be received after this life. *Viz.* of Heaven, and of Hell, but of Purgatory is not one word spoken. Purgatory was wont to be called a Fire, as hot as Hell, but not so long enduring. But now the Defenders of Purgatory within this Realm, be ashamed go to say: Nevertheless they say, it is a third place. Where or What it is, they confess themselves they can not tell. And of God's word they have nothing to show neither, Where it is, nor What it is, nor That it is. But all is feigned of their own brains without authority of Scripture.

Likewise a Master, that has an unthrifty Servant, which out of his Master's sight does nothing but riot and disorder himself, if he forgive his servant, and for the love he bears to him, and the desire he has to see him corrected and reformed, he will command him never to be out of his sight: this Command, although indeed it be a great pain to the servant, yet the Master doth it not to punish those faults, which before he had pardoned and forgiven, but to keep him in stay [check], that he fall no more to like disorder. But these examples and cases of punishment here in this life, can in no wise be wrested and drawn to the life to come. And so in no wise can serve for Purgatory.

And further more, seeing that the Scriptures so often and so diligently teaches us, almost in every place, to relieve all them that are in necessity, to feed the hungry, to clothe the naked, to visit the sick and the prisoner, to comfort the sorrowful; and so to all others that have need of our help: and the same in no place makes mention, either of such pains in Purgatory, or what comfort we may do them; it is certain that the same is feigned for lucre, and not grounded upon God's word. For else the Scripture in some place would have told us plainly what case they stood in that be in purgatory, and what relief and help we might do unto them. But as for such as God's word speaks not one word of neither of them both, my counsel shall be, that you keep not the Bishop of *Rome's* Decrees, that you may come to purgatory, but keep God's laws, that you may come to heaven. Or I promise you assuredly, that you shall never escape Hell. Now to your next Article.

Your tenth Article is this,
We will have the Bibles, and all Books of Scripture in English, to be called in again. For we be informed, that otherwise the Clergy shall not of long time confound the Heretics.

Alas! it grieves me to hear your Articles: and much I rue and lament your ignorance: praying God made earnestly once to lighten your eyes, that you may see the truth. What Christian heart would not be grieved to see you so ignorant, (for willingly and willfully, I trust, you do it not) that you refuse Christ, and join your selves with Antichrist. You refuse the holy Bible, and all holy Scriptures so much, that you will have them called in again; and the Bishop of *Rome's* Decrees you will have advanced and observed. I may well say to you as Christ said to *Peter, Turn back again, for you favour not godly things.*

Although you savour so little of godliness, that you like not to read his word with your Eyes, you ought not to be So malicious and envious, to let them that be more godly, and would gladly read it to their comfort and edification. And if there be an *English* Heretic, how will you have him confuted, but in *English*? And whereby else, but by Gods word? Then it follows, that to confute *English* Heretics, we must have God's word in *English*, as all other Nations have it in their own native language. *S. Paul* to the *Ephesians* teaches all men, as well Lay men, as priests, to arm themselves, and to fight against all Adversaries with God's word: Without the which we cannot be able to prevail, neither against subtle Heretics, puissant [powerful] Devils, this deceitful world nor our own sinful selves. And therefore until God's word came to light, the Bishop of *Rome*, under the Prince of darkness, reigned quietly in the world: and his Heresies were received and allowed for the true Catholic Faith. And it can none otherwise be, but that Heretics must reign, where the right of God's Word drives not away our darkness.

[. . .]

Your thirteenth Article is this,
We will that no Gentlemen shall have any more servants than one, to wait upon him, except he may dispend one hundred mark land [without a landed income of one hundred marks, i.e., £33 6s 4d]. *And for every hundred we think it reasonable he should have a man.*

For was it ever seen in any country since the world began, that Commons did appoint the Nobles, and gentlemen, the number of their Servants? Stands it with any reason to turn upside down the good order of the whole world, that is every where, and ever has been? That is to say, The Commoners to be governed by the Nobles; and the Servants by their Masters. Will you now have the Subjects to govern their King, the Villains to rule the Gentlemen, and the Servants their Masters? If men would suffer this, God will not; but will take vengeance on all them, that will break his order; as he did of *Dathan* and *Abiram* although for a time he be a God of much sufferance and hides his indignation under his mercy; That the evil of themselves may repent, and be their own folly.

Your fourteenth Article is this,
We will that the half part of the Abbey lands, and Chantry lands in every man's possession, howsoever he came by them, be given again to two places, where two of the chief Abbeys were within every County. Where such half part shall be taken out; and there to be established a place for devout persons, which shall pray for the King and the Common wealth. And to the same we will have all the Alms of the Church box given for these seven years.

At the beginning you pretended, that you meant nothing against the King's Majesty, but now you open your selves plainly to the world, that you [are] now about to pluck the Crown from his head: and against all justice and equity, not only to take from him Such lands as be annexed unto his Crown, and be parcel of the same: but also against all right and reason, to take from all other men Such lands, as they came to by more just title, by gift, by fare [purchase], by exchange, or otherwise. There is no respect, nor difference had among you, whether they come to them by right, or by wrong. Be you so blind, that you cannot see how justly you proceed, to take the sword in your hand against your prince, and to dispossess just Inheritors without any cause? Christ would not take upon him to judge the right and title of lands betwixt two brethren; and you arrogantly presume, not only to judge, but unjustly to take away all men's right titles; yea, even from the King himself. And do you not tremble for fear, that the Vengeance of God shall fall upon you, before you have grace to repent?

116

Further reading

Michael Bennett, *Lambert Simnel and the Battle of Stoke* (New York, 1987).
Douglas Bush, *The Renaissance and English Humanism* (Toronto, 1939).
S.B. Chrimes, *Henry VII* (New Haven, CT, 1999).
Eamon Duffy, *The Stripping of the Altars* (London, 1992).
Anthony Fletcher and Diarmaid MacCulloch, *Tudor Rebellions* (4th edn, New York 1997).
Jennifer Loach, *Edward VI* (New Haven, CT, 1999).
R. Rex, *Henry VIII and the English Reformation* (London, 1993).
J.J. Scarisbricke, *Henry VIII* (London, 1968).
Joan Thirsk, ed., *The Agrarian History of England and Wales, Volume 4: 1500–1640* (Cambridge, 1991).

8

THE LATER TUDORS

THE MARIAN MARTYRS (1553–8)

Mary Tudor (1516–58), Henry VIII's eldest child, enjoyed a privileged existence until she reached adolescence. Heir apparent to the English throne, she was well educated and the centre of her own household as Princess of Wales. But the collapse of her parent's marriage destroyed the idyll: by 1534 she was the king's bastard daughter, deprived of her rank and subject to harassment for her refusal to abandon her mother's cause or her faith. The birth of her siblings, Elizabeth in 1534 and Edward in 1537, further eclipsed Mary. Henry grew increasingly angry with her for her tenacious grip on Catholicism, and she was shunted farther and farther from the court, subject to increased pressure, and, at times, in fear of her life. The accession of Edward VI in 1547 did little to improve her situation. The new king was in fact far more radical in his religious views than Henry had ever been, and he continued to pressure Mary to conform to Protestantism. But the years of mistreatment and psychological duress had only confirmed Mary in her devotion to Rome, and when Edward died in 1553, she came to the throne determined to restore England to the true faith.

With the support of her new husband, Philip II, King of Spain, and the invaluable assistance of the pope's legate, Reginald Pole, cardinal archbishop of Canterbury, the queen set about the monumental task of ending the English schism. Reproduced here are Mary's instructions to Pole in 1554, revealing her plans for reconciliation. Pressure on Protestants to return to Catholicism grew as time passed. By 1555 the government had launched a more thorough campaign to root out heresy, and some of its first victims were those Mary held personally responsible for leading her subjects astray. Among the most prominent of these were Nicholas Ridley (1500?–1555), bishop of Rochester, and Hugh Latimer (1485?–1555), former bishop of Worcester. Their refusal to recant their views led to their execution at Oxford, described here by John Foxe, the author of *Acts and Monuments of these Latter and Perilous Days*, better known as the 'Book of Martyrs'. Published first in Latin and then, in 1563, in English, it compiled the stories of Christian martyrs throughout the ages, including those executed under Mary. The book became a fundamental text of the Protestant Church of England,

and copies were available in every parish church. Here is Foxe's account of Ridley and Latimer's last moments.

Opinion of the most serene Queen of England which she wrote with her own hand, and gave to his right reverend lordship the legate; cardinal Pole

First – I should wish that all the Church property, which for the discharge of our conscience, the King my husband,* and I have totally renounced, should be distributed as shall seem best to my Lord Cardinal and to the rest of you, so that what has been commenced for the increase of the religion in this kingdom, may produce its due effect.

Secondly – I desire, that the preachers by their piety and doctrine do smother and extinguish all those errors and false opinions disseminated and spread abroad by the late preachers, making provision at the same time, that no book be printed sold or purchased, or brought into the kingdom, without our licence, and under very strict penalties.

Thirdly – I should deem it well, for the churches and universities of this kingdom, to be visited by such persons as my Lord Cardinal and we may know to be fit and sufficient, to execute what is required in this matter.

Fourthly – Touching the punishment of heretics, I believe it would be well to inflict punishment at this beginning, without much cruelty or passion, but without however omitting to do such justice on those who choose by their false doctrines to deceive simple persons, that the people may clearly comprehend that they have not been condemned without just cause, whereby others will be brought to know the truth, and will beware of letting themselves be induced to relapse into such new and false opinions. And above all, I should wish that no one be burned in London, save in the presence of some member of the Council; and, that during such executions, both here and elsewhere, some good and pious sermons be preached, &c.

Fifthly – I really believe it to be by no means fitting, for a plurality of benefices to be placed in the hands of one individual, but that they should be so distributed that each priest may be resident, and have care of his flock, whereas at present, quite the reverse is seen, to which I attribute so great a lack of preachers throughout this kingdom; nor are they of such a sort as they ought to be, so as by their doctrine to overcome the diligence of false preachers in the time of schism, and also by leading an exemplary life, without which in my opinion, their sermons would not be of so much profit as I could wish; and in like manner, as their good example will through them, effect great good, so I acknowledge myself to be very greatly bound on my part also to give the like example by aiding in the disposition and maintenance of such

* Phillip II of Spain.

persons, that they may perform their office and duty well; not forgetting on the other hand, to have those punished who shall do the contrary, that it may serve as a very evident example to the whole of this kingdom, of how I discharge my conscience in this matter, and administer justice by doing so.

The behaviour of Dr. Ridley and Master Latimer at the time of their, death, which was the 16th of October, 1555

Upon the north side of the town,* in the ditch over against Balliol College, the place of execution was appointed and for fear of any tumult that might arise, to let [delay] the burning of them, the lord Williams was commanded, by the queen's letters, and the householders of the city, to be there assistant, sufficiently appointed. And when every thing was in a readiness, the prisoners were brought forth by the mayor and the bailiffs.

Master Ridley had a fair black gown furred . . . such as he was wont to wear being bishop, and a tippet of velvet furred likewise about his neck, a velvet night-cap upon his head, and a corner cap upon the same, going in a pair of slippers to the stake, and going between the mayor and an alderman, etc.

After him came Master Latimer in a poor Bristol frieze frock all worn, with his buttoned cap, and kerchief on his head, all ready to the fire, a new long shroud hanging over his hose, down to the feet: which at the first sight stirred men's hearts to rue upon them, beholding on the one side, the honour they sometime had, and on the other, the calamity whereunto they were fallen.

Master Doctor Ridley, as he passed toward Bocardo,† looked up where Master Cranmer did lie, hoping perhaps to have seen him at the glass-window, and to have spoken to him. But then Master Cranmer was busy with friar Soto and his fellows, disputing together, so that he could not see him, through that occasion. Then Master Ridley, looking back espied Master Latimer coming after, to whom he said, 'Oh, be ye there?' 'Yea,' said Master Latimer, 'have after as fast as I can follow.' So he, following a pretty way off, at length they came both to the stake, the one after the other, where first Dr. Ridley entering the place, marvellously earnestly holding up both his hands, looked towards heaven. Then shortly after espying Master Latimer, with a wonderous cheerful look he ran to him, embraced, and kissed him; and, as they that stood near reported, comforted him, saying, 'Be of good heart, brother, for God will either assuage the fury of the flame, or else strengthen us to abide it.'

With that went he to the stake, kneeled down by it, kissed it, and effectually prayed, and behind him Master Latimer kneeled, as earnestly calling upon God as he. After they arose, the one tarried with the other a little while, till

---

* Oxford.
† The Oxford gaol.

they which were appointed to see the execution, removed themselves out of the sun. What they said I can learn of no man.

Then Dr. Smith, of whose recantation in king Edward's time you heard before, began his sermon to them upon this text of St. Paul, 'If I yield my body to the fire to be burnt, and have not charity, I shall gain nothing thereby.' Wherein he alleged that the goodness of the cause, and not the order of death, makes the holiness of the person; which he confirmed by the examples of Judas, and of a woman in Oxford that of late hanged herself, for that they, and such like as he recited, might then be adjudged righteous, which desperately sundered their lives from their bodies, as he feared that those men that stood before him would do. But he cried still to the people to beware of them, for they were heretics, and died out of the church. And on the other side, he declared their diversity in opinions, as Lutherans, Œlocompadians, Zwinglians,* of which sect they were, he said, and that was the worst: but the old church of Christ, and the catholic faith believed far otherwise. At which place they lifted up both their hands and eyes to heaven, as it were calling God to witness of the truth: the which countenance they made in many other places of his sermon, where they thought he spoke amiss.

He ended with a very short exhortation to them to recant, and come home again to the church, and save their lives and souls, which else were condemned. His sermon was scant; in all, a quarter of an hour.

Dr. Ridley said to Master Latimer, 'Will you begin to answer the sermon, or shall I?' Master Latimer said, 'Begin you first, I pray you.' 'I will,' said Master Ridley.

Then, the wicked sermon being ended, Dr. Ridley and Master Latimer kneeled down upon their knees towards my lord Williams of Thame, the vice-chancellor of Oxford, and divers other commissioners appointed for that purpose, who sat upon a form [bench] thereby; to whom Master Ridley said, 'I beseech you, my lord, even for Christ's sake, that I may speak but two or three words.' And whilst my lord bent his head to the mayor and vice-chancellor, to know (as it appeared) whether he might give him leave to speak, the bailiffs and Dr. Marshall, vice-chancellor, ran hastily unto him, and with their hands stopped his mouth, and said, 'Master Ridley, if you will revoke your erroneous opinions, and recant the same, you shall not only have liberty so to do, but also the benefit of a subject; that is, have your life.' 'Not otherwise?' said Master Ridley. 'No,' quoth Dr. Marshal. 'Therefore if you will not so do, then there is no remedy but you must suffer for your deserts.' 'Well,' quoth Master Ridley, 'so long as the breath is in my body I will never deny my Lord Christ, and his known truth: God's will be done in me!' And with that he rose up, and said with a loud voice, 'Well then; I commit our cause, to Almighty God, which shall indifferently judge all.' To whose saying, Master Latimer

* Referring to supporters of the continental reformers Luther, Œlocompadius, and Zwingli.

added his old posy, 'Well there is nothing hid but it shall be opened.' And he said, he could answer Smith well enough, if he might be suffered.

Incontinently [immediately] they were commanded to make them ready, which they with all meekness obeyed. Master Ridley took his gown and his tippet, and gave it to his brother-in-law Master Shipside, who all his time of imprisonment, although he might not be suffered to come to him [Ridley], lay there at his own charges to provide him necessaries, which from time to time he sent him by the sergeant that kept him. Some other of his apparel that was little worth, he gave away; others the bailiffs took.

He gave away besides, divers other small things to gentlemen standing by, and divers of them pitifully weeping, as to Sir Henry Lea he gave a new groat;* and to divers of my lord Williams's gentlemen some napkins, some nutmegs, and pieces of ginger; his dial, and gifts to such other things as he had about him, to every one that stood next him. Some plucked the points off his hose. Happy was he that might wear any rag of him.

Master Latimer gave nothing, but very quietly suffered his keeper to pull off his hose, and his other array, which to look unto was very simple: and being stripped into his shroud, he seemed as comely a person to them that were there present, as one should lightly see; and whereas in his clothes he appeared a withered and crooked silly old man, he now stood bolt upright, lightly behold!

Then Master Ridley, standing as yet in his truss, said, to his brother, 'It were Best for me to go in my truss still.' 'No,' quoth his brother, 'it will put you to more pain: and the truss will do a poor man good.' Whereunto Master Ridley said, 'Be it, in the name of God;' and so unlaced himself. Then, being in his shirt, he stood upon the aforesaid stone, and held up his hand and said, 'O heavenly Father, I give unto you that most hearty thanks, for that thou hast called me to be a Professor of that, even until death. I beseech thee, Lord God, take mercy upon this realm of England and deliver the same from all her enemies.'

Then the smith took a chain of iron, and brought the same about both Dr. Ridley's, and Master Latimer's middle: and, as he was knocking in a staple, Dr. Ridley took the chain in his hand, and staked the same, for it did gird in his belly, and looking aside to the smith, said, 'Good fellow, knock it in hard, for the flesh will have his course.' Then his brother did bring him gunpowder in a bag, and would have tied the same about his neck. Master Ridley asked, what it was. His brother said. 'Gunpowder'. 'Then,' said he, 'I will take it to be sent of God; therefore I will receive it as sent of him. And have you any,' said he, 'for my brother,' meaning Master Latimer. 'Yea sir, that I have,' quoth his brother. 'Then give it unto him,' said he, 'betime [quickly] lest ye come too late.' So his brother went; and carried of the same gunpowder to Master Latimer.

Then they brought a faggot, kindled with fire, and laid the same down at

* A coin worth fourpence.

Dr. Ridley's feet. To whom Master Latimer spoke in this manner: 'Be of good comfort, Master Ridley, and play the man. We shall this day light such a candle, by God's grace, in England, as I trust shall never be put out.'

And so the fire being given unto them, when Dr. Ridley saw the fire flaming up towards him, he cried with a wonderful loud voice, 'In manus tuas, Domine, commendo spiritum meum: Domine recipe spiritum meum.' And after, repeated this latter part often in English, 'Lord, Lord, receive my spirit;' master Latimer crying as vehemently on the other side, 'O Father of heaven, receive my soul!' who received the flame as it were embracing of it. After that he had stroked his face with his hands, and as it were bathed them a little in the fire, he soon died (as it appeared) with very little pain or none. And thus much concerning the end of this old and blessed servant of God, Master Latimer, for whose labourious travails, fruitful life, and constant death, the Whole realm hath cause to give great thanks to Almighty God.

But Master Ridley, by reason of the evil making of the fire unto him, because the wooden faggots were laid about the gorse, and over-high built, the fire burned first beneath, being kept down by the wood; which when he felt, he desired them for Christ's sake to let the fire come unto him. Which when his brother-in-law heard, but not well understood, intending to rid him out of his pain (for the which cause he gave attendance), as one in such sorrow not well advised what he did, heaped faggots upon him, so that he clean covered him, which made the fire more vehement beneath, that it burned clean all his nether parts, before it once touched the upper, and that made him leap up and down under the faggots, and often desire them to let the fire come unto him, saying, 'I cannot burn.' Which indeed appeared well; for, after his legs were consumed by reason of his struggling through the pain (whereof he had no release, but only his contentation in God), he showed that side toward us clean, shirt and all untouched with flame. Yet in all this torment he forgot not to call unto God still, having in his mouth, 'Lord have mercy upon me,' intermingling his cry, 'Let the fire come unto me, I cannot burn.' In which pangs he laboured till one of the standers by with his bill pulled off the faggots above, and where he saw the fire flame up he wrested himself unto that side. And when the flame touched the gunpowder, he was seen to stir no more but burned on the other side, falling down at Master Latimer's feet; which, some said, happened by reason that the chain loosed; others said, that he fell over the chain by reason of the poise of his body and the weakness of the nether limbs.

Some said, that before he was like to fall from the stake, he desired them to hold him to it with their bills. However it was, surely it moved hundreds to tears, in beholding the horrible sight; for I think there was none that had not clean exiled all humanity and mercy, which would not have lamented to behold the fury of the fire so to rage upon their bodies. Signs there were of sorrow on every side. Some took it grievously to see their deaths, whose lives they held full dear: some pitied their persons, that thought their souls had no need thereof. His brother moved many men, seeing his miserable case, seeing

(I say) him compelled to such infelicity, that he thought then to do him best service, when he hastened his end. Some cried out of the fortune, to see his endeavour (who most dearly loved him, and sought his release) turn to his greater vexation and increase of pain. But whoso considered their preferments in time past, the places of honour that they some time occupied in this commonwealth, the favour they were in with their princes, and the opinion of learning they had in the university where they studied, could not choose but sorrow with tears, to see so great dignity, honour, and estimation, so necessary members sometime accounted, so many godly virtues, the study of so many years, such excellent learning, to be put into the fire, and consumed in one moment. Well! dead they are, and the reward of this world they have already. What reward remains for them in heaven, the day of the Lord's glory, when he cometh with his saints, shall shortly, I trust, declare.

THE SPANISH ARMADA (1588)

Elizabeth I (1533–1603) became embroiled in war with Spain unwillingly. War was costly and unpredictable; moreover, England's principal allies were the Dutch, a people in rebellion against their lawful sovereign. Elizabeth was a Protestant, as were her allies, but she was also a monarch. The war came gradually, as relations between Elizabeth and her former brother-in-law Philip II soured. When she inherited the throne in 1558, Philip actually toyed with the idea of marrying Elizabeth – a proposal she would not have welcomed. The start of the Dutch Revolt in 1568, a papal bull excommunicating the queen in 1572, and Elizabeth's execution of her cousin Mary, Queen of Scots in 1587 were all important milestones in the decay of Anglo-Spanish relations. Elizabeth could not countenance Spain's triumph in the Low Countries, and Philip could not win there without first defeating England. A Spanish invasion was the solution. Troops assembled in the Low Countries would be ferried to England in the summer of 1588 by the Armada, and the duke of Parma, Spain's general, would conquer the island for his master.

The defeat of the Spanish Armada occupies a special place in the English national consciousness. Many myths surround the story; for example, the Spanish fleet was not larger than the English, and more Spanish ships foundered as a result of storms and poor navigation than were actually lost to enemy gunfire. But whatever the reality, the perception, in England and abroad, was of a great victory – and indeed, the Armada was a colossal failure for Spain. The queen's ships performed better in combat, and England decisively prevented invasion. As important was the impact of the victory on Elizabeth's image and the English outlook upon the world. The queen transformed herself from penny-pinching, reluctant warrior, to a female David. This transformation was by no means unstudied, as the queen's words to her troops at Tilbury, printed here, demonstrate. Speaking to thousands of hastily assembled militiamen, Elizabeth defied Philip and put herself at the head of a people whose invincibility was insured by their devotion to their monarch. Richard Hakluyt's day-by-day account of the Armada's agony is another example of the way in which the campaign came to symbolize England's role as a providentially inspired nation. The heroics of her captains, such as Sir Francis Drake, the godliness of her people, and the steadfast courage of her queen were marks of divine favour. Hakluyt's story became a central feature of the English self-image for the rest of the early modern period.

My loving People, we have been persuaded by some that are careful of our safety, to take heed how we commit our self to armed multitudes, for fear of treachery; but I assure you, I do not desire to live to distrust my faithful and loving people. Let tyrants fear. I have always so behaved my self, that under God, I have placed my chiefest strength and safeguard in the loyal hearts and good will of my subjects, and therefore I am come amongst you, as you see, at this time, not for my recreation and disport, but being resolved, in the midst and heat of the battle, to live or die amongst you all, to lay down for my God, and for my Kingdom, and for my People, my honor, and my blood, even in the dust. I know I have the body but of a weak and feeble woman, but I have the heart and stomach of a King, and of a King of England too, and think foul scorn that Parma or Spain, or any Prince of Europe should dare to invade the borders of my Realm; to which, rather than any dishonor shall grow by me, I my self will take up arms, I my self will be your general, judge, and rewarder of every one of your virtues in the field. I know, already for your forwardness, you have deserved rewards and crowns; and we do assure you, in the word of a Prince, they shall be duly paid you.

The miraculous victory achieved by the English Fleet . . . Upon the Spanish Armada sent in the year 1588, for the invasion of England

Having part declared the strange and wonderful events of the year eighty eight, which hath been so long time foretold by ancient prophecies; we will now make relation of the most notable and great enterprise of all others which were in the foresaid year achieved, in order as it was done. Which exploit (although in very deed it was not performed in any part of the low Countries) was intended for their ruin and destruction. And it was the expedition which the Spanish king, having a long time determined the same in his mind, and having consulted thereabout with the Pope, set forth and undertook against England and the low Countries. To the end that he might subdue the Realm of England, and reduce it unto his catholic Religion, and by that means might be sufficiently revenged for the disgrace, contempt and dishonour, which he (having 34 years before enforced them to the Pope's obedience) had endured of the English nation, and for divers other injuries which had taken deep impression in his thoughts. And also for that he deemed this to be the most ready and direct course, whereby he might recover his hereditary possession of the low Countries . . .

At length when as the French king about the end of May [1588] signified unto her Majesty in plain terms that she should stand upon her guard, because he was now most certainly informed, that there was so dangerous an invasion imminent upon her realm, that he feared much lest all her land and sea-forces would be sufficient to withstand it, &c. then began the Queen's Majesty more carefully to gather her forces together, & to furnish her own ships of war, & the principal ships of her subjects with soldiers, weapons, and other necessary provision. The greatest and strongest ships of the whole navy she sent onto Plymouth under the conduct of the right honourable Lord Charles Howard, lord high Admiral of England, &c. Under whom the renowned Knight Sir Francis Drake was appointed Vice-admiral. The number of these ships was about a hundred. The lesser ships being 30 or 40 in number, and under the conduct of the lord Henry Seymour were commanded to lie between Dover and Calais.

On land likewise throughout the whole realm, soldiers were mustered and trained in all places, and were committed unto the most resolute and faithful captains. And whereas it was commonly given out that the Spaniard having once united himself unto the duke of Parma, meant to invade by the river of Thames, there was at Tilbury in Essex over-against Gravesend, a mighty army encamped, and on both sides of the river fortifications were erected, according to the prescription of Frederico Genebelli an Italian engineer. Likewise there were certain ships brought to make a bridge, though it were very late first. Unto the said army came in proper person the Queens most royal Majesty . . . Also there were other such armies levied in England.

The principal catholic Recusants (least they should stir up any tumult in the time of the Spanish invasion) were sent to remain at certain convenient places, as namely in the Isle of Ely and at Wisbech. And some of them were sent unto other places, to wit, unto sundry bishops and noblemen, where they were kept from endangering the state of the common wealth, and of her sacred Majesty, who of her most gracious clemency gave express commandment, that they should be treated with all humanity and friendship . . .

Upon Tuesday which was the three and twenty of July, the navy being come over against Portland, the wind began to turn northerly, insomuch that the Spaniards had a fortunate and fit gale to invade the English. But the Englishmen having lesser and nimbler Ships, recovered again the vantage of the wind from the Spaniards, whereat the Spaniards seemed to be more incensed to fight than before. But when the English Fleet had continually and without intermission from morning to night, beaten and battered them with all their shot both great and small: the Spaniards uniting themselves, gathered their whole Fleet close together into a roundel, so that it was apparent that they meant not as yet to invade others, but only to defend themselves and to make haste unto the place prescribed unto them, which was near unto Dunkirk, that they might join forces with the duke of Parma, who was determined to have proceeded secretly with his small ships under the shadow and protection of the great ones, and so had intended circumspectly to perform the whole expedition.

This was the most furious and bloody skirmish of all, in which the lord Admiral of England continued fighting amidst his enemy's Fleet, and seeing one of his Captains afar off, he spoke unto him in these words: Oh George what doest thou? Wilt thou now frustrate my hope and opinion conceived of that? Wilt thou forsake me now? With which words he being inflamed, approached forthwith, encountered the enemy, and did the part of a most valiant Captain. His name was George Fenner, a man that had been conversant in many Sea-fights.

In this conflict there was a certain great Venetian ship with other small ships surprised and taken by the English.

The English navy in the mean while increased, whereunto out of all Havens of the Realm resorted ships and men: for they all with one accord came flocking thither as unto a set field, where immortal fame and glory was to be attained, and faithful service to be performed unto their prince and country.

In which number there were many great and honourable personages, as namely, the Earls of Oxford, of Northumberland, of Cumberland, &c. with many Knights and Gentlemen . . . And so it came to pass that the number of the English ships amounted unto a hundred: which when they were come before Dover, were increased to an hundred and thirty, being notwithstanding of no proportionable bigness to encounter with the Spaniards, except two or three and twenty of the Queens greater ships, which only, by reason of their presence, bred an opinion in the Spaniards minds concerning the power of the English Fleet: the mariners and soldiers whereof were esteemed to be twelve thousand . . . And albeit there were many excellent and warlike ships in the English fleet, yet scarce were there 22 or 23 among them all which matched 90 of the Spanish ships in bigness, or could conveniently assault them. Wherefore the English ships using their prerogative of nimble steerage, whereby they could turn and wield themselves with the wind which way they listed, came often times very near upon the Spaniards, and charged them so sore, that now and then they were but a pike's length apart & so continually giving them one broadside after another, they discharged all their shot both great and small upon them, spending one whole day from morning till night in that violent kind of conflict, until such time as powder and bullets failed them. In regard of which want they thought it convenient not to pursue the Spaniards any longer, because they had many great vantages of the English, namely for the extraordinary bigness of their ships, and also for that they were so nearly conjoined, and kept together in so good array, that they could by no means besought withal one to one. The English thought therefore, that they had right well acquitted themselves, in chasing the Spaniards first from Calais, and then from Dunkirk, and by that means to have hindered them from joining with the Duke of Parma his forces, and getting the wind of them, to have driven them from their own coasts.

The Spaniards that day sustained great loss and damage having many of their ships shot through and through, and they discharged likewise great store of ordnance against the English; who indeed sustained some hindrance, but not comparable to the Spaniard's loss: for they lost not any one ship or person of account. For very urgent inquisition being made, the English men all that time wherein the Spanish Navy sailed upon their seas, are not found to have wanted above one hundred of their People: albeit Sir Francis Drake's ship was pierced with shot above forty times, and his very cabin was twice shot thorough, and about the conclusion of the fight, the bed of a certain gentleman lying weary thereupon, was taken quite from under him with the force of a bullet. Likewise, as the Earl of Northumberland and Sir Charles Blunt were at dinner upon a time, the bullet of a demiculverin broke thorough the midst of their cabin, touched their feet, and struck down two of the standers by, with many such accidents befalling the English ships, which it were tedious to rehearse. Whereupon it is most apparent, that God miraculously preserved the English nation. For the L. Admiral wrote unto her Majesty that in all human reason, and according to the judgement of all men (every circumstance being duly considered) the English men were not of any such force, whereby they might, without a miracle, dare once to approach within sight of the Spanish Fleet: insomuch that they freely ascribed all the honour of their victory unto God, who had confounded the enemy, and had brought his counsels to no effect . . .

While this wonderful and puissant Navy [the Armada] was sailing along the English coasts, and all men did now plainly see and hear that which before they would not be persuaded of, all people throughout England prostrated themselves with humble prayers and supplications unto God . . . knowing right well, that prayer was the only refuge against all enemies, calamities, and necessities, and that it was the only solace and relief for mankind, being visited with affliction and misery. Likewise such solemn days of supplication were observed throughout the united Provinces.

Also a while after the Spanish Fleet was departed, there was in England, by the commandment of her Majesty, and in the united Provinces, by the direction of the States, a solemn festival day publicly appointed, wherein all persons were enjoined to resort unto the Church, and there to render thanks and praises unto God: and the Preachers were commanded to exhort the people thereunto. The foresaid solemnity was observed upon the 29 of November; which day was wholly spent in fasting, prayer, and giving of thanks.

Likewise, the Queen's Majesty herself, imitating the ancient Romans, rode into London in triumph, in regard of her own and her subject's glorious deliverance. For being attended upon very solemnly by all the principal Estates and officers of her Realm, she was carried thorough her said City of London in a triumphant chariot, and in robes of triumph, from her Palace unto the Cathedral Church of Saint Paul, out of the which the ensigns and colours of the vanquished Spaniards hung displayed. And all the Citizens of London in their Liveries stood on either side the street, by their several Companies, with their ensigns and banners: and the streets were hanged on both sides with Blue cloth, which, together with the foresaid banners, yielded a very stately and gallant prospect. Her Majesty being entered into the Church, together with her Clergy and Nobles gave thanks unto God, and caused a public Sermon to be preached before her at Paul's Cross; wherein no other argument was handled, but that praise, honour, and glory might be rendered unto God, and that God's name might be extolled by thanksgiving. And with her own princely voice she most Christianly exhorted the people to do the same: whereby upon the people with a loud acclamation wished her a most long and happy life, to the confusion of her foes.

Thus the magnificent, huge, and mighty fleet of the Spaniards (which themselves termed in all places invincible) such as sailed not upon the Ocean sea many hundred years before, in the year 1588 vanished into smoke; to the great confusion and discouragement of the authors thereof . . .

Further reading

Simon Adams and M.J. Rodriguez-Salgado, eds, *England, Spain, and the Grand Armada* (London, 1991).
D.M. Loades, *Mary Tudor: A Life* (Oxford, 1989).
Garrett Mattingly, *The Armada* (New York, 1972).
Thomas F. Mayer, *Reginald Pole, Prince and Prophet* (Cambridge, 2000).
Geoffrey Parker, *The Grand Strategy of Philip II* (New Haven, CT, 2000).
Robert Tittler, ed., *The Reign of Mary I* (London, 1991).

9

THE EARLY STUARTS
AND CIVIL WAR

THE GUNPOWDER PLOT (1605)

English Catholics greeted James I's (1566–1625) accession to the throne with great hope. They viewed his mother, Mary, Queen of Scots, as a martyr for the faith, and though James himself was Protestant, as king of Scotland he had shown no inclination towards persecution. He maintained cordial relations with the papacy, and was well known for his dislike of the more extreme forms of Puritanism. After their sufferings under Elizabeth, many recusants saw James as a deliverer. They were disappointed. Although James had no plan to extirpate Catholicism root and branch, he was aware that recusants presented a greater potential threat in England than in Scotland. Moreover, reaffirming the laws against Catholics was popular with many of his new subjects, whose anti-Catholic views had only grown stronger since the defeat of the Armada. Those laws equated Catholicism with treason; they punished priests as foreign spies, and those who sheltered them also faced ruin or death. Catholic homes could be ransacked by searches for priests or religious paraphernalia like rosaries, and recusants' fortunes dwindled under the burden of the monthly £20 fines imposed on those who refused to attend church. Although the laws were only enforced sporadically, they nevertheless imposed great hardship upon the Catholic population.

In his first year on the throne James did nothing to dash recusants' hopes, but by early 1604 he began to act more forcefully, ordering priests out of the country and insisting upon the enforcement of recusancy laws. It was in this context that the plan to destroy the king and most of the Protestant establishment was hatched, principally by Robert Catesby (1573–1605) and Thomas Percy (1560–1605), Catholic gentlemen who believed that direct action was the only way to end persecution. They gathered together a small band of conspirators and worked towards their goal: the overthrow of King and Parliament at their meeting in November 1605.

Excerpted here are two documents connected with the plot. The first is from the pen of Father John Gerard (1564–1637), a Jesuit priest whom the government identified as a mastermind of the plan. Gerard's role was in fact less central, but it is clear that he was aware of a treasonous conspiracy. Here he explains what drove Catesby and his fellows to act: the merciless hounding of innocent Catholics. The second is Guy (or Guido, as he was known at the time) Fawkes's (1570–1606) confession. Extracted under torture, Fawkes's story is correct in most of its details, and cemented him in the popular mind as the 'Devil of the Vault'. Although he was not the leader of the conspiracy, it was Fawkes who the authorities caught in Parliament's cellars, preparing to ignite thousands of pounds of gunpowder. Along with the other plotters, he was convicted of treason and executed.

The Gunpowder Plot became another crucial milestone in English history. Like the Armada, it reaffirmed popular fear and hatred of Catholics, who were inextricably connected with treason. More positively, it once again demonstrated England's uniqueness as a nation watched over by God. Every 5 November the pulpits rang with denunciations of Romish treason and praise for God's mercy in delivering a Protestant people from the hands of its enemies.

The state of persecuted Catholics at the Queen's death and the King's entry, with their hopes of relaxation by him, whereof they failed

I was desirous by the former chapter to make known unto you the state of things, how they passed in England until the end of Queen Elizabeth's reign; wherein though I was more long than I had thought to be, yet little methinks is said in comparison of that feeling which we must needs have that live here, and see daily before our eyes 'abominationem desolationis stantem in loco sancto',* that have so many causes to put us often in mind of the glory and splendour of the Church robbed and spoiled by the first schism under King Henry, overthrown and defaced by heresy, beginning to prevail under King Edward; and wholly trodden upon and cruelly persecuted during all the long reign of Queen Elizabeth, in which all means were used that policy could invent, or power perform, to root out all Catholics and Catholic religion out of England.

To which effect they continually devised and imposed all kinds of penalties upon such as would profess the Roman Faith. They made sundry and most severe statutes against all practice of Catholic religion. They made it death to receive the absolution of a Priest; yea, death to harbour a Priest in [a] house, or to give him a cup of drink, or any assistance in his need; death to persuade any to the Catholic religion . . .

True it is that most Catholics had great hope and expectation of this lying James, then King of Scotland only. And this hope [survived], as a human help of no small force did join with God's grace and bring some comfort with it, amidst the many discomforts sustained under the long continued reign of Queen Elizabeth.

* 'The abomination of desolation standing in the holy place' (Matthew 24. 5).

First, they did, and might, expect that the son of such a mother* (who not only lived a Catholic in her kingdom and in prison, but died, also because she was a Catholic) would himself also be a friend to Catholics at least, if he would not be a follower of Catholic religion . . .

But now what shall we think to have been the state of all Catholic minds when all these hopes did vanish away; and as a flash of lightning, giving for the time a pale light unto those that sit in darkness, doth afterwards leave them in more desolation? What grief may we imagine they felt generally, when not only no one of these hopes did bring forth the hoped fruit, nor any promise was performed, but when, on the contrary side, His Majesty did suffer himself to be guided and as it were governed by those that had so long time inured their hands and hardened their hearts with so violent a persecution; yea, when he did not only confirm the former laws with which we were afflicted, but permitted new and more grievous vexations to fall upon us than before we had felt, and prepared yet more and more heavy whips wherewith to scourge us? Truly the event proved contrary to all our hopes. For, first, it was observed that some weeks after his being In England, he began to use far different speech of and against Catholics than was expected from the son of such a mother. And when soon afterward there ensued his first Parliament, he made a bitter speech (now extant in print) against them all; but especially, to our greater increase of grief and despair of comfort, against the see Apostolic, much different from that was expected, where so great favours and tokens of love had been received . . .

The increase of persecution, and all kind of molestations unto Catholics, with their failing of all hopes, procured by the puritan faction

Such as be acquainted with the state of affairs in England cannot be ignorant that there be many at this time of the Puritan faction put in authority and place of government especially concerning the persecution of Catholics. All which, as they be further gone in heresy than the ordinary sort of moral Protestants be, so are they More violent enemies against all Catholics and, Catholic proceedings . . .

Now if we should stand upon the particular enumeration of the calamities which fall upon Catholics by private persons, and especially Puritans put in authority over them, the many insolences and molestations which are offered in the searches which are used in most odious manner, and so have been ever since this first Parliament, it would much afflict the hearts of the pious readers. And it is to be thought that many particulars thereof are not known to His Majesty, though all exercised and executed in his name, and under his

---

* Mary Queen of Scots, executed by Elizabeth in 1587.

authority. What a thing is it for a Catholic gentleman to have his house suddenly beset on all sides with a number of men in arms both horse and foot, and not only his house and gardens and such inclosed places all beset, but all highways laid for some miles near unto him, that none shall pass but they shall be examined! Then are these searchers ofttimes so rude and barbarous that, if the doors be not opened in the instant when they would enter, they break open the doors with all violence, as if they were to sack a town of enemies won by the sword, which is a strange proceeding, and proper only to our persecuted state at this time, for it is not used elsewhere, but with us so Common that no man can have assurance of one hour's quiet or safety within the walls of his own habitation, which yet in just and peaceable commonwealths should be his fortress and castle . . .

Briefly, their insolences are so many and so outrageous, and thereby the miseries and afflictions of Catholics were so much increased and multiplied, that It seemed to many very intolerable to be long endured; The only hope might be that which at those times Priests did labour to persuade, and divers of the graver Catholics were yet content to believe, might be possible (as in darkness, the least glimpse of light, though but far off, doth bring some comfort, in hope it may come nearer), and that was the memory of His Majesty's faithful promises, which, being given on the word of a Prince, they thought could not be violated, unless they should hear himself to speak the contrary. This only hope did yet live in some, though many apparent proofs to the contrary did continually weaken it. But this little spark of light also was soon after clean put out, no doubt by the industry and malicious procurement of the Puritans, whose custom it is to incense the King against Catholics by some false information, and thereby to draw from His Majesty certain bitter speeches and invectives against Catholics, Which then themselves are forward to publish, thereby to put Catholics the more in despair, and by despair into some cause giving of further afflictions, like him that will beat a child to make him cry, and then beat him because he crieth . . .

Guy Fawkes's Confession

I confess that a practice, in general, was first broken unto me against His Majesty, for relief of the Catholic cause, and not invented or propounded by myself. And this was first propounded unto me about Easter last was twelvemonth, beyond the seas, in the [Spanish] Low Countries, by Thomas Winter, who came thereupon with me into England, and there we imported our purpose to three other gentlemen more, namely, Robert Catesby, Thomas Percy, and John Wright; who all five consulting together of the means how to execute the same; and taking a vow among ourselves for secrecy, Catesby propounded to have it performed by gunpowder, and by making a mine under the upper House of Parliament, which place we made choice of the rather, because religion having been unjustly suppressed there, it was fittest that justice and punishment should be executed there. This being resolved amongst us, Thomas Percy hired a house at Westminster for that purpose, near adjoining to the Parliament House, and there we began, to make our mine about the 11th of December, 1604. The five that first entered into the work were Thomas Percy, Robert Catesby, Thomas Winter, John Wright, and myself; and soon after we took another unto us, Christopher Wright, having sworn him also, and taken the sacrament for secrecy. When we came to the very foundation of the wall of the house, which was about three yards thick, and found it a matter of great difficulty, we took unto us another gentleman, Robert Keyes, in like manner, with the oath and sacrament as aforesaid. It was about Christmas when we brought our mine under the wall, and about Candlemas we had wrought the wall half through; and while they were in working I stood as sentinel, to descry any man that came near; whereof I gave them warning, and so they ceased, until I gave notice again to proceed. All we seven lay in the house, and had shot and powder being resolved to die in that place before we should yield or be taken. Whilst they were a working upon the wall they heard a rushing in a cellar of removing of coals, whereupon we feared we had been discovered, and they sent me to go to the cellar, who, finding that the coals were a selling, and that the cellar was to be let, viewing the commodity thereof for our purpose, Percy went and hired the same for yearly rent. We had before this provided and brought into the house twenty barrels of powder, which we removed into the cellar, and covered the same with billets and faggots which we provided for that purpose. About Easter the Parliament being prorogued till October next, we dispersed ourselves and I returned into the Low Countries, lest by my longer stay I might have grown suspicious, and so have come in question. In the mean time Percy having the key of the cellar, laid in more powder and wood into it. I returned, about the beginning of September next, and then, receiving the key again of Percy, we brought in more powder and billets to cover the same again, and so I went for a time into the country, till the 30th of October. It was further resolved amongst us that the same day that this act should have been performed, some other of our confederates should have surprised the person of the Lady Elizabeth, the King's eldest daughter, who was kept in Warwickshire, at the Lord Harrington's house, and presently have proclaimed her queen, having a project of a proclamation ready for that purpose; wherein we made no mention of altering religions, nor would have avowed the deed to be ours until we should have had our power enough to make our party good, and then we would have avowed both. Concerning Duke Charles, the King's second son, we had sundry consultations how to seize on his person; but because we found no means how to compass it, the Duke being kept near London, where we had not forces enough, we resolved to serve our turn with the Lady Elizabeth . . .

THE GRAND REMONSTRANCE (1641)

The passage of the Grand Remonstrance on 23 November 1641 marked a key moment in Britain's descent into civil war. In 204 articles the Remonstrance catalogued the accumulated grievances of Charles I's reign, beginning with the assembly of his first Parliament only weeks after his accession in 1625. Primarily the work of John Pym (1583–1643) and his allies, it was less a demonstration of the opposition's strength than a measure of its desperation. King Charles's partisans in the Long Parliament had grown steadily in numbers since the execution of the royal friend and counsellor the earl of Strafford (b. 1593) in May 1641. The explosive outbreak of rebellion in Ireland further increased pressure upon Pym. He could, and repeatedly did, use it as dramatic evidence of the Catholic conspiracy that threatened the state. But the king, as commander-in-chief, would lead an army to suppress the rebels, and with soldiers at his command he might well act against his English enemies as well. The Grand Remonstrance was part of Pym's plan to undercut Charles's revived political hopes; it reminded the people of the king's failures and more importantly demanded that Parliament should play a role in choosing royal counsellors. The Remonstrance further divided the nation. It passed the House of Commons with a narrow majority: 159 to 148 votes, and was then printed and distributed throughout the country, despite the bitter complaints of its opponents and members of the House of Lords.

Reproduced here is the petition that accompanied the lengthy Remonstrance, which sums up its contents and the opposition's demands, and the king's reply. Charles's firm rejection of the Remonstrance's premises and of the key demands it contained is a mark of his own confidence in his position and of the strength he could muster to maintain it.

The grand remonstrance, with the petition accompanying it

The Petition of the House of Commons, which accompanied the Remonstrance of the state of the kingdom, when it was presented to His Majesty at Hampton Court, December 1, 1641

Most Gracious Sovereign

Your Majesty's most humble and faithful subjects the Commons in this present Parliament assembled, do with much thankfulness and joy acknowledge the great mercy and favour of God, in giving your Majesty a safe and peaceable return out of Scotland into your kingdom of England, where the pressing dangers and distempers of the State have caused us with much earnestness to desire the comfort of your gracious presence, and likewise the unity and justice of your royal authority, to give more life and power to the dutiful and loyal counsels and endeavours of your Parliament, for the prevention of that eminent ruin and destruction wherein your kingdoms of England and Scotland are threatened. The duty which we owe to your Majesty and our country, cannot but make us very sensible and apprehensive, that the multiplicity, sharpness and malignity of those evils under which we have now many years suffered, are fomented and cherished by a corrupt and ill-affected party, who amongst other their mischievous devices for the alteration of religion and government, have sought by many false scandals and imputations, cunningly insinuated and dispersed amongst the people, to blemish and disgrace our proceedings in this Parliament, and to get themselves a party and faction amongst your subjects, for the better strengthening themselves in their wicked courses, and hindering those provisions and remedies which might, by the wisdom of your Majesty and counsel of your Parliament, be opposed against them.

For preventing whereof, and the better information of your Majesty, your Peers and all other your loyal subjects, we have been necessitated to make a declaration of the state of the kingdom, both before and since the assembly of this Parliament, unto this time, which we do humbly present to your Majesty, without the least intention to lay any blemish upon your royal person, but only to represent how your royal authority and trust have been abused, to the great prejudice and danger of your Majesty, and of all your good subjects.

And because we have reason to believe that those malignant parties, whose proceedings evidently appear to be mainly for the advantage and increase of Popery, is composed, set up, and acted by the subtle practice of the Jesuits and other engineers and factors for Rome, and to the great danger of this kingdom, and most grievous affliction of your loyal subjects, have so far prevailed as to corrupt divers of your Bishops and others in prime places of the Church, and also to bring divers of these instruments to be of your Privy Council, and other employments of trust and nearness about your Majesty, the Prince, and the rest of your royal children.

And by this means have had such an operation in your counsel and the most important affairs and proceedings of your government, that a most dangerous division and chargeable preparation for war betwixt your kingdoms of England and Scotland, the increase of jealousies betwixt your Majesty and your most obedient subjects, the violent distraction and interruption of this Parliament, the insurrection of the Papists in your kingdom of Ireland, and bloody massacre of your people, have been not only endeavoured and attempted, but in a great measure compassed and effected.

For preventing the final accomplishment whereof, your poor subjects are enforced to engage their persons and estates to the maintaining of a very expensive and dangerous war notwithstanding they have already since the beginning of this Parliament undergone the charge of £150,000 sterling, or thereabouts, for the necessary support and supply of your Majesty in these present and perilous designs. And because all our most faithful endeavours and engagements will be ineffectual for the peace, safety and preservation of your Majesty and your people, if some present, real and effectual course be not taken for suppressing this wicked and malignant party:

We, your most humble and obedient subjects, do with all faithfulness and humility beseech your Majesty,

1. That you will be graciously pleased to concur with the humble desires of your people in a parliamentary way, for the preserving the peace and safety of the kingdom from the malicious designs of the Popish party:

For depriving the Bishops of their votes in Parliament, and abridging their immoderate power usurped over the Clergy, and other your good subjects, which they have perniciously abused to the hazard of religion, and great prejudice and oppression to the laws of the kingdom, and just liberty of your people.

For the taking away such oppressions in religion, Church government and discipline, as have been brought in and fomented by them:

For uniting all such your loyal subjects together as join in the same fundamental truths against the Papists, by removing some oppressive and unnecessary ceremonies by which divers weak consciences have been scrupled, and seem to be divided from the rest, and for the due execution of those good laws which have been made for securing the liberty of your subjects.

2. That your Majesty will likewise be pleased to remove from your council all such as persist to favour and promote any of those pressures and corruptions wherewith your people have been grieved; and that for the future your Majesty will vouchsafe to employ such persons in your great and public affairs, and to take such to be near you in places of trust, as your Parliament may have cause to confide in; that in your princely goodness to your people you will reject and refuse all mediation and solicitation to the contrary, how powerful and near soever.

3. That you will be pleased to forbear to alienate any of the forfeited and escheated lands in Ireland which shall accrue to your Crown by reason of this rebellion, that out of them the Crown may be the better supported, and some satisfaction made to your subjects of this kingdom for the great expenses they are like to undergo [in] this war.

Which humble desires of ours being graciously fulfilled by your Majesty, we will, by the blessing and favour of God, most cheerfully undergo the hazard and expenses of this war, and apply ourselves to such other courses and counsels as may support your real estate with honour and plenty at home, with power and reputation abroad, and by our loyal affections, obedience and service, lay a sure and lasting foundation of the greatness and prosperity of your Majesty, and your royal posterity in future times.

The King's answer to the petition accompanying the grand remonstrance

We having received from you, soon after our return out of Scotland, a long petition consisting of many desires of great moment, together with a declaration of a very unusual nature annexed hereunto, we had taken some time to consider of it, as befitted us in a matter of that consequence, being confident that your own reason and regard to us, as well as our express intimation by our comptroller* to that purpose, would have restrained you from the publishing of it till such time as you should have received our answer to it; but, much against our expectation, finding the contrary, that the said declaration is already abroad in print, by directions from your House as appears by the printed copy, we must let you know that we are very sensible of the disrespect. Notwithstanding, it is our intention that no failing on your part shall make us fail in ours of giving all due satisfaction to the desires of our people in a parliamentary way; and therefore we send you this answer to your petition, reserving ourself in point of the declaration which we think unparliamentary, and shall take a course to do that which we shall think fit in prudence and honour.

To the petition, we say that although there are divers things in the preamble of it which we are so far from admitting that we profess we cannot at all understand them, as of 'a wicked and malignant party prevalent in the government'; of 'some of that party admitted to our Privy Council and to other employments of trust, and nearest to us and our children; of endeavours to sow among the people false scandals and imputations, to blemish and disgrace the proceedings of the Parliament'; all, or any of them, did we know of, we should be as ready to remedy and punish as you to complain of, so that the prayers of your petition are grounded upon such premises as we must in no wise admit; yet, notwithstanding, we are pleased to give this answer to you.

To the first, concerning religion, consisting of several branches, we say that, for preserving the peace and safety of this kingdom from the design of the Popish party, we have, and will still, concur with all the just desires of our people in a parliamentary way: that, for the depriving of the Bishops of their votes in Parliament, we would have you consider that their right is grounded upon the fundamental law of the kingdom and constitution of Parliament. This we would have you consider; but since you desire our concurrence herein in a parliamentary way, we will give no further answer at this time.

As for the abridging of the inordinate power of the clergy we conceive that the taking away of the High Commission Court hath well moderated that; but if there continue any usurpations or excesses in their jurisdictions, we therein neither have nor will protect them.

Unto that clause which concerns corruptions (as you style them) in religion, in Church government, and in discipline, and the removing of such unnecessary ceremonies as weak consciences might check at: that for any illegal innovations which may have crept in, we shall willingly concur in the removal of them: that, if our Parliament shall advise us to call a national

* Sir Thomas Jermyn.

synod, which may duly examine such ceremonies as give just cause of offense to any, we shall take it into consideration, and apply ourself to give due satisfaction therein; but we are very sorry to hear, in such general terms, corruption in religion objected, since we are persuaded in our consciences that no Church can be found upon the earth that professes the true religion with more purity of doctrine than the Church of England doth, nor where the government and discipline are jointly more beautified and free from superstition, than as they are here established by law, which, by the grace of God, we will with constancy maintain (while we live) in their purity and glory, not only against all invasions of Popery, but also from the irreverence of those many schismatics and separatists, Herewith of late this kingdom and this city abounds, to the great dishonour and hazard both of Church and State, for the suppression of whom we require your timely aid and active assistance.

To the second prayer of the petition, concerning the removal and choice of councillors, we know not any of our Council to whom the character set forth in the petition can belong: that by those whom we had exposed to trial, we have already given you sufficient testimony that there is no man so near unto us in place or affection, whom we will not leave to the justice of the law, if you shall bring a particular charge and sufficient proof against him; and of this we do again assure you, but in the meantime we wish you to forbear such general aspersions as may reflect upon all our Council, since you name none in particular.

That for the choice of our councillors and ministers of state, it were to debar us that natural liberty all freemen have; and as it is the undoubted right of the Crown of England to call such persons to our secret counsels, to public employment and our particular service as we shall think fit, so we are, and ever shall be, very careful to make election of such persons in those places of trust as shall have given good testimonies of their abilities and integrity, and against whom there can be no just cause of exception whereon reasonably to ground a diffidence; and to choices of this nature, we assure you that the mediation of the nearest unto us hath always concurred.

To the third prayer of your petition concerning Ireland, we understand your desire of not alienating the forfeited lands thereof, to proceed from much care and love, and likewise that it may be a resolution very fit for us to take; but whether it be seasonable to declare resolutions of that nature before the events of a war be seen, that we much doubt of. Howsoever, we cannot but thank you for this care, and your cheerful engagement for the suppression of that rebellion; upon the speedy effecting whereof, the glory of God in the Protestant profession, the safety of the British there, our honour, and that of the nation, so much depends; all the interests of this kingdom being so involved in that business, we cannot but quicken your affections therein, and shall desire you to frame your counsels, to give such expedition to the work as the nature thereof and the pressures in point of time require;

and whereof you are put in mind by the daily insolence and increase of those rebels.

For conclusion, your promise to apply yourselves to such courses as may support our royal estate with honour and plenty at home, and with power and reputation abroad, is that which we have ever promised ourself, both from your loyalties and affections, and also for what we have already done, and shall daily go adding unto, for the comfort and happiness of our people.

THE ANSWER TO THE NINETEEN
PROPOSITIONS (1642)

The descent into civil war after the Grand Remonstrance was gradual, but inexorable. Conflict was hastened by the king's failed attempt to arrest Pym and four other members of Parliament early in January 1642. Both sides sought to secure the high moral ground as well as the arms and ammunition needed for the coming clash. Parliament's Nineteen Propositions of 1 June was a comprehensive statement of its position and demands. King Charles, in York marshalling his forces, seized upon the Propositions as damning evidence of parliamentary radicalism. His answer, drafted by John Colepepper (1600–60) and Lucius Carey, Lord Falkland (c.1610–43), repudiated Parliament's ambitions. The Propositions insisted that Charles surrender most of his sovereign power: Parliament would henceforth approve the king's ministers, command the militia, ratify royal marriage treaties, and even supervise the education of the king's children.

Charles's answer did not spare his adversaries from abuse: they were 'cabalists' engaged in 'bold-faced treason' – but it also strove to present the king as the moderate defender of the traditional constitution. Most importantly it advanced the idea of English government as a balance between the three estates of King, Lords, and Commons. Each estate had the responsibility of checking the ambitions of its fellows, thereby defending the interests of the kingdom at large. How far Charles actually subscribed to this notion is unclear, for it would have limited royal powers in ways that he had always resisted. Nevertheless, the studied moderation of the answer won Charles the support of wavering moderates. More importantly, the argument became a precedent for the future, and would become an established theme in Anglo-American political thought.

His Majesties Answer to the nineteen propositions of both
Houses of Parliament

. . . We suppose these demands By this time to appear such as the Demanders cannot be supported to have any such real care of us as hath been long pretended, they are too much in the style, not only of equals, but of Conquerors, and as little to be intended for removing of jealousies. But we call God witness, that as for our Subject's sake these Rights are vested in us, so for their sake, as well as for our own, We are resolved not to quit them nor to subvert, (though in a parliamentary way) the ancient, equal, happy, well-poised and never enough commended Constitution of the Government of this Kingdom, nor to make Our self of a King of England a Duke of *Venice*, and this Kingdom a Republic.

There being three kinds of Government amongst men, Absolute Monarchy, Aristocracy and Democracy, and all these having their particular conveniences and inconveniences. The experience and wisdom of your Ancestors hath so molded this out of a mixture of these, as to give this Kingdom (as far as our Precedents provide) the conveniences of all three, without the inconveniences of any one, (as long as the Balance hangs even between the three Estates and run jointly on in their proper Chanell) begetting verdure and Fertile Meadows on both sides and the overflowing of either one entails deluge or Inundation. The ill of absolute Monarchy is Tyranny, the ill of Aristocracy is faction and division, the ills of Democracy are Tumults, violence and licentousness. The good of Monarchy is the uniting a Nation under one head to resist Invasion from abroad, and Insurrection at home: the good of Aristocracy is the Conjunction of Counsel in the able persons of a State for the public benefit: The good of Democracy is Liberty and the Courage and Industry which Liberty begets.

In this Kingdom the *Laws* are jointly made by a King, by a House of Peers, and by a House of Commons chosen by the People, all having free Votes and particular *Privileges*: The Government according to these Laws is trusted to the King, power of Treaties of war and Peace, of making Peers, of choosing Officers and Counsellors for State, Judges for Law, Commanders for Forts and Castles, giving Commissions for raising men to make War abroad or to prevent or provide against Invasions, or Insurrections at home, benefit of Confiscations, power of pardoning, and some more of the like kinds are placed in the King. And the kind of regulated Monarchy having this power to preserve that Authority, without which it would be disabled to preserve the Laws in their Force, and the Subjects in their liberties and properties, is intended to draw to him such a Respect and Relation from the great Ones, as may hinder the ills of Division and Faction, and such a Fear and Reverence from the people, as may hinder Tumults, Violence and licenciousness. Again, that the Prince may not make use of this high and perpetual power to the hurt of those for whose good [he has] it, make use of the name of public Necessity for the gain of his private Favorites and followers, to the detriment of his people, the House of Commons (an excellent conserver of Liberty, but never intended for any share in Government, or the choosing of them that should govern) is solely entrusted with the first Propositions concerning the Levies of Money (which is the sinews as well of Peace as War) and the impeaching of those, who for their own ends, though countenanced by any surreptitiously gotten Command of the King, have violated that Law, which he is bound (when he knows it) to protect, and to the protection of which they were bound to advise him, at least not to serve him in the Contrary. And the Lords being trusted with a Judicial power, are an excellent Screen and Bank between the Prince and people, to assist each against any Encroachments of the other, and by just Judgements to preserve that law, which ought to be the rule of every one of the three. For the better enabling them in this, beyond the Examples of any of Our Ancestors, We were willing contented to oblige Our self both to call a Parliament every three years, and not to dissolve it in fifty days, and for the present exigent, the better to raise Money, and avoid the pressure (no less grievous to us than them) Our people must have suffered by a longer continuance of so vast a Charge as too great Armies, and for their greater certainty of having sufficient time to remedy the inconveniences arisen during so long an absence of Parliament and for the punishment of the Causers and ministers of them We yielded up Our Right of dissolving this Parliament, expecting an extraordinary moderation from it in gratitude for so unexampled a Grace, and little looking that any Malignant Party should have been encouraged or enabled to have persuaded them, first to continue the Injustices and indignities We have endured, and then by a new way of Satisfaction for what was taken from us, to demand of us at once to Confirm what was so taken and to give up almost all the rest.

Since therefore the power Legally placed in both Houses is more than sufficient to preserve and restrain the power of Tyranny, and without the power which is now asked us, we shall not be able to discharge that trust which is the end of monarchy, since this would be a total Subversion of the Fundamental Laws, and that excellent Constitution of this Kingdom which hath made this Nation so many years both famous and happy to a great degree of Envy since the power of punishing (which is already in your hands according to Law) if the power of preferring be added, We shall have nothing left for us, but to look on; since the encroaching of one of these Estates upon the power of the other is unhappy in the effects both to them and all the rest; since this power [is] at most a joint [one]. Government in us with our Councellors (or rather our Guardians) will return us to the worst kind of minority and make us despicable both at home and abroad, and beget eternal action and Dissention as destructive to public happiness as War both in the chosen and those that choose them, and the people who choose the Choosers; since so new a power will [un]doubtedly intoxicate persons who were not born to it and beget not only divisions among them as equals, but in them contempt of us as become an equal to them, and Insolence and Injustice towards our people, as now so much their inferiors, which will be the more grievous unto them, as suffering from those who were so lately of a nearer degree to themselves, and being to have redress only from those that placed them and fearing they may be inclined to preserve what they have made, both out of kindness and policy; since all great changes are extremely inconvenient and almost infallibly beget yet greater Changes, which beget yet greater Inconveniences.

Since as great a one in the Church must follow this of the kingdom, Since the second estate would in all probability follow the fate of the first and by some of the same turbulent spirit jealousies would be soon raised against them, and the like propositions for reconciliation of Differences would be then sent to them, as they have joined to send to us, till (all power being vested the House of Commons and their number making them incapable of transacting affairs of State with the necessary secrecy and expedition; those being restricted to some close Committee) at last the Common people (who in the mean time must be battered, and to whom Licence must be given in all their wild humours, how contrary soever to established Law, or their own real good) discover this *Arcanum imperii*, that all this was done by them but not for them, grow weary of journey-work, and set up for themselves, call Parity and independence, Liberty; devour that Estate which had devoured the rest; destroy all Right and properties, all distinctions of Families and men. And by this means this splendid and excellently distinguished form of Government end in a dark equal chaos of confusion, and the long line of our many noble Ancestors in a Jack Cade or Wat Tyler . . .*

CHARLES I'S TRIAL AND EXECUTION (1649)

Although Parliament destroyed the king's army on the battlefield at Naseby in June 1645, Charles's determination to continue the fight remained as strong as ever. In the months following his defeat he continued to play his shifty game, convinced that there was no need to keep faith with rebels. He negotiated with the increasingly divided leaders of Parliament and the New Model Army, as well as anyone else who might serve his purposes: the Scots, the Irish – both Catholic and Protestant – the French, the Spanish. He encouraged the royalist uprisings of 1648 that came to be called the Second Civil War. Once again defeat in the field did not extinguish the king's hopes. Some Members of Parliament, desperate for a peace that would reduce the ominous power of their own army, continued to negotiate a treaty. The soldiers, increasingly radicalized by the hostility of their erstwhile allies, and in an ideological ferment encouraged by Levellers and agitators, concluded that an honourable peace could only be secured by bringing Charles to justice.

Seized by his enemies, Charles prepared for his final performance upon the political stage. What follows are several documents related to the work of the High Court of Justice, the 150-odd officers and Members of Parliament picked by

* Leaders of medieval peasant rebellions in England.

the Army's commanders for a task that most people, even some members of the court itself, viewed as a monstrous one. The court's charge against the king carefully catalogues the battles at which Charles had been present, 'levying war against his people'. Witnesses stood ready to testify against the king. The court's intention was clear: Charles Stuart, 'that man of blood' deserved punishment, but the trial, with its procedure and through sworn testimony, must justify such radical action to the nation.

The king's answer, which he was not allowed to present in full, was soon published, and proved a highly successful piece of political propaganda. While the court's death warrant might have represented its last word on the subject, the king's argument, with its defence of the 'ancient constitution' persuaded many, even among his former enemies, that he had justice on his side.

The charge against the king

That the said Charles Stuart, being admitted King of England, and therein trusted with a limited power to govern by and according to the laws of this land and not otherwise; and by his trust, oath, and office, being obliged to use the power committed to him for the good and benefit of the people, and for the preservation their rights and liberties; yet, nevertheless, out of a wicked design to erect and uphold in himself an unlimited and Tyrannical power to rule according to his will, and to overthrow the rights and liberties of the people, yea, to take away and make void the foundations thereof, and of all redress and remedy of misgovernment, which by the fundamental constitutions of this kingdom were reserved on the people's behalf in the right and power of frequent and successive Parliaments, or national meetings in Council; he, the said Charles Stuart, for accomplishment of such his designs, and for the protecting of himself and his adherents in his and their wicked practices, to the same ends has traitorously and maliciously levied war against the present Parliament, and the people therein represented, particularly upon or about the 30th day of June, in the year of our Lord 1642, at Beverley, in the County of York; and upon or about the 24th day of August in the same year, at the County of the Town of Nottingham, where and when he set up his standard of war . . . and upon or about the 8th day of June, in the year of our Lord 1645, at the Town of Leicester; and also upon the 14th day of the same month in the same year, at Naseby-field, in the County of Northampton. At which several times and places, or most of them, and at many other places in this land, at several other times within the years aforementioned, and in the year of our Lord 1646, he, the said Charles Stuart, hath caused and procured many thousands of the free people of this nation to be slain; and by divisions, parties, and insurrections within this land, by invasions from foreign parts, endeavoured and procured by him, and by many other evil ways and means, he, the said Charles Stuart, has not only maintained and carried on the said war both by land and sea, during the years before mentioned, but also has renewed, or caused to be renewed, the said war against the Parliament and good people of this nation in this present Year 1648. By which cruel and unnatural wars, by him, the said Charles Stuart, levied, continued, and renewed as aforesaid, much innocent blood of the free people of this nation has been spilt, many families have been undone, the public treasure wasted and exhausted, trade obstructed and miserably decayed, vast expense and damage to the nation incurred, and many parts of this land spoiled, some of them even to desolation . . . All which wicked designs, wars, and evil practices of him, the said Charles Stuart, have been, and are carried on for the advancement and upholding of a personal interest of will, power, and pretended prerogative to himself and his family, against the public interest, common right, liberty, justice, and peace of the people of this nation by and from whom he was entrusted as aforesaid.

By all which it appears that the said Charles Stuart hath been, and is the occasioner, author, and continuer of the said unnatural, cruel and bloody wars; and therein guilty of all the treasons, murders, rapines, burnings, spoils, desolations, damages and mischiefs to this nation, acted and committed in the said wars, or occasioned thereby.

The king's reasons for declining the jurisdiction of the High Court of Justice

Having already made my protestations, not only against the illegality of this pretended Court, but also, that no earthly power can justly call me (who am your King) in question as a delinquent, I would not any more open my mouth upon this occasion, more than to refer myself to what I have spoken, were I in this case alone concerned: but the duty I owe to God in the preservation of the true liberty of my people will not suffer me at this time to be silent: for, how can any free-born subject of England call life or anything he possesses his own, if power without right daily make new, and abrogate the old fundamental laws of the land which I now take to be the present case? Wherefore when I came hither, I expected that you would have endeavoured to have satisfied me concerning these grounds which hinder me to answer to your pretended impeachment. But since I see that nothing I can say will move you to it (though negatives are not so naturally proved as affirmatives) yet I will show you the reason why I am confident you cannot judge me, nor indeed the meanest man in England: for I will not (like you) without showing a reason, seek to impose a belief upon my subjects.

There is no proceeding just against any man, but what is warranted, either by God's laws or the municipal laws of the country where he lives. Now I am most confident this day's proceeding cannot be warranted by God's laws; for, on the contrary, the authority of obedience unto Kings is, clearly warranted, and strictly commanded in both the Old and New Testament, which, if denied, I am ready instantly to prove.

And for the question now in hand, there it is said, that where the word of a King is there is power; and who may say unto him, what dost thou?' Eccles. viii. 4. Then for the law of this land, I am no less confident, that no learned lawyer will affirm that an impeachment can lie against the King, they all going in his name: and one of their maxims is, that the King can do no wrong. Besides, the law upon which you ground your proceedings must either be old or new: if old, show it; if new, tell what authority, warranted by the fundamental laws of the land, has made it, and when. But how the House of Commons can erect a Court of Judicature, which was never one itself (as is well known to all lawyers) I leave to God and the world to judge. And it were full as strange, that they should pretend to make laws without King or Lords' House, to any that have heard speak of the laws of England.

And admitting, but not granting, that the people of England's commission could grant your pretended power, I see nothing you can show for that; for certainly you never asked the question of the tenth man in the kingdom, and in this way you manifestly wrong even the poorest ploughman, if you demand not his free consent; nor can you pretend any colour for this your pretended commission, without the consent at least of the major part of every man in England of whatsoever quality or conditions, which I am sure you never went about to seek, so far are you from having it. Thus you see that I speak not for my Own right alone, as I am your King, but also for the true liberty of all my subjects, which consists not in the power of government, but in living under such laws, such a government, as may give themselves the best assurance of their lives, and property of their goods; nor in this must or do I forget the privileges of both Houses of Parliament, which this day's proceedings do not only violate, but likewise occasion the greatest breach of their public faith that (I believe) ever was heard of, with which I am far from charging the two Houses . . .

Then for anything I can see, [the] higher House is totally excluded; and for the House of Commons, it is too well known that the major part of them are detained or deterred from sitting; so as if I had no other, this were sufficient for me to protest against the lawfulness of your pretended Court. Besides all this, the peace of the kingdom is not the least in my thoughts; and what hope of settlement is there, so long as power reigns without rule or law, changing the whole frame of that government under which this kingdom has flourished for many hundred years (nor will I say what will fall out in case this lawless, unjust proceeding against me do go on) and believe it, the Commons of England will not thank you for this change; for they will remember how happy they have been of late years under the reigns of Queen Elizabeth, the King my father, and myself, until the beginning of these unhappy troubles, and will have cause to doubt, that they shall never be so happy under any new: and by this time it will be too sensibly evident, that the arms I took up were only to defend the fundamental laws of this kingdom against those who have supposed my power has totally changed the ancient government.

Thus, having showed you briefly the reasons why I cannot submit to your pretended authority, without violating the trust which I have from God for the welfare and liberty of my people, I expect from you either clear reasons to convince my judgment, showing me that I am in an error (and then truly I will answer) or that you will withdraw your proceedings.

This I intended to speak in Westminster Hall, on Monday, January 22, but against reason was hindered to show my reasons.

The death warrant of Charles I

At the High Court of Justice for the trying and judging of Charles Stuart, King of England, Jan. 29, Anno Domini [1698]

Whereas Charles Stuart, King of England, is, and stands convicted, attainted, and condemned of high treason, and other high crimes; and sentence upon Saturday last was pronounced against him by this Court, to be put to death by the severing of his head from his body; of which sentence, execution yet remains to be done; these are therefore to will and require you to see the said sentence executed in the open street before Whitehall, upon the morrow, being the thirtieth day of this instant month of January, between the hours of ten in the morning and five in the afternoon of the same day, with full effect. And for so doing this shall be your sufficient warrant. And these are to require all officers, soldiers, and others, the good people of this nation of England, to be assisting unto you in this service.
To Col. Francis Hacker, Col. Huncks, and Lieut.-Col. Phayre, and to every of them.
Given under our hands and seals.
John Bradshaw.
Thomas Grey.
Oliver Cromwell.
&c. &c.

Further reading

Charles Carlton, *Charles I, the Personal Monarch* (2nd edn, London, 1995).
Anthony Fletcher, *The Outbreak of the English Civil War* (New York, 1981).
Antonia Fraser, *Faith and Treason: The Gunpowder Plot* (London, 1996)
S.R. Gardiner, *History of England from the Accession of James I to the Outbreak of the Civil War* (London, 1894–96).
S.R. Gardiner, *What Gunpowder Plot Was* (London, 1897).
Ann Hughes, *The Causes of the English Civil War* (2nd edn, New York, 1998).

Maurice Lee, *Great Britain's Solomon: James VI and I in his Three Kingdoms* (Champaign, IL, 1990).

Richard Ollard, *The Image of the King* (New York, 1979).

Conrad Russell, *The Fall of the British Monarchies* (Oxford, 1991).

C.V. Wedgewood, *The Trial of Charles I* (London, 1964).

10

RESTORATION TO REVOLUTION

THE RESTORATION (1660)

Though in hindsight the momentum towards a restoration of the monarchy in early 1660 seems irresistible, the exiled Stuart court was apprehensive. Charles II (1630–85) and his advisors feared that powerful interests might yet unite to frustrate the king's return. These worries were uppermost in the mind of Sir Edward Hyde (1609–74), soon to be earl of Clarendon, when he drafted the Declaration of Breda. Hopes for a restoration grew as political chaos overwhelmed the English state in the winter of 1659–60. The king moved from Catholic France to the Protestant Low Countries, distancing himself from his Catholic mother and cousin Louis XIV. The Declaration Charles issued at Breda was an important step towards a formal restoration. It offered reassurance and promised reconciliation rather than vengeance. Soldiers of the revolutionary army would be paid, old political conflicts buried, and religious persecution forbidden. Further, those who had bought royalist lands in good faith would remain in possession. In fact the promise of the Declaration was not entirely fulfilled thanks to the ferocious royalist backlash that followed the assembly of the Cavalier Parliament (1661–79), but its soothing words helped insure that less than a month after it was issued, Parliament invited Charles II home to assume his throne.

The universal enthusiasm that greeted the king's return is the subject of *England's Joy*, one of dozens of pamphlets and broadsheets published to celebrate the event. It breathlessly recounts the king's journey to London and revels in the resurrection of a social order once condemned as unnecessary and dangerous. The reappearance in force of the nobility and gentry – as well as the apparent absence of the king's former enemies – sets the scene for the uncompromising Restoration settlement to come.

The Declaration of Breda

Charles R.
Charles, by the grace of God, king of England, Scotland, France and Ireland, Defender of the Faith, &c. To all our loving subjects, of what degree or quality soever, greeting.

If the general distraction and confusion which is spread over The whole kingdom does not awaken all men to a desire And longing that those wounds which have so many years together, been kept bleeding, may be bound up, all we can say will be to no purpose; however, after this long silence, we have thought it our duty to declare how much we desire to contribute thereunto; and that as we can never give over the hope, in Good time, to obtain the possession of that right which God and Nature hath made our due, so we do make it our daily suit to The Divine Providence, that He will, in compassion to us And our subjects, after so long misery and sufferings, remit and put us into a quiet and peaceable possession of that our right, with as little blood and damage to our people as is possible; nor do we desire more to enjoy what is ours, than that all our subjects may enjoy what by law is theirs, by a full and entire administration of justice throughout the land, and by extending our mercy where it is wanted and deserved.

And to the end that the fear of punishment may not engage any, conscious to themselves of what is past, to a perseverance in guilt for the Future by opposing the quiet and happiness of their country, in the restoration of King, Peers and people To their just, ancient and fundamental rights, we do, by these Presents, declare, that we do grant a free and general pardon, which we are ready, upon demand, to pass under our Great Seal of England, to all our subjects, of what degree or quality soever, who, within forty days after the publishing hereof, shall lay hold upon this our grace and favour, and shall, by any public act, declare their doing so, and that they return to the loyalty and obedience of good subjects; excepting only such persons as shall hereafter be Excepted by Parliament, those only to be excepted. Let all our subjects, how faulty soever, rely upon the word of a king, solemnly given by this present declaration, that no crime whatsoever, committed against us or our royal father before the publication of this, shall ever rise in judgment, or be brought in question, against any of them, to the least endamagement of them, either in their lives, liberties or estate, or (as far forth as lies in our power) so much as to the prejudice of their reputations, by any reproach or term of distinction from the rest of our best subjects; we desiring and ordaining that henceforth all notes of discord, separation and difference of parties be utterly abolished among all our subjects, whom we invite and conjure to a perfect union among themselves, under our protection, for the resettlement of our just rights and-theirs in a free Parliament, by which, upon the word of a King, we will be advised.

And because the passion and uncharitableness of the times have produced several opinions in religion, by which men are engaged in parties and animosities against each other (which, when they shall hereafter unite in a freedom of conversation, will be composed or better understood), we do declare a liberty to tender consciences, and that no man shall be disquieted or called in question for differences of opinion in matter of religion, which do not disturb the peace of the kingdom; and that we shall be ready to consent to such an Act of Parliament, as, upon mature deliberation, shall be offered to us, for the full granting that indulgence.

And because, in the continued distractions of so many years, and so many and great revolutions, many grants and purchases of estates have been made to and by many officers, soldiers and others, who are now possessed of the same, and who may be liable to actions at law upon several titles, we are likewise willing that all such differences, and all things relating, to such grants, sales and purchases, shall be determined in Parliament, which can best provide for the just satisfaction of all men who are concerned.

And we do further declare, that we will be ready to consent to any Act or Acts of Parliament to the purposes aforesaid, and for the full satisfaction of all arrears due to the officers and soldiers of the army under the command of General Monck; And that they shall be received into our service upon as good pay and conditions as they now enjoy.

Given under our Sign Manual and Privy Signet, at our Court at Breda, this 4/14 of day of April, 1660, in the twelfth year of our reign.

England's Joy

Being come aboard one of the fairest of those ships which attended at Sluce [*Helvoetsluys*] for wafting him [Charles II] over from the Hague in Holland; and therein having taken leave of his sister, the Princess Royal; he set sail for England on Wednesday evening, May 23rd, 1660. And having, during his abode at sea, given new names to that whole navy (consisting of twenty-six goodly vessels), he arrived at Dover on the Friday following [May 25th] about 'two o'clock in the afternoon.

Ready on the shore to receive him, stood the Lord General MONK, as also the Earl of WINCHELSEA Constable of Dover Castle, with divers persons of quality on the one hand; and the Mayor of Dover, accompanied by his brethren of that Corporation of the other, with a rich canopy. As soon as he had set foot on the shore, the Lord General presenting himself before him on his knee, and kissing his royal hand; was embraced by his Majesty: and received divers gracious expressions of the great sense he had of his loyalty, and in being so instrumental in his Restoration.

There also did the Corporation of Dover, and the Earl of WINCHELSEA do their duties to him in like sort; all the people making joyful shouts: the great guns from the ships and castle telling aloud the happy news of this his entrance upon English ground.

From thence, taking coach immediately, with his royal brothers, the Dukes of YORK and GLOUCESTER, he passed to Barham Down – a great plain lying betwixt Dover and Canterbury – where were drawn up divers gallant Troops of horse, consisting of the nobility, knights and gentlemen of note, clad in very rich apparel; commanded by the Duke of BUCKINGHAM, Earls of

OXFORD, DERBY, NORTHAMPTON, WINCHELSEA, LICHFIELD, and the Lord Viscount MORDAUNT:

As also the Several foot regiments of the Kentish men. Being entered [on] the Down on horseback where multitudes of the country people stood making loud shouts, he rode to the head of each troop – they being placed on his left hand, three deep – who bowing to him, kissed the hilts of their swords, and then flourished them above their heads, with no less acclamations; the trumpets in the meantime also echoing the like to them.

In the suburbs of Canterbury stood the Mayor and Aldermen of that ancient city, who received him with loud music, and presented him with a cup of gold of two hundred and fifty pounds value Whence, after a speech made to him by the Recorder, he passed to the Lord CAMPDEN'S house, the Mayor carrying the sword before him.

During his stay at Canterbury (which was till Monday morning) he knighted the Lord General MONK, and gave him the ensigns of the most honourable Order of the Garter: And by Garter Principal King of Arms sent the like unto Lord Admiral MONTAGUE, then aboard the navy, riding in the Downs. There likewise did he knight Sir WILLIAM MAURICE, a member of the House of Commons; whom he constituted one of his principal Secretaries of State.

From Canterbury he came on Monday to Rochester, where the people had hung up, over the midst of the streets, as he rode, many beautiful garlands, curiously made up with costly scarves and ribbons, decked with spoons and bodkins of silver and small plate of several sorts; and some with gold chains, in like sort as at Canterbury: each striving to outdo the other in all expressions of joy.

On Tuesday, May the 29th (which happily fell out to be the anniversary of his Majesty's birthday) he set forth from Rochester in his coach; but afterwards took horse on the farther side of Blackheath: on which spacious plain he found divers great and eminent troops of horse, in a most splendid and glorious equipage; and a kind of rural triumph, expressed by the country swains, in a morris dance with the old music of tabor and pipe; which was performed with all agility and cheerfulness imaginable.

And from this Heath these troops marched off before him; viz. Major General BROWN, the Merchant Adventurers, Alderman ROBINSON, the Lord MAYNARD, the Earls of NORWICH, PETERBOROUGH, CLEVELAND, DERBY, Duke of RICHMOND, and His Majesty's own Life Guards.

In this order proceeding towards London, there were placed in Deptford, on his right hand – as he passed through the town – above an hundred proper maids, clad all alike in white garments, with scarves about them, who having prepared many baskets covered with fine linen, and adorned with rich scarves and ribbons; which Baskets were full of flowers and sweet herbs, strewed the way before him as he rode.

From thence passing on he came into Saint George's Fields in Southwark, where the Lord Mayor and Aldermen of London in their scarlet, with the Recorder and other City Council[men], waited for him in a large tent, hung with tapestry; in which they had placed a chair of State, with a rich canopy over it. When he came thither the Lord Mayor presented him with the City sword, and the Recorder made a speech to him; which being done, he alighted and went into the tent, where a noble banquet was prepared for him.

From this tent the proceeding was thus ordered, viz. First, the City Marshal, to follow in the rear of His Majesty's Life Guards. Next the Sheriff's trumpets. Then the Sheriff's men in scarlet cloaks, laced with silver on the capes, carrying javelins in their hands. Then divers eminent citizens well mounted, all in black velvet coats, and chains of gold about their necks, and every one his footman, with suit, cassock and ribbons of the colour of his Company: all which were made choice of out of the several Companies; in this famous City and so distinguished: and at the head of each distinction the ensign of that Company.

After these followed the City Council, by two and, two, near the Aldermen; then certain Noblemen and Noblemen's sons, Then the King's trumpets. Then the Heralds at Arms.

After them the Duke of BUCKINGHAM. Then the Earl of LINDSEY, Lord High Chamberlain of England, and the Lord General MONK. Next to them Garter Principal King of Arms; the Lord Mayor on his right hand bearing the City sword, and a Gentleman Usher on his left, and on each side of them the Sergeants at Arms with their maces.

Then the King's Majesty with his equerries and footmen on each side of him; and at a little distance on each hand his royal brothers, the Dukes of York and GLOUCESTER: and after them divers of the King's servants who came with him from beyond sea. And in the rear of all, those gallant troops, viz. The Duke of BUCKINGHAM, Earls of OXFORD, NORTHAMPTON, WINCHELSEA, LICHFIELD, and Lord MORDAUNT, as also five regiments of horse belonging to the army.

In this magnificent fashion, His Majesty entered the Borough of Southwark, about half-past three o'clock in the afternoon; and within an hour after, the City of London, at the Bridge: where he found the windows and streets exceedingly thronged with people to behold him, and the walls adorned with hangings and carpets of tapestry and other costly stuff and in many places sets of loud music; all the conduits as he passed running claret wine; and the several Companies in their liveries, with the ensigns belonging to them; as also the trained bands of the city standing along the streets as he passed, welcoming him with loyal acclamations.

And within the rails where Charing Cross formerly was, a stand of six hundred pikes, consisting of knights and gentlemen, as had been officers in the armies of his late Majesty, of blessed memory: the truly noble and valiant Sir JOHN STOWELL, Knight of the Honourable Order of the Bath [and]

Paterson (famous for his eminent acts and sufferings) being in the head of them.

From which place, the citizens in velvet coats and gold Chains being drawn up on each hand, and divers companies of foot soldiers; his Majesty passed betwixt them, and entered White Hall at seven o'clock, the people making loud shouts and the horse and foot several volleys of shots, at this his happy arrival. There the House of Lords and Commons of Parliament received him, and kissed his royal hand.

At the same time likewise, the Reverend Bishops of ELY, SALISBURY, ROCHESTER and CHICHESTER in their episcopal habits, with divers of the long oppressed orthodox clergy; met in That royal Chapel of King HENRY the SEVENTH of Westminster and there also sung *Te DEUM &c.*, in praise and thanks to Almighty GOD, for this His unspeakable mercy, in the deliverance of his Majesty from many dangers, and so happily restoring him to rule these kingdoms, according to his just and undoubted right.

THE REVOLUTION OF 1688

Charles II's unexpected death in February 1685 brought his brother James, Duke of York (1633–1702), to the throne. James's religion had been the essential element in British politics since the early 1670s, when his conversion to Roman Catholicism became clear. Party politics, embodied in the struggle between Whigs and Tories, had their origins in the fears surrounding the possible accession of a Catholic king. Tories, remembering the Civil Wars, defended James's hereditary rights, while Whigs, fearful of popery, favoured limits on his authority – or the duke's exclusion from the succession altogether. Charles II's unwavering support for the Tories insured that Exclusion failed, and James became king. Within months he triumphed over the rebellion led by his bastard nephew, the duke of Monmouth (1649–85), and presided over parliamentary elections that returned an overwhelmingly Tory House of Commons.

But James was not a party politician. He was, he believed, placed by God upon his throne, and God had shown his favour by defeating Exclusion and Monmouth's rebels. James II's God was, moreover, a Catholic deity, and He expected the king to relieve the suffering of His people. Although at his accession James promised to respect the Protestant Church of England, of which he was the head, his actions belied those assurances. The king intended to support his co-religionists. Through the controversial use of his prerogative powers to suspend and dispense statute law, James began to appoint Catholics to office in the state and army. He forced the universities, whose foremost task was to train Protestant ministers, to accept Catholic fellows. James's policies created profound unease throughout the country, even among Tories, for whom defence of the Church of England was as important as defence of the monarchy. Embassies to Rome, Catholic advisors, and indulgence towards dissenters of all sorts, from Quakers to

Catholics – effectively destroyed the close link between James and his strongest supporters.

The king's embrace of his old enemies, the Protestant Dissenters, and, in late 1687, news of the queen's pregnancy, were the final straws for many. Prominent peers sought the support of William of Orange (1650–1702). The Protestant *stadthouder* of Holland and husband of James's eldest daughter, Mary (1662–94), he had a keen interest in English affairs. For years he had expected Mary to inherit the English crown, and the possible birth of a prince threatened that legacy. William seized his chance, and invaded England in November 1688, promising a free Parliament and the security of Protestantism. His real intention, which he kept to himself, was to replace his father-in-law on the throne.

What follows here are two documents representing each view. Gilbert Burnet (1643–1715), later bishop of Salisbury, was a friend of the Prince and Princess of Orange, and closely associated with the leaders of the Exclusionist party. His *History of My Own Times* is a first-hand account of events surrounding the Revolution. His bias against James II is obvious, but reflects the views of many of the king's opponents. The second document is a letter James wrote from his French exile in January 1689. Denying any malign intent, James seeks to project an image of injured moderation. William and his allies have deluded the kingdom, and James reminds his subjects of the cost of rebellion by referring to the execution of Charles I.

Gilbert Burnet, 'History of My Own Times'

. . . Thus ended the second year of this reign, with the destruction of all law by the substitution of a dispensing power; with the institution of an Ecclesiastical Commission, to proceed arbitrarily against the clergy; with the Obtrusion of Popery upon the nation, the suspension of an English bishop, and the infringement of the rights and privileges of both universities; and it was easy to see that there was no maintaining such proceedings without a standing army.

The occasion of the late rebellion* had raised one, and instead of disbanding it, the King was willing now to make a parade with it; and to inject more terror into the nation, ordered the troops to encamp on Hounslow Heath, and to be exercised all the summer long. This was done with great magnificence, and at a vast expense. But that which abated the King's joy in seeing so brave an army about him was, that it appeared visibly on all occasions that his soldiers had as strong an aversion to his religion as had the rest of his subjects, and that this encampment gave them an opportunity of encouraging one another, and forming combinations never to depart from the Protestant religion.

The veil was now pulled off, and the King's design of converting the nation

* The failed effort of James's bastard nephew, James, Duke of Monmouth, to seize the throne in the summer of 1685.

to Popery was too manifest to be concealed; and therefore the priests advised him to take heart, and no longer manage a correspondence with Rome privately, but to send a proper person invested with a public character. The person the King made choice of was Palmer, Earl of Castlemaine, a man hot and eager in all his notions, and whose success in the negotiation was answerable to all the other unfortunate passages of his life . . .

The King, being conscious that he had lost the Church of England by his bad usage of them, was now looking out for a counterpoise, and making strong application to the Dissenters to persuade them to accept of the favour he intended them, and to concur with him in his designs. The Dissenters at that time were divided into four main bodies – the Presbyterians, the Independents, the Anabaptists, and the Friends, or Quakers. The two former had not the visible distinction of different rites. That wherein they chiefly differed was, that the Presbyterians were not so adverse to Episcopal ordination and a Liturgy, and were friends to civil government and a limited monarchy; whereas the Independents were for a commonwealth in the State, and a popular government in the Church, and no set form of worship; but both were enemies to the repeal of the Tests and the toleration of Popery. The Anabaptists were generally men of virtue and universal charity; but, being at too great a distance from the Church of England, they were for a toleration of all religions, as the only means to capacitate themselves for favour And employments. And the Friends or Quakers, had set up such a visible distinction in the matter of the hat, and their odd forms of speech, besides the great difference in many points of doctrine, that they were generally supposed, for the same reason, to be for the toleration.

These were the men that the King had now taken under his wing; and, to give them a specimen of what favours he intended for them in England, he sent down a proclamation to Scotland, wherein he repealed all the severe laws that were passed in his grandfather's name during his infancy; all that lay an inability on his Roman Catholic subjects; all that imposed tests on those who were in employments; and all that were made against moderate Presbyterians; wherein he promised never to force his subjects to change their religion, and required only that they would renounce the principles of rebellion, and oblige themselves to support him in his absolute power against any opponents. But this proclamation being found liable to many just exceptions, another was sent down, whereby full liberty was granted to all Presbyterians to set up conventicles in their own way. This was received with great rejoicing, and as an extraordinary work of Providence that had moved the heart of a prince from whom they expected an increase of the severities under which they laboured to grant them an unconfined liberty of conscience, but few were so ignorant as not to know what the intent of all this indulgence was.

To put both nations under the same regulation, the King sent out in April [1687] a Declaration of Toleration and Liberty of Conscience for England, wherein he expressed his aversion to persecution on account of religion; suspended all penal and sanguinary laws in matters of this nature; suppressed all oaths and tests that excluded any of his subjects from employments; and renewed his promise of maintaining the Church of England and all his subjects in their properties, and particularly in the possession of the abbey lands.* The mention of abbey lands made it believed that the design of setting up Popery was well-nigh accomplished, and that the King concluded he had a sure game in his hand; but, for all that, the Dissenters were very full of their acknowledgments, and seemed to outvie all that had gone before them in the abject strains of submission and flattery . . .

The King began his progress, and went from Salisbury all round as far as Chester. But in most places where he came he saw such a visible coldness, both in the nobility and gentry (though he himself was very obliging to all that came near him – to Dissenters especially, and those who were thought Republicans), that he shortened his journey, and returned to the Queen at Bath, having left behind him everywhere injunctions to choose such parliament men as Could ratify the toleration he had granted, and repeal the tests as he had done.

When the King came back, he changed the magistracy in most of the cities in England in favour of the Dissenters, but was surprised to find that the new Lord Mayor and aldermen of London took the Test, and ordered the observation of Gunpowder Treason day to be continued, that they disowned the invitation of the Pope's nuncio to dinner, and entered it in their books that he came without their knowledge, and that they continued the service of the Church of England in Guildhall Chapel, notwithstanding the King sent them a permission to use what form of worship they pleased.

The ill success he found in the orders he sent to the lord lieutenants of counties to examine the gentlemen and freeholders upon these questions, viz. whether, in case they should be chosen to serve in Parliament, they would consent to repeal the penal laws and tests?, Whether they would vote for men who would engage to repeal them, and whether they would maintain the King's Declaration [of indulgence]? For in most counties the lord lieutenants themselves either declared against those questions, and refused it put them at all, or they did it in so negligent a manner that it was plain they did not desire to be answered in the affirmative. Many counties, too, answered boldly in the negative, and others refused to answer anything, as did the Lord Mayor of London, and most of the new aldermen; and, for this contempt, many were turned out of their commissions . . .

Whether the King imagined that he Could vacate the force of the laws by his repeated insults over them, or was willing to bring the clergy either Under contempt for compliance, or under penalties for disobedience to his injunctions, but so it was that, about the end of April [1688], he thought fit to renew his last year's Declaration of Liberty of Conscience, with an addition that he

* Monastic lands seized in the Reformation.

would adhere firmly to it, and put none in employment but such as would concur in maintaining it; and with an order of Council, requiring the bishops to send copies thereof to their clergy, and to enjoin them to read it on several Sundays in time of Divine service . . .

Sancroft, Archbishop of Canterbury, acted on this occasion a part suitable to his post and character. He wrote to all the bishops of his province to come up and consult about this matter of great importance; and of such as could not, he desired their opinions. Eighteen bishops, and the main body of the clergy, concurred in the resolution against reading the Declaration; and he and six more signed a petition to the King, containing their reasons for not obeying the order of Council that I had been sent them, viz: – That their refusal proceeded not from any disrespect to his Majesty, or unwillingness to show favour to Dissenters; but, the Declaration being founded on a dispensing power which was known to Be illegal and destructive both to Church and State, they could not in prudence, honour, and conscience make themselves so far parties to it as the publication of it in time of Divine service must amount to . . .

After the fortnight's consultation, violent counsels seemed to agree best with the king's temper and resentment, and so the bishops were cited to appear before the Council, where, after, being examined whether the petition was of their penning, and owning it – whether of their publication, and denying it – they were asked at last whether they would enter into bonds to appear at the King's Bench, and answer to an information of misdemeanour; but, upon their right of peerage, refusing to do it, they were sent to the Tower.

Never was the City, in the memory of man, in such a fermentation as upon this occasion. The banks of the river (for the bishops went by water) were crowded with people, kneeling down, and asking their blessings, and with loud shouts expressing their good wishes and hearty concern for their preservation. In the Tower the soldiers and officers did the same, and a universal consternation appeared in all people's faces.

The Bishop's defence was, that having received an order to which they could not pay obedience, they thought it incumbent on them to lay before the King their reasons for it; that, as subjects, they had a right to petition; as peers, and of his great Council, they had a further claim; and, as bishops, they were concerned to look after matters of religion; and that the King's Declaration being of that nature, and founded on a power that was contrary to law, they thought it both their right and duty to make such representation to him. But the sacredness of the King's authority, and the seditiousness of petitioning in any point of government out of Parliament, were much objected on the other side. They were, however, at last acquitted, to the inexpressible joy of the City, the army, and the whole nation . . .

Things were now come to that pass, and the King, by assuming to himself a power to make laws void, had so broken the government and legal administration of it, that it was high time for the nation to look to its preservation. Admiral Russell had a sister in Holland, and under pretence of coming to see her, he was desired by some men of great power and interest in England to wait on the Prince,* to acquaint him with disposition of the nation, and to know his resolution what he proposed to do. And the thing was pressed with greater earnestness at that time, because the Queen's confinement of a son, which was generally through to be an imposture, had dissatisfied people's minds more and more.

However this may be, the Prince of Orange thought it proper to send over Zulestein, both to congratulate upon this occasion and to feel the pulse of the nobility and chief gentry with relation to his Coming over; and, upon his return, Zulestein brought such advices and assurances to the Prince, as Determined his resolution. It was advised that the Prince Could never hope for a more favourable conjuncture; that the proceedings against the bishops and the pretended birth of a prince had made people imagine that the ruin of their religion was intended, and Popery and slavery entailed upon the nation; that the army continued well affected; the seamen showed the same inclination; and the whole nation, in short, was now in a proper disposition to be made use of. The army, indeed, were so exasperated against the Papists that were among them, that the King found it necessary to part them by breaking up the camp, and sending them into winter quarters . . .

The Prince resolved to carry over to England an army of nine thousand foot, and four thousand horse and dragoons . . . and prevailed with the States to settle a fund for nine thousand seamen, and to have their naval preparations in such condition that they might be ready to put to sea upon the first orders . . .

The Protestant wind came at last, which both locked the English ships up in the river, and carried the Dutch fleet out to sea. On the 1st of November, O.S., we sailed out with the evening tide, and having the sea clear and a fair navigation, shaped our course to the west. On the 3rd we passed between Dover and Calais, and before it grew night came in sight of the Isle of Wight. The next was the anniversary of the day on which the Prince was born and married, and to land on that day he fancied would seem auspicious, and animate the soldiers; but the day following, it was thought (being Gunpowder Treason day), would most sensibly affect the English. Torbay was thought the best place for the fleet to lie in, and it was proposed to land the army as near as possible; but when it was perceived next morning that we had overrun it, and had nowhere to go now but to Plymouth, where we could promise ourselves no favourable reception, the Admiral began to give up all for lost, till the wind abating, and turning to the south, with a soft and gentle gale carried the whole fleet into Torbay in the space of four hours.

* William of Orange.

His Majesties late letter in vindication of himself;
Dated at St. Germans en Laye, the Fourteenth of this instant
January, 1689

James R.

My Lords when I saw that it was no longer safe for Us to remain within Our Kingdom of England, and that thereupon We had taken Our resolutions to withdraw for some time: We left to be communicated to you and to all Our Subjects, the Reasons of Our withdrawing; And were likewise resolved at the same time to leave such Orders behind Us to you of our Privy Council; as might best suit with the present state of Affairs. But that being altogether unsafe for us at that time, We now think fit to let you know, that though it has been Our constant care since Our first Accession to the Crown to Govern Our People with that Justice and Moderation as to give, if possible, no occasion of Complaint; yet more particularly upon the late Invasion, seeing how the Design Was laid; and fearing that Our People, who could not be destroyed but by themselves might by little imaginary grievances, be cheated into a certain ruin. To prevent so great mischief, and to take away not only all just cause of Discontent; We freely, and of Our own accord redressed all those Things that were set forth as the cause of that invasion; And that We might be informed by the Counsel and Advice of Our Subjects themselves, which way We might give them a further and a full satisfaction; We resolved to meet them in a Free Parliament; And in order to it; We first laid the foundation of such a Free Parliament, in restoring the City of *London* and the rest of the Corporations to their ancient Charters and Privileges; and afterwards actually appeared the writs to be issued out for the Parliament Meeting on the 15th of January; But the Prince of Orange seeing all the Ends of his Declaration answered, the People beginning to be undeceived, and they returning apace to their ancient Duty and Allegiance; and well foreseeing that if the Parliament should meet at the time appointed, such a settlement in all probability would be made, both in Church and State, as would totally defeat his ambitious and unjust Design, resolving by all means possible to prevent the Meeting of the Parliament; And to do this the most effectual way, he thought fit to lay a restraint on Our Royal Person; for as it were absurd to call that a Free Parliament, where there is any Force on either of the Houses, so much less can that Parliament be said to act Freely where the Sovereign, by whose Authority they Meet and Sit, and from whose Royal Assent all their Acts receive their Life and Sanction, is under actual Confinement. The hurrying of Us under a Guard from Our City of *London*, whose returning Loyalty We could no longer Trust, and the other Indignities We suffered in the Person of the Earl of *Feversham* when sent to him [William of Orange] by Us; and in that barbarous Confinement of Our own Person, We shall not here repeat; because they are, We doubt [not], very well known; and may We hope, if enough considered and reflected upon; together with his other Violation &

160

Breaches of the laws and Liberties of England, which by this Invasion he pretended to restore, be sufficient to open the Eyes of all Our Subjects, and let them plainly see what every one of them may expect, and what Treatment they shall find from him, if at any time it may serve his purpose, from whose hands a Sovereign prince, an Uncle, and a Father could meet with no better Entertainment. However the sense of these Indignities, and the just apprehension of further Attempts against Our Person by them who already endeavoured to murder Our Reputation by Infamous Calumnies (as if We had been capable of a supposed Prince of *Wales*) which was incomparably more Injurious, then the Destroying of Our Person it self, together with a serious reflection on a Saying of Our Royal Father of Blessed Memory, when he was in the like Circumstances, *That there is little difference between the Prison and the Graves of Princes* (which afterwards proved too true in His Case) could not but persuade Us to make use of that which the Law of Nature gives to the meanest of Our Subjects of freeing Our selves by all means possible from that unjust Confinement and Restraint. And this, We did not more for the Security of Our own Person, than that thereby We might be in a better Capacity of transacting and providing for every thing that may Contribute to the Peace and Settlement of Our Kingdom. For as on the one hand, no change of Fortune shall ever make Us forget Our selves, so far as to Condescend to any thing unbecoming that High and Royal Station, in which God Almighty by Right of Succession has placed Us: so on the other hand, neither the Provocation or Ingratitude of Our own Subjects nor any other Consideration whatsoever, shall ever prevail with Us to make the least step contrary to the True Interest of the *English* Nation; which we ever did, and ever must look upon as Our own, OUR WILL and Pleasure therefore is, that you of Our Privy Council take care to make therefore Our Gracious intentions known to the Lords Spiritual & Temporal in & about Our cities of *London, Westminster*, to the Lord Mayor and Commons of Our City of *London*, and to all Our Subjects in general; And to assure them, that We desire nothing more, than to return and hold a Free Parliament wherein We may have the best opportunity of undeceiving Our People, and showing the Sincerity of those Protestations We have often made of the preserving the Liberties and properties of Our Subjects and the Protestant Religion; more especially the Church of England as by Law Established, with such Indulgence for those that Dissent from Her, as We have always thought Ourselves in Justice and Care the general Welfare of Our People, bound to produce for them. And in the mean time You of Our Privy-Council (who can Judge better by being upon the place) are to send Us your Advice, what is fit to be done by Us towards Our Returning and the Accomplishing those Good Ends. And We do require you in Our Name, and by Our Authority, to Endeavour to Suppress all Tumults and Disorders, that the Nation in general, and every one of Our Subjects in particular, may not receive the least prejudice from, the present Distraction that is possible. So, not doubting of your Dutiful Obedience to these Our Royal Commands, We bid you Heartily Farewell. Given at St. *Germans an Laye* the 14th of January, 1681, And of Our Reign the Fourth Year.

THE ANGLO-SCOTTISH UNION (1707)

The Union of England and Scotland brought about by James VI and I's accession in 1603 was a strictly personal one. Though James had pressed hard for a formal 'incorporating' union that would combine the two states, and Cromwell had briefly created one by force, by 1707 all that held the two kingdoms together was the fragile life of the last Stuart monarch, Queen Anne (1665–1714).

Anglo-Scottish relations rarely ran smoothly; since 1603 they generally alternated between periods of frosty neglect and outright hostility. Concern about the state of the relationship preoccupied English politicians even before Anne's reign began. The English Act of Settlement (1701), granting the crown to the House of Hanover if Anne died childless, enraged Scottish opinion. The Act carried with it the implication that the Scottish throne would as a matter of course follow the English – and yet Scots were not consulted at all. In 1704 the Scots Parliament passed the Act of Security, which, by boldly asserting Scotland's right to make its own arrangements following the queen's death, brought the Scottish succession question to the fore in London. English ministers feared that Scotland might award the crown to Anne's exiled half-brother, James Edward (1688–1766), the 'Old Pretender'. This would recreate the British world before 1603, with two dynasties ruling on the island, and with the Scottish Crown an ally, or worse, a dependant, of France. Forestalling this possibility was crucial for the English.

A Treaty of Union, negotiated by commissioners appointed by the queen from both England and Scotland, was placed before the Scottish Parliament in 1706. Although in many respects generous to Scotland, preserving its distinct religious and legal structures, as well as granting it equal footing in English trade, it was vehemently opposed by many – perhaps most – Scots. A propaganda war raged for months over the union; two contributions to the battle are excerpted here.

A Letter Concerning Trade, attributed to Daniel Defoe (1661?–1731), typifies the Unionist approach. This side stressed the potential financial rewards of union. Defoe and other unionists appealed to merchants and gentlemen who hoped to share in the growing prosperity of English trade, both within the British Isles, and particularly, the empire. Anti-unionists, represented here by John Hamilton, Lord Belhaven (1656–1708), took a very different tack. Belhaven's speech, delivered to the Scots Parliament as it considered the treaty, played to Scottish patriotism. The indignities of playing second fiddle to England and the long proud history of an independent Scotland made Belhaven's appeal a powerful one. In the end, Parliament, much influenced by the unionist ministry, ratified the treaty. But Belhaven's ringing words inspired resistance to the union that would last for another generation.

A letter concerning trade,
From several Scots-Gentlemen that are Merchants in England,
To their Country-Men that are Merchants in Scotland

Gentlemen, this Affair of the Union, has been the Subject of many of our Thoughts: And the prosperity of our native Country is what we earnestly wish for, and if we are extremely deceived, the Union is the most desirable thing that ever was offered to *Scotland*.

We have just now read one Printed Paper, Entitled, *Some Considerations in relation to Trade*, humbly offered &c. And also another to the same purpose, Entitled, *A short View of our present Trade and Taxes*. We shall beg leave to give you our Thoughts on the Matter that are advanced in both these Pamphlets . . .

We wish, the Gentlemen who frame these Arguments against the union with a great deal of Art, would lay aside private Interest and Party, and weigh things in the Balance of Reason and Justice, and not put false Colours on them to impose upon ignorant People, or to promote other Ends and Designs, than what they publicly mention.

If half the Art were applied to recommend, that's used to discommend the Union, these ingenious Gentlemen would soon make Proselytes of all their Country.

Upon this sudden occasion, we shall not pretend regularly to answer Objections against, or make Arguments for the Union, but we shall mention some Materials or Heads for Arguments and Answers, which by any Men that is not already pre-engaged, may with ease be effectually applied to that End.

To pretend to be Friends to the Union, and yet to raise all Objections right or wrong, to say all that you can against it, and nothing for it, to calculate all the Debt and none of the Credit, to make Demands that are unjust and unequal, and cannot be granted; this is under the colour of Friends to the Union, to be the worst of Enemies.

The Taxes of *England*, especially those on Trade and things of Necessity, used to be small and low; the Malt Taxes, and many other Taxes were never known till this War,* and this War is only a contest for Trade, and we hope it has almost reached its good End, and in truth both Malt-Tax and Land-Tax are now expired, the K. of *France* suing for a Peace, which we hope 12 Months will bring about, and after Peace, by the Treaty of Union you will come to be entirely free of the Land-Tax or Cess which you can never be, except there is an Union. Gentlemen you know all this as well as we; In your Considerations and Views, &c. you might have had some Consideration or View of these things.

You mightily aggravate the high Duties on Wine, Brandy, Raisins, Almonds, &c. Neither the Poor nor Rich in Scotland would be the worse (but much the better) if these Trades were Discouraged, and instead of changing

---

* The War of the Spanish Succession, 1702–13.

your Product for things of luxury (that are Consumed amongst you, and Perish in the Using) you would Barter it in *Africa* for Gold, or in *America* for Silver, or that which would bring in Silver, you would be much greater Gainer: It's true, you would Drink less Wine and Brandy, &c. but to the great Encouragement of Tillage, you would Drink more Ale, and Aquavitæ [Scotch whisky] (if you would be Advised by us) we would have you be Contented with, till you double your Estates . . .

We are glad your heads are kept above Water, but if this Union be not Concluded, restrictions and Prohibitions will be put faster upon Export[s], than you can Put upon them upon your Import, and this we fear will quite Sink you . . .

When you have as much freedom and as many Advantages by Trade as the *English* have, you will be as able to Pay the Taxes and Customs as they are: You see we Thrive under them all and get Money, you will not have the Trade for fear of the Customs; you will not Catch Fish for fear you wet your Feet, what wise *Scotsman* would be afraid to change the Trade and Policy of *Scotland* for that of *England*, let us judge of them both, according to what they have Produced these Hundred Years past?

The Union will produce three times the Encouragement that there now is for your Manufactures, for your Grating [resale], for the Consumption, and Exportation of your Corn and Cattle, and for your Navigation, so will the Product of your Land be exceedingly increased.

Your Miserable unhappy Poor, that are used more like Slaves than Christians, and are deluded to oppose their own happiness, will have twice as much Wages, twice as good Victuals, and have equal Justice, Liberty and Property With their Masters; And therefore, will not need to leave you, and wander Abroad as they are forced to do, or if they are disposed to Travel, they may come to *England*, where they then will have a Right to these Blessings, although now they have a Right to nothing: We do not wonder, that Great and Cunning Men who foresee all this, and are unwilling to lose their absolute Sovereignty over these poor Ignorant Creatures, to impose on their Ignorance, and delude them to that degree, that they Pine for Chains and Yokes for their own Necks.

Consider the great Expence the *English* have been at, in Maintaining and Settling Trade all over the World, in Armies, Forts, Factories, all which are already Bought, Paid for and Fitted; And you are let into them.

What wild and unjust Calculations do Gentlemen make, who mention all the Taxes and Charges in the time of this Expensive War, when *England* Pays above £6,000,000 annually. And yet they take no Notice of the great Expectations of future Profit, nor yet of the present Advantages that are Enjoyed. Even this very *Newfoundland* Trade, which is used as an Objection, must either turn to no account at all, or else to the Advantage of *Scotland* more than of *England*.

Then, Consider the *English* Trade to *Holland*, *Sweden*, *Denmark* and the *Baltic*

Sea, which Trades as they are now by the more Northerly parts of *England* carried away from the more Southerly parts, so after the Union *Scotland* will get them and keep them, till Freight Labour and Food come to be as Dear in *Scotland* as in *England*, we might Instance many other particulars, *viz*.

The *Linen Cloth to be Exported to* England *and the Plantations*.

The Scots *Coal to be Exported to* England.

The *Trade to* Guinea, *and the other parts of* Africa.

The *Income by Coarse Woolen and Worsteds*.

The *Income by the Fisheries*.

The *Income of Gloves, Stockings, and all sorts of thin Leather*.

The *Income of all manner of Coarse Manufactures*.

Gentlemen, from these and other such particulars, we could make far more just Calculations than you have made.

But since Calculations are in fashion, we will pass by all the above mentioned particulars of very profitable Trades, and from which we could Calculate vast Advantages to *Scotland*, and for brevity make use of the single Example of the *Plantation* Trade, from which alone we can show the real Advantage that *Scotland* will reap by the Union, will far surmount their Imaginary losses in your Calculations.

For Example, the *Virginia* Trade Employs Annually 300 Sail of Ships, the *Islands* above 500 Sail, the far greater part of the Commodities that their Ships Export, are such as the Product and Manufacture of *Scotland* can afford Cheaper than *England*, and what is Imported from thence is Tobacco, Sugar, Cotton, &c.

Now it can be imputed to nothing but Laziness or Stupidity, if you that have greater Encouragements have not a proportionable Share of that Trade, but suppose you had but one 8th Part, that is 100 Ships, *viz*. 50 to *Virginia*, &c. and 50 to the *Islands*, what a vast quantity of your Native Product and Manufacture will those Carry off! And I hope at least, three Fourths of what is Imported by these Ships will be Exported and the Duty Drawn Back, so we will suppose only 2000 Hogsheads is Exported and Sold at 5 *sh* [shillings] per Pound, and say each Hogshead Containing 4 or 500 *lib*. [pound] and make £10. The Export of Tobacco at this modest and under-Reckoning Amounts to about £20,000. Then these 50 Ships from the *Islands*, they will be almost twice the Value, and for brevities' sake we'll say the Amount of the whole that's Exported makes but £400,000 *per Annum*, This we think you may really get every Year by the Tobacco and Sugar, which you bring into Scotland; Whereas now, by your own Confessions and Calculations you cannot be supposed to lose less than £20,000 annually by what you Import of those Commodities.

And the Things that you carry abroad to the Plantations to produce this £400,000 are of such Natures, that the making and carrying them out does as much real good to the Nation, as the bringing in of what they produce does – not to mention the great Wealth that *Scotsmen* who have already settled in the

Plantations would bring to *Scotland* in returning thither their Persons, or their Money and rents, how will this one Branch of Trade swallow up all your Objections, and over balance all your pretended Losses?

It is not because there are no other Trades but the Plantation Trade that we insist upon none of the other above named profitable Trades that the Union will bring you, it's rather because they are obvious, and you yourselves if you please, may demonstrate the advantages of them as well as we, for from every one of them many 1000 Pounds annual Advantage may easily accrue to the Nation.

For instance, in one of the least considerable of them *viz.* The Trade to *Guinea*, we think that after the Union, *Scotland* may in exchange for Lead, coarse Spirits of Malt, old Sheets, and the Pladden [plaid cloth] and Linens, reasonably get from *Guinea* yearly £50,000 in Gold, besides the other advantages in Trading there for Slaves, allspice, and dye Woods, &c.

And as to our calculation of the annual Expence of your Country we think that from what we have said, it were more just to make it as follows, than as the Author of the *Short View* has made it.

The Imposition on Trade (when by means of the Union Draw backs are allowed, and Trades that are prejudicial to the Nation discouraged or prohibited) will not, we believe amount to above £50,000

The Excise upon Beer and Ale, will not be increased till the Consumption is increased, so we will call it £40,000

The Excise upon Malt being new, and now not in force, and not like to be continued above a Year should not be charged.

As to the Excise on Brandy, we think that for the encouragement of Tillage, Spirits should be used instead of it, and so the sixteenth part of what is now used would serve £110

Of the Land Tax we say the same as of the Malt-tax £90,110

But admitting that one or two Years, the Malt-Tax and Land-Tax and other high Impositions should continue, this War cannot last much longer, consider what *England* is Fighting for, and what a vast deal it has cost *England*, and what vast advantage a Peace and Union will bring to you all.

Gentlemen, what we have written is from the best of our Beliefs and Judgment, and with hearty attention to every *Scotsman* and to our native Country, we assure you we have no by Ends nor private Interests, further or other, than what are common to all of us; and no consideration on Earth would tempt us to betray or mislead you. We do from our Hearts believe, that this Union will bring Honour, Peace, Strength and Riches, to you as Men, and Moderation, Piety, Charity and Love, amongst you as Christians; and as you receive so you to *England* will give the same Blessings: Which that it may be so, is the hearty Prayers of your Friends, Country Men and Acquaintances, this 23 Day of *November* 1706, met together on purpose to put these our Sentiments in Writing, to the end the same may be communicated to you with our best Wishes.

The Lord Bellhaven's Speech

When I consider this Affair of an Union betwixt the two Nations, as it is expressed in the several *Articles* thereof, and now the Subject of our Deliberation at this time; I find my Mind crowded with variety of very Melancholy Thoughts, and I think it my Duty to disburden my self of some of them, by laying them before, and exposing them to the Serious Consideration of this Honourable House.

I think, I see a *Free and Independent Kingdom* delivering up That, which all the World hath been Fighting for, since the days of *Nimrod*; yea That for which most of all the empires, Kingdoms, States, Principalities and Dukedoms of *Europe*, are at this very time engaged in the most Bloody and Cruel Wars that ever were, to wit, A Power to Manage their own Affairs by themselves, without the Assistance and Counsel of any [. . .]

I think I see a *National Church*, founded upon a rock, secured by a *Claim of Right*, hedged and fenced about by the strictest and pointesest legal Sanction that Sovereignty could contrive, voluntarily descending into a Plain, upon equal Level with *Jews, Papists, Socinians, Arminians, Anabaptists*, and other Sectaries, &c.

I think, I see *the Noble and Honourable Peerage of Scotland*, whose Valiant predecessors Led Armies against their Enemies upon their own proper Charges and Expenses, new divested of their Followers and Vassals, and put upon such an equal Foot with their Vassals, that I think, I see a petty *English* Excise-man receive more Homage and Respect . . .

I think, I see *the present Peers of* Scotland, whose Noble Ancestors Conquered Provinces, over-run Countries, reduced and subjected Towns, and fortified Places, exacted Tribute through the greatest part of *England*, now walking in the Court of Requests like so many *English* Attorneys, laying aside their Walking-Swords when in Company with the *English* Peers, lest their self-defence should be found Murder.

I think, I see *the Honourable Estate of Barons*, the bold Asserters of the Nation's Rights and Liberties in the worst of Times, now setting a Watch upon their Lips, and a Guard upon their Tongues, lest they be found guilty of *Scandalum Magnatum*.*

I think, I see the *Royal State of Burrows* [boroughs], walking their desolate Streets, hanging down their Heads under Disappointments; Wormed out of all the Branches of their old Trade, uncertain what hand to turn to [forced] to become Apprentices to their Unkind Neighbours; and yet after all, finding their [English] Trade so fortified by Companies, and secured by Prescriptions, that they despair of any Success therein.

I think, I see *our Learned Judges* laying aside their Practices and Decisions,

---

* Libelling a Peer of England.

studying the Common Law of *England*, gravelled with Certioraries, *Nisi prius's*, Writs of Error, Verdicts indovar, Ejectione firme, Injunction, Demurrers, &c. and frightened with Appeals and Avocations, because of new Regulations and Rectifications they may meet with.

I think, I see *the Valiant and Gallant Soldiery* either sent to learn the Plantation Trade Abroad; or at Home Petitioning for a small Subsistence as the Reward of their Honourable Exploits, while their old corps [regiments] are broken, the common Soldiers left to Beg, and the youngest *English* corps kept standing.

I think, I see *the Honest Industrious Trades* man loaded with new Taxes, and Impositions, drinking Water in place . . . of Ale, eating his fastless Pottage, Petitioning for Encouragement to his Manufactures, and Answered by Counter petitions.

In short, I think, I see *the Laborious Plow-man*, with his Corn spoiling upon his Hands, for want of Sale, Cursing the day of his birth, dreading the Expense of his Burial, and uncertain whether to Marry or do worse.

I think, I see the Incurable Difficulties of the *Landed-men*, their pretty Daughters Petitioning for want of Husbands, and their Sons for want of Employments.

I think, I see *Mariners* delivering up their Ships to their *Dutch* Partners; and what through Presses and Necessity, earning their Bread [as] underlings in the Royal *English* Navy.

But above all; My Lord, I think we see our Ancient Mother CALEDONIA, like *Ceasar*, sitting in the midst of our Senate, Ruefully looking round about Her, Covering Herself with Her Royal Garment attending the Fatal Blow, and breathing out Her last . . .

Are not these, *My Lord*, very afflicting Thoughts? And yet they are but the least Part suggested to me by these Dishonourable Articles. Should not the Consideration of these Things vivify [these] *dry Bones* of ours? Should not the Memory of our Noble Predecessors' Valour and Constancy, rouse up our drooping Spirits? Are our Noble Predecessors Souls got so far into the *English Cabbage-Stock and Cauliflowers*, that we should show the least Inclination that way? Are our Eyes so Blinded? Are our Ears so Deafened? Are our Hearts so Hardened? Are our Tongues so Faltered? Are our hands so Fettered, *That in this our day*, I say, My Lord, *That in this our day, we should not mind the things, that concern the very Being, and Well-being of our Ancient Kingdom, before they be hid from our Eyes!*

No, *My Lord*, GOD *forbid: Man's Extremity is* GOD's *opportunity. He is a present Help in time of need, and a Deliverer, and that right early.* Some unforeseen Providence will fall out, that may cast the Balance. Some *Joseph* or other will say, *Why do ye strive together, since you are Brethren.* None can Destroy *Scotland*, save *Scotland*'s self; hold your hands from the Pen, you are Secure . . .

That I may [show] a Way, My Lord, to a full, calm and free Reasoning upon this Affair, which is of the last Consequence unto this Nation, I shall [re]mind this Honourable House, That we are the Successors of our Noble Predecessors who founded our Monarchy, framed our Laws, amended altered and corrected them from time to time, as the Affairs and Circumstances of the Nation did require, without the Assistance or Advice of any Foreign Power or Potentate, and who during the time of 2000 years, have handed them down to us a free Independent Nation, with the Hazard their Lives and Fortunes; Shall not we then argue for that which our Progenitors have purchased for us at so dear a Rate, and with so much Immortal Honour and Glory? GOD forbid. Shall the Hazard of a Father unbind the Ligaments of a Dumb Son's Tongue; and that we hold our Peace, when our *Patria* is in Danger! I Speak this, *My Lord*, that I may encourage every individual Member of this House, to speak their Mind freely. There are many Wise and Prudent Men amongst us who think it not worth their While to open their Mouths; there are Others, who can speak very well and [to] good Purpose, who shelter themselves under the shameful Cloak of Silence, from a Fear of the Frowns of Great Men and Parties. I have observed, *My Lord*, by my Experience, the greatest number of Speakers in the most Trivial Affairs; and it will always prove so, while we come not to the right understanding of our Oath *de fideli*, whereby we are bound not only to give our Vote, but our faithful Advice to the Parliament, as we must *Answer to GOD*; and in our Ancient Laws, the Representatives of the Honourable Barons and the Royal Boroughs are termed Spokesmen: It lies upon your Lordships therefore, particularly to take Notice of such, whose Modesty makes them Bashful to Speak. Therefore I shall leave it upon you and conclude this Point, with a very Memorable Saying, of an honest private Gentleman, to a Great *Queen*, upon occasion of a State Project, contrived by an able Statesman and the Favorite to a Great *King*, against a Peaceable Obedient People because of the Diversity of their Laws and Constitutions. *If at this time thou hold thy peace Salvation shall come to the People from another place, but thou and thy House shall Perish.* I leave the Application to each particular Member of this House.

My Lord, I come now to consider our Division. We are under the Happy Reign (blessed be GOD) of the *Best of Queens*, Who has no evil Design against the Meanest of Her Subjects, Who Loves all Her people, and is equally beloved by them again; and yet that under the happy influence of our most Excellent *Queen*, there should be such Divisions and Factions, more dangerous and threatening to Her Dominions, than if we were under an Arbitrary Government, is most strange and unaccountable. Under an Arbitrary Prince, all are willing to Serve; because all are under a necessity to Obey, whether they will or not. He chooses therefore whom he will; without respect to either Parties or Factions; and if he think fit to take the Advices of his Councils or Parliaments, every Man speaks his Mind freely, and the Prince receives the faithful Advice of his People, without the mixture of Self-designs. If he prove a Good Prince, the Government is easy, if Bad, either Death or a Revolution brings a deliverance: Whereas here, *My Lord*, there appears no End of our Misery, if not prevented in time. Factions are now become Independent, and

have got Footing in Councils, in Parliaments, in Treaties, in Armies, in corporations, in Families, among Kindred; yea Man and Wife are not free from
their Political Jars . . .

Now *My Lord*, from those Divisions there has got up a kind of *Aristocracy*,
something like the Famous Triumvirate at *Rome*, they are a kind of
Undertakers and Pragmatic Statesmen, who finding their Power and Strength
great and answerable to their Designs, will make Bargains with our Gracious
Sovereign; they will serve Her faithfully, but upon their own Terms: they
must have their own Instruments, their own Measures; this Man must be
turned out, and that Man put in, and then they'll make Her the most *Glorious
Queen in Europe.*

Where will this end, *My Lord?* Is not her Majesty in Danger by such a
Method? Is not the Monarchy in Danger? Is not the Nation's Peace and
Tranquility in Danger? Will a Change of Parties make the Nation more
Happy? No. *My Lord*, The Seed is sown, that is like to afford us a perpetual
Increase; it's not an Annual Herb, it takes deep Root, it Seeds and Breeds; and
if not timely prevented by Her Majesty's Royal Endeavours, will split the
whole stand in two.

My Lord, I think, considering our present Circumstances at this time, the
Almighty GOD has reserved this Great Work for us: We may bruise this
Hydra of Division, and crush this *Cockatrice's* Egg. Our Neighbours in *England*
are not yet fitted for any such thing, they are not under the Afflicting Hand of
Providence, as we are: Their Circumstances are Great and Glorious, their
Treaties are Prudently Managed both at Home and Abroad, their Generals
Brave and Valorous, their Armies Successful and Victorious, their Trophies and
Laurels Memorable and Surprising; Their Enemies Subdued and Routed, Their
Strong Holds Besieged and Taken, Sieges relieved, Marshals killed and Taken
Prisoners; Provinces and Kingdoms are the Results of their Victories; the
Royal Navy is the Terror of *Europe*, their Trade and Commerce extended
through the Universe, encircling, the whole habitable World, and rendering
their own Capital City the *Emporium*, for the whole Inhabitants of the Earth;
and which is yet more than all these things, the Subjects freely bestowing their
Treasury upon their Sovereign; and above all, their vast Riches, the Sinews of
War, and without which, all the Glorious Success had proven Abortive, these
Treasures are managed with such Faithfulness and Nicety, that they Answer
seasonably all their Demands, though at never so great a Distance. Upon these
Considerations, *My Lord*, How hard and difficult a thing will it prove, to per-
suade our Neighbours to a self-denyal Bill?

It is quite otherwise with us, *My Lord*, we are an Obscure Poor People,
though formerly of better Account, removed to a remote Corner of the World,
without Name and without Alliances; our Posts mean and precarious: so that
I profess, I don't think any one Post of the Kingdom worth the arguing
after . . .

What hinders us then My Lord, to lay aside our Divisions, to unite Cordially and Heartily together in our present Circumstances, when our All is at the Stake? *Hannibal, My Lord*, is at our Gates, *Hannibal* is come within our Gates, *Hannibal* is come the length of this Table, he is at the foot of this Throne, he will demolish this Throne; if we take not Notice, he'll seize upon these *Regalia*, he'll take them as our *spolia opima*, and whip us out of this House never to return again.

For the Love of GOD then, *My Lord*, for the Safety and Welfare of our Ancient Kingdom, where sad Circumstances, I hope, we shall yet convert unto Prosperity and Happiness! We want no Means, if we Unite, *GOD blesses the Peace-makers*; we want neither Men nor Sufficiency of all manner of things necessary, to make a Nation happy: All depends upon Management, *Concordia res parve crescunt* [concord turns weakness into strength]. I fear not these Articles, though they were ten times worse then they are; if we once Cordially forgive one another, and that according to our Proverb, *Bygones be bygones and fair Play to come*. For my part, in the sight of GOD, and in the presence of this Honourable House, I heartily forgive every Man; and beg, That they may do the same to me. And I do most humbly Propose, That His Grace *My Lord Commissioner* [the marquis of Queensbury] may appoint an *Agape*, may order a Love Feast for this Honourable House, that we lay aside all self designs; and that after our Fasts and Humiliations, we may have a day of Rejoicing and Thankfulness, may eat our Meat with Gladness, and our Bread with Merry Heart: then *shall we sit each Man under his own fig-tree*, and *the Voice of the Turtle shall be heard in our Land*, a Bird famous for Constancy and Fidelity.

My Lord, I shall make a Pause here, and stop going on further in my Discourse till I see further, if His Grace, *My Lord Commissioner* receive any Humble Proposals, for removing Misunderstandings among us, and putting an End to our Fatal Divisions; upon Honour, I have no other Design, and Content to beg the Favour upon my bended Knees . . .

Further reading

Edward Gregg, *Queen Anne* (London, 1980).
Ronald Hutton, *The Restoration* (Oxford, 1987).
Ronald Hutton, *Charles II* (Oxford, 1989).
Jonathan Israel, ed., *The Anglo-Dutch Moment* (Cambridge, 1991).
J.R. Jones, *The Revolution of 1688 in England* (London, 1972).
Brian P. Levack, *The Formation of the British State* (Oxford, 1987).
John Miller, *The Restoration and the England of Charles II* (London, 1997).
P.W.J. Riley, *The Union of England and Scotland* (Manchester, 1978).
William A. Speck, *Reluctant Revolutionaries* (Oxford, 1988).

SOURCES

Calendar of Letters Despatches and State Papers Relating to the Negotiations Between England and Spain, Preserved in the Archives at Simancas and Elsewhere. vol. 1. G.A. Bergenroth, editor. London, 1862, pp. 159–60; 163–4; 168; 177–8.

England as Seen by Foreigners in the Days of Elizabeth and James the First. William Brenchley Rye, editor. London, 1865, pp. 103–7.

The Court of Queen Elizabeth: Originally Written by Sir Robert Naunton under the Title of 'Fragmenta Regalia'. James Caulfield, editor. London, 1814, pp. 1; 5–6; 9; 11–12; 15, 16.

Edward Hyde, Earl of Clarendon. *Characters and Episodes of the Great Rebellion.* G.D. Boyle, editor. Oxford, 1889, pp. 223–5; 227.

Sir William D'Avenant. *The Dramatic Works of Sir William D'Avenant.* vol. 2. Edinburgh, 1872, pp. 310; 312–15; 321–7.

Charles II. *A Proclamation for the Better Ordering of Those Who Repair to the Court for Their Cure of the Disease Called The King's Evil.* London, 1662.

John Churchill, Duke of Marlborough. *Memoirs of the Duke of Marlborough.* vol. 2. William Coxe, editor. London, 1848, pp. 2–4; 8; 10–11.

Original Letters Illustrative of English History. First Series, vol. 2. Sir Henry Ellis, editor. London, 1846, pp. 90–1; 101–3.

Original Letters Illustrative of English History. Third Series, vol. 2. Sir Henry Ellis, editor. London, 1846, pp. 159–61.

Acts of the Privy Council of England, New Series, vol. 8, 1571–1575. John Roche Dasent, editor. London, 1894, pp. 94; 112; 114–16; 196–8.

Calendar of Treasury Books April 1705 to September 1706. vol. 20, part II. William A. Shaw, editor. London, 1952, pp. 1–2; 6; 16–18. By permission of Her Majesty's Stationery Office.

Select Cases before the King's Council in the Star Chamber. Publications of the Selden Society, vol. 16. London, 1902, pp. 50–1; 164–8.

William Sheppard. *The Court-Keeper's Guide.* London, 1649, pp. 84–94.

The Full and True Relation of all the Proceedings at the Assizes Holden at Maidstone for the Countie of Kent. 1680.

The Oak Book of Southampton. vol. 1. P. Studer, editor. Publications of the Southampton Record Society, Southampton, 1910, pp. 117–19; 121–2; 130–1; 134–5; 145–6.

Orders and Directions, Together With a Commission for the Better Administration of Justice and More Perfect Information of His Majestie. London, 1630.

A Compleat Journal of the Votes. Speeches, and Debates, Both of the House of Lords and House of Commons Throughout the Whole Reign of Queen Elizabeth of Glorious Memory. Sir Simonds D'Ewes, editor. London, 1693, pp. 285–88.

Henry Elsynge. *Memorials of the Method and Maner of Proceedings in Parliament in Passing Bills*. London, 1658, pp. 6–7; 21–2; 24; 26–7.

A Smith and Cutler's Plain Dialogue about Whig and Tory. [London, c.1690.]

Charles Davenant. *The True Picture of a Modern Whig*. Sixth edition, London, 1701, pp. 3–5; 14–18; 22–3.

Acts of the Privy Council of England. New Series, vol. 1, 1542–1547. John Roche Dasent, editor. London, 1890.

Acts of the Privy Council of England. vol. 32, 1601. John Roche Dasent, editor. London, 1907, pp. 102–4.

Calendar of the State Papers Relating to Ireland of the Reign of Elizabeth. 1 November 1600–31 July 1601. Ernest George Atkinson, editor. London, 1905, pp. 438; 441–2.

The Register of the Privy Council of Scotland. vol. 11, 1616–1619. David Masson, editor. Edinburgh, 1894, pp. 14–15.

Polydore Vergil. *The Anglica Historia of Polydore Vergil*. Denys Hay, translator and editor. Camden Third Series, vol. 74. London, 1950, pp. 13–27. Used with kind permission of the Royal Historical Society.

Chronicle of King Henry VIII of England. Martin A. Sharpe Hume, translator and editor. London, 1889, pp. 1; 3–4; 10–15.

Tudor Constitutional Documents A.D. 1485–1603. J.R. Tanner, editor. Cambridge, 1922, pp. 47–50.

Three Chapters of Letters Relating to the Supression of Monasteries. Thomas Wright, editor. Publications of the Camden Society, vol. 26. London, 1843, pp. 85; 103–7.

Tudor Economic Documents. vol. 1. R.H. Tawney and Eileen Power, editors. London, 1924, pp. 39–44.

Thomas Cranmer. *Memorials of the Most Reverend Father in God, Thomas Cranmer*. John Strype, editor. London, 1694. Appendix, pp. 86–8; 92–4; 97–112.

J.M. Stone. *The History of Mary I. Queen of England*. New York, 1901, pp. 503–4.

John Foxe. *The Acts and Monuments of John Foxe: A New and Complete Edition*. vol. 7. Stephen Reed Cattley, editor. London, 1838, pp. 547–51.

J.E. Neale. *Essays in Elizabethan History*. New York, 1959, p. 104.

Richard Hakluyt. *Voyages and Documents*. Janet Hampden, editor. Oxford, 1958, pp. 358–9; 369–70; 377–9; 386–8; 395–7.

John Gerard. *The Condition of Catholics under James I*. John Morris, editor. London, 1872, pp. 15–16; 20–1; 25; 31; 34–6; 39–40.

Criminal Trials. vol. 2, *The Library of Entertaining Knowledge*. London, 1835, pp. 141–3.

The Constitutional Documents of the Puritan Revolution 1625–1660. Samuel Rawson Gardiner, editor. Third edition, Oxford, 1906, pp. 202–5; 233–6; 371–6; 380; 465–7.

Charles I. *His Maiesties Answer to the XIX Propositions of Both Houses of Parliament*. London, 1642.

Stuart Tracts 1603–1693. C.H. Firth, editor. Westminster, 1903, pp. 427–30.

Gilbert Burnet. *An Abridgment of Bishop Burnet's History of His Own Times*. Thomas

Stackhouse, editor. London, 1906, pp. 254; 259–61; 265–8; 271–2; 282.

James II. *His Majesties Late Letter in Vindication of Himself*. London, 1689.

[Daniel Defoe]. *A Letter Concerning Trade*. Edinburgh, 1706, pp. 1; 7–15.

John Hamilton, Lord Belhaven. *The Lord Beilhaven's {sic} Speech in Parliament*. Edinburgh, 1706, pp. 1–3; 5–8.

INDEX

Privy Council 1, 27, 28, 57, 63;
attendance lists 1; consolidation of
power 27, 31; Elizabethan 31–5;
members 31; range of business 32; royal
attendance 32; Scotland 81, 85–6;
stabilising function 32; texts 32–5,
85–6; and Wales 8–3
Privy Seal office 28
purgatory, doctrine of 114–15
Puritanism 42, 130, 132, 133
Pym, John 135, 140

Quakers 156

rebellions: Cranmer's answers to 107,
110–16; economic and social causes
106–7; Ireland 65–6, 69, 70, 80, 83–5,
136, 139; religious demands 110–16;
western England 106–7
recusancy laws 64, 130, 131, 132–3, 156
recusants 48, 64, 126, 130; see also Roman
Catholicism
Reformation 64, 96; Court of
Augmentations 27; Henrician
Reformation (1529–36) 64, 96–106;
monasteries, dissolution of the 97,
103–6
Reformation Parliament 97, 100–3
Regnans in excelsis (papal bull, 1570) 65
relics 103
Restoration (1660) 63, 64, 149–54;
Declaration of Breda (text) 149–51;
England's Joy (text) 151–4
Richard III 5, 91
Richard, Lewis 15
Ridley, Nicholas 118, 120–4
rioting 43–5, 57, 73, 86
Rochester, earl of 22, 24
Roman Catholicism: extinction of papal
authority in England 101–3; fear and
hatred of 63, 64, 65–8, 70, 111,
113–14, 115, 130, 131, 136, 137, 154;
and the Gunpowder Plot 130–1;
Marian period 118; recusancy laws 64,
130, 131, 132–3, 156; Tory allegiances
74
royal service 28; personal ties and
patronage 28, 29, see also central
government

Saint Bennet's of Holme (abbey) 42
Sancroft, Archbishop William 158

Schwartz, Martin 94, 95, 96
Scotland 80, 81; Anglo-Scottish Union
(1707) 63, 81, 162–71; ecclesiastical
rights 81, 85; government 27; judicial
authority 40; Parliament 63, 162;
patriotism 162, 167–71; Privy Council
81, 85–6; succession question 162; text
85–6
Second Civil War (1648) 143
Seymour, Lord Henry 126
sheriffs 53
Simnel, Lambert 91–6
Six Articles 111
Slawata, William 10
Southampton 54–7
Spanish Armada (1588) 124–9
Star Chamber 40; abolition 42;
membership 41; popularity 41; powers
41–2; royal attendance 41; texts 41–5
Statue of Labourers 57, 59
status and hierarchy 1
Stephen, King 106
Stoke, Battle of (1487) 91, 95
Stowell, Sir John 153–4
Strafford, Thomas Wentworth, 1st earl of
135
Stuart, James Francis Edward ('Old
Pretender') 162
Sunderland, Charles Spencer, 3rd earl of
22, 23, 24–5
Symonds (Simons), Richard 91, 92, 96

tax rebellions 6
taxation 8, 35, 64, 163–4, 166
three Estates 140, 141–3
Tories 22, 64, 73–8, 154
torture 32
trade 54; A Letter Concerning Trade (text)
162, 163–7; and Anglo-Scottish union
162, 163–7; colonial trade 165–6; corn
trade 33–4; corporate privileges 54;
wool trade 106
transportation 49
Treasury 27; texts 36–9
Tyler, Wat 143
Tyrone, Hugh O'Neill, 2nd earl of 83, 84,
85
tythingmen 53

Urswick, Christopher 94

vagrancy 60, 61, 106

179